PRAISE FOR MICHAEL CLARKSON

Quick Fixes for Everyday Fears

"I find Clarkson's research fascinating. There is a lot of insecurity in achievers, but they overcome their fears where others do not."

—Ted Turner, CNN founder

"Michael Clarkson got to the next millennium before the rest of us did. His theories on psychology and how to concentrate under intense pressure are ahead of his time."

—The Amazing Kreskin

"Michael Clarkson's work and theories are truly superb."
—Dr. Edward M. Hallowell, professor of psychiatry, Harvard Medical School, and bestselling author

"I admire Michael Clarkson's clear-sightedness and guts in telling it like it is."
—Dr. Mihaly Csikszentmihalyi, professor of psychology, Claremont University, and bestselling author

"Michael Clarkson's perspectives on fear and the use of emotions intrigues us."
—Dr. Benjamin Spock

Competitive Fire

"This book is a stepping stone toward personal mastery—be it in athletics, martial endeavors or life itself."
—Arthur C. Anderson in the *Journal of Asian Martial Arts*

Pressure Golf

"Clarkson is right on the money with everything he writes about the mental and emotional sides of golf."

—Nick Price, three-time majors winner

THE Age OF Daredevils

THE Age OF Daredevils

MICHAEL CLARKSON

Little
a

Text copyright © 2016 Michael Clarkson

Published by Little A, New York
www.apub.com

Amazon, the Amazon logo, and Little A are trademarks of Amazon.com, Inc., or its affiliates.

ISBN-13: 9781503935426 (hardcover)
ISBN-10: 1503935426 (hardcover)
ISBN-13: 9781503935419 (paperback)
ISBN-10: 1503935418 (paperback)

Cover design by Adil Dara

Printed in the United States of America

First edition

To Beatrice Hill and Annie Taylor

CHAPTER ONE
A DAY MOST LIKELY TO COME

On this cloudless afternoon of August 5, 1951, Bill listens intently to try to hear her voice, her rumble. He shuts both eyes, asks people around him to please hush a moment, and focuses on his second sense. From this far away on the edge of a river bordering the sleepy village of Chippawa, her rumble should be faint, a roll of distant thunder from a mile and a half away as the crow flies, but if breezes allow, it will carry across the long, restless water to where he is situated—hiding under a stone bridge. He needs to hear her. Next to him, anchored to shore but bobbing slightly in calm water as he touches its side, is a peculiar vessel designed to take him to the rumble and beyond; the only way to describe it is a homemade rubber barrel of thirteen oversize inner tubes lashed together with fishnet and hope. The rumble is Horseshoe Falls, and everyone has heard her, been swooned by her sights and legend, as well as her sounds. Not everyone, though, is conscious of the fact (or admits) that much of the beauty and allure of the falls, of the alpha female, is the thrill of being frightened by her beast.

One person who does is William Red Hill Jr.—Bill to his family and close friends. On this day most likely to come, Hill is preparing to nose-dive off the top of the falls in the contraption right out of a Boy Scout weekend that he has christened *The Thing*. He and his assistants have been forced to conceal *The Thing* from police—who will try to halt the stunt and throw him in the slammer overnight to protect him from himself—and from the hydroelectric officials, who would reduce the flow over the falls and ground *The Thing* on rocks in the Horseshoe Rapids, which gallops above the booming waterway. In other daredevil escapades over the past five decades, two people have perished in barrels over the big cataract and four others have drowned in the Great Whirlpool below it (although some others have survived stunts, apparently by the grace of the good Lord). Before there were rocket ships and bungee cords, there were barrels . . . and people off Main Street to climb into them—a teacher, a poolroom operator, a barber, a machinist, a short-order cook, a war veteran, and now Bill, whose last job was in an aircraft factory, making fuselages for Allied training missions in World War II. The stench of the war is finally dissipating, but people remember, and they are sick of living and dying; it's best these days to leave it up to people like Bill. This is the sixth stunt on the river since 1945. During the war, there were none. It's becoming the age of watching others, like in that new trendy invention, television, and you can even keep track of those untrustworthy Reds from the USSR each evening on the boob tube.

As far as Hill knows, at this moment the Keystone Kops are tailing his understudy, a fake Bill Hill, who roared away from home an hour ago in a '39 DeSoto with noisy gears and tinted windows. They could pass for brothers—five eight, 150, thinning red hair, and expressions suitable for high-stakes poker. *Shhh!* He thinks he hears it, that off-and-on rumble in the distance, a thunderstorm that doesn't quit on the ground. It relaxes him. The rumble has been poking him for most of his thirty-seven years—when he was a child, it would waft through his bedroom window to keep him tossing at night, then tease him at the breakfast table to convince him to skip school, to get him flying on his red bicycle, to draw him to the threshold of the world, where the fast white water of the upper rapids faints 165 feet into a cauldron just as deep and treacherous. The falls remains quite mad with the roar that never stops, and it can take you to the loony bin along with it if you stay long enough, or live close enough by. Today, waiting for the wind to reverse from the north so he can feel its moist breath on his nose, he can't positively identify the far-off voice as being the falls. It might be his strong heart. He knows, however, that Horseshoe Falls is there, waiting, in no big rush, fearing no one. Even from here he can see its mist spiraling into the skies like Indian smoke signals before a bloody battle.

Physically, he feels a little out of sorts today; Bill and his assistants are staying so quiet under the small stone bridge on the Niagara Parkway that his favorite brunch of pork chops and deep-fried potatoes is lingering, grumbling in his belly. To pass time until everything is go for the launch, Bill looks critically at his barrel of inner tubes, and he looks at the river, then back to his barrel again. When his mind wanders into dark places, he gently pats his black spaniel, Pal, and forces himself to remember the promise of last night—from the blond waitress at the Foxhead Inn, who will be there for him in street clothes when he defeats the falls. She is trim and pretty (Molly was her name, he thinks), resembling the rising new actress Marilyn Monroe, who is to make a feature for the silver screen at Niagara with big-name actors. After this day, after Bill has appeared in all the newsreels from Tampa to Timbuktu, even Marilyn might want to look him up. As sad as it sounds, Bill has to look beyond his wife, Alice; she probably doesn't want him anymore, partly because he can't go out and earn three thousand a year, like everybody else. Who knows where she is on this important day in his life? His strokes along Pal's neck become softer, longer.

Wait, there it is again. No doubt about it this time—the rumble of the falls is filling his ears! It has an even more intense voice today because today he will finally meet his destiny; he will marry the historic river in one way or another—to live forever in the annals of daredevils initiated by his late great father, William Red Hill Sr., or succumb to its green waters and descend forever to the bottom. Bill tries not to reveal it to anyone around him, but he is frightened, and downed a couple of bottles of ale before noon. He wants to pull the plug, but how does he do that with so many people converging around *The Thing*? *Dad,* he keeps reassuring himself, recalling a deathbed promise. "Dad." Then something else snatches his attention: listen, there is a second sound coming from the area of the falls—a buzzing, like a whole lot of people talking at the same time, like when you're trying to sleep in the divorced man's room at the Rapids Tavern and the patrons below are having a grand old time, but you can't tell exactly who they are gossiping about. Or you could give another meaning to it—they are talking about you, and you want to hear more. Down at the falls, even strangers are talking about you, wondering what Red Hill Jr. is going to try next. Whatever meanings and emotions are bubbling in Hill's gut start to feel good, but suddenly one of his assistants, Al Sedore, breaks the spell. "You look like you're deep in thought, but I'm reporting back . . ." Sedore has just returned by pickup truck from the brink of the falls, weaving in and out of parked cars like an Indy 500 participant to get here. "You wouldn't believe the thousands and thousands of goddam people! All around the safety railing and below in the gorge. Who's ever seen such a crowd!" While Hill seems perfectly calm, Sedore is practically hyperventilating. "They're waiting for you, go get 'em!" Sedore offers Hill a cigarette, and he takes it. In the heat of battle Sedore is usually calm; he recently won a Carnegie lifesaving medal for rescuing three young boys above the falls.

"Good, but no need for cussin', Al. No need for panic, buddy." Hill squints into the sun and rubs the sweat off his tanned forehead, his hairline receding much like the Horseshoe rock bed eroding backward from Lake Ontario. Then he lights up, but keeps the cigarette at his side, away from people.

On this sweltering Sunday afternoon, church pews have emptied early and pastors have finished their warnings to accept Jesus before it's too late and everybody from miles around is pushing to get closer to the brink of Niagara Falls—in canvas hats and binoculars, sipping Coca-Cola through straws, gay and festive, but not to ooh and aah at the waterfall as they normally do. Already, newspaper reporters are estimating the crowd to be anywhere from one hundred and fifty to three hundred thousand; goodness, there are even fifty reporters.

"Who's there?" Hill says to Sedore. "Ma? Major?"

"Everybody—Corky, Major, your mother."

"So, Major . . ."

"Major isn't going over the falls today," Sedore interrupts emphatically. Bill's younger brother, Major, has retooled his own steel barrel, *Jiggs' Jinx*, which got trapped at the brink of the falls last year before he was dramatically rescued, and has been talking about finally completing his stunt on this day. "Even Wes came. I thought he was up north after moose?"

"So did I. What about Sander?" A New York interior designer, Leslie Sander, has told the media that he, too, will go over Niagara Falls today in a twelve-foot steel barrel with a double hull and a double billing on the marquee.

"No word. He's all talk."

"I'm still a little concerned," Hill says. "I saw a boat acting strange on the American side. By the way, was Alice there?"

"Sorry, didn't see her. But I wasn't lookin'. Let's go now."

"Can't. The wind." Hill and his team must wait until the wind turns into a zephyr and the currents shift so he won't be blown ashore like Major last year.

Suddenly, a camera crew shows up and starts filming Bill putting out his cigarette. He smiles for them and pats his dog for them and says something to Norm Chandler, a bespectacled, spindly middle-aged man who designed *The Thing* on a limited budget. "Everything will be all right, Normie." Other people close to Hill are showing up under the bridge. The deepest crowd, though, has gathered way down in the basin directly below Horseshoe Falls on the Canadian shore, swirling with spray, shorebirds, and salty language. Even the seaweed smells acceptable when you know something grand is about to happen, when the seagulls start to scream bloody murder. Convertibles and other excited automobiles have jammed the streets of both Niagara Falls, Ontario, and Niagara Falls, New York, and standing room is nowhere to be found within a mile of the falls; not even Mayor Ernest Hawkins of Niagara Falls, Ontario, can manage preferential viewing. There has been so much hyperbole in the papers and on radio and television prior to this day's event, the crowd keeps swelling. Along with those at the Maid of the Mist docks, tens of thousands are lining up along the top of the gorge, in the windows of the Foxhead, on the Rainbow Bridge, and even over on Goat Island on the American side, enjoying a jumbo hot dog and some midsummer hoopla. Almost to a person, they are all dressed up in their Sunday best, in freshly ironed white shirts and midcalf skirts, though tormented by the breeze and boys kicking up dust in their Buster Brown shoes.

Bill's mother, Beatrice, is at the Maid of the Mist, along with his younger brothers Major, Corky, and Wesley, and the tall ghost of their father, William Sr. Not to be dismissed, Major and Corky have already enjoyed some renown in daring the devil, and are planning more stunts. The curly-haired, pretty boy Corky is a strapping swimmer, eager to smash his late father's record for power stroking across the river below the falls, which Bill has twice failed to eclipse. But now, as he sits by his barrel upriver, Bill thinks, *So what?* Most brothers engage in rivalry: first to ride a two-wheeler, first to get kissed, first to smash a bottle with a .22. The Hills have done these things, too, but the real bragging rights are settled in scrapbooks crammed with newspaper and magazine accounts of their exploits at the falls. The skinny but sneaky-strong Major has twice dashed in a barrel down the fast and precarious Whirlpool Rapids below the falls. Junior has matched that number. So what? Major boasts many wounds from parachute jumps into enemy lines in Europe for the Allies during the Second World War, nearly equaling his father's military record, while Junior spent the war locally as an air raid warden in a white helmet. So what? Nothing else counts now but Bill's life, and his family is trembling at the base of the falls. Over the years, they have waited so many times for barrel jumpers or would-be barrel jumpers to come over the watery cliff, Major calls it the Waiting Room. Major, Corky, and Wesley are here to save their brother. *Come out alive, Bill, and we'll settle this in another way.* Major is afraid of the falls, but it won't let him rest until he rides it to the bottom; one of the Hills *has* to beat it (after that, he hopes to make the stunt safe enough for tourists paying a pretty penny). Lately, he's been referring to himself as Red Hill, after his Pa, although on a good day in his uniform, Major looks more like the actor Jimmy Stewart. He watches the brink of the falls as though he expects Nazis to come storming over.

William Red Hill Sr. is a celebrated name to live up to; his obit mentioned four bravery medals, not including those he earned as a sniper in the bloody battle of Vimy Ridge in France in 1917 in the war to end all wars. He also earned the title *daredevil* with three barrel adventures into the Whirlpool. He made *Time* magazine. They were going to bury Red with all his medals, but then thought better of it. Beatrice usually wears one around her neck to her sons' stunts—and it helps balance her scowl—but she doesn't today. Now Bill is going to accomplish something even his father had dreaded. Over the years, Red Hill Sr. had been a helper or witness to some incredible derring-do at the falls—in 1901 as a thirteen-year-old, he watched as the first man to go over the cataract was a woman—and later he scrambled in rowboats as two men died in barrels. "Fool's game," Red had told everyone he wanted to listen; privately, though, at night under the streetlamp puffing a Camel, he thought he could beat the falls if the barrel was right and the river was on a kind day. If Bill can beat the fool's game, he will not have to be Bill anymore or even Red Hill Jr. but simply Red Hill. Why, he even has red hair; Major doesn't anymore, if he ever really did. Bill is proud of his hair; as a youth, he let his sisters rinse it with barley soup.

Stunting at Niagara and the exploits of the Hill family are front-page news in any country with a printing press, especially in the United States and Europe, and the British royal family asks to see the Hills whenever they come on a tour of North America. Tourism is growing with all the headlines, and businessmen are constructing wax museums to honor Red Sr. and other celebrities, and they ask police to please tone it down when considering their arrest of daredevils. Until now, the Hills have not been able to make a full-time living off the river, but after this day, Bill hopes to be in a position to build a proper memorial to his father and buy enough yellow roses for Ma to keep the smell of the seaweed out of her kitchen for a month.

The day keeps getting hotter, but Beatrice Hill is cold and dank, a graying fifty-nine-year-old with hair desperately holding its permanent in the breezes of the Waiting Room. The mist of water drifts in as fog oozes into her eyelashes, and she has to keep mopping her face. Bea feels very small down here, and it would not take much of a sudden wave to carry her away, but it's better than standing up on the brink, where you can hurt fingers squeezing the railing. Gazing up at the falls makes her light-headed, a tiny figure in one of those glass ornaments you flip upside down to get the sparkles going nuts in liquid—which is just the opposite of the way she feels at home, especially in her kitchen, where it takes two big brutes to knock her off her feet. Bea hates the falls. She and her family have survived two incredible world wars, the Depression, and disease, but the falls still looks down at her, taunts her; it is the only thing that does not live out its evil, and it has been going merrily along for twelve thousand years, evolution's phenomenon left over from the Ice Age. This morning before a packed congregation at All Saints, Rev. Percival Mayes said with a glowing face that God created all the beautiful things on heaven and earth. "Baloney," Bea mutters to herself, using a handkerchief to wipe her brow. From where she now stands at the boat docks, she doesn't see the angelic side of the falls, as the tourists do, as it poses for a thousand Brownie cameras with its sparkling waters changing hue among blue, green, and white beneath the big blue sky, with its rainbows and its handsome physique.

People flock here from Washington and Wichita to fall in love with its rawness, as well as one another. With sunshine turning everything white gold, today they are in heaven. Up close, however, Bea knows the water has toxic streaks snaking through it; when her husband Red died at age fifty-four, it had not been so much from war wounds as from his life upon the restless river. Saving the lost and foolish and risking his neck to recover suicide bodies for their relatives while receiving little more than a firm handshake had drained him and poisoned him more effectively than the mustard gas at Vimy. *Friendly fire* they had called that, describing how the Allies' mustard gas had blown back in the face of sniper Hill, landing him in the hospital for eighteen months in 1917–1918. But it was the angelic river that carved ravines into his face, stole the baby blue from his eyes, and mummified him better than any undertaker, she believes. And the same river has sent two of her sons practically mad while stripping their savings, putting their marriages on the rocks, and even landing them behind bars on occasion. "They say it's a great river and it is," Bea is oft to say. "It takes more than it gives." Even her daughters are not immune—her eldest, Edith, who is with her today, has been offered money to go over the falls by an enterprising company seeking publicity. Bill has mused about the possibility of Edith and him one day being the first daredevil brother and sister team, the Flying Wallendas of the waterways. All is not lost, however—Bea is proud that her sons are all sporting white shirts on this Sunday, and Lloyd ("Major" to his fans and everybody else) even has a necktie, but she knows that under their clothes are bathing suits; that's how she can always tell if something is up at the river. And now, friendly fire at Niagara Falls is threatening to claim her firstborn. As spectators toss pennies into the world's most revered fountain for good fortune, bookies are taking bets of seven to two that Bill will not survive his adventure in the inner tubes. In anticipation of a successful barrel trip, Corky and Major are accepting handshakes from total strangers and scribbling their names on postcards while they try to maintain focus as unofficial members of their brother's rescue team; they are watching driftwood come off the falls to predict where *The Thing* will break surface. They know that down in the lower basin, the river is dense and hard to move, like a whale. Up top, just above the falls, it is shallow and quick on its feet, a shark. You hope the shark doesn't do so much to you that you have nothing left to deal with the whale.

If only Bill's contrivance holds together in the angry river. If one is to win the fool's game, a design of heavy rubber is the way to go, according to Hill's late father, because it has the best chance to bounce off the rocks. Oh, yes, the rocks. Surviving the turbulence of the upper rapids and the harrowing plunge over Horseshoe, holding your last breath all the way, are just two issues—dealing with the rocks and boulders sadistically hidden by spray at the bottom of the falls is quite another. The rocks have crushed barrels and boats over the years. The rocks haven't always conspired beneath the falls, but they have appeared at times throughout history as the falls cuts a deep gorge southward—it has dug itself seven miles backward since the Ice Age and cares little about what is in its path. Of course, Horseshoe doesn't have to crush your organs—it can hold you captive behind its thick curtain of water and slowly smother you, as it did with one of the daredevils. Bill has seen much of this; he was witness with his father for three barrel jumps when he should have been in summer school for his failing grades, but is there better education than watching men live or die? And so, Bill has surrounded himself with what he thinks is the best in barrel design—the rubber inner tubes all teamed up. Some of the barrels of his predecessors ended up in the back of his family's souvenir store. He didn't care so much why those people got into barrels, rather if they were safe enough to protect them—their physical and psychological needs. On lonely nights, Alice sometimes found him sleeping in them, strapped in a harness, fidgeting nervously in a dream.

"Why would you ever want to defy death?" she once asked him.

"Define death," he said. It could be working nine to five, six days a week, for a buck ten an hour and an employee number at the Fleet Aircraft plant. In any event, Hill has dismissed the steel and wooden barrels of the souvenir store in favor of much-lighter rubber. It matters not that it smells like an old garage; such a barrel should be tossed clear of the rocks below the falls before currents of air sweeping down to the basin catch it, nurture it, and place it safely down on the surface, avoiding the rocks. "The long and wide tubes will be like shock absorbers," he told the papers. Hill does not want to be dragged beneath the surface into what he calls the *plunge pool*, where he could be trapped for hours by big underwater surf, where there is lots of air mixed with the water, preventing him from swimming. Should he be flung from the barrel, bubbles of the plunge pool might block out the sunlight and lead to disorientation. He thinks of such things now, as he waits in Chippawa, so that he doesn't worry he will never again hear the two other sounds he cherishes: "Hi, Honey," and from his daughter, Sally: "Daddy, can I sit in the barrel with you?" Easier said than done, but he can't afford to think of such matters.

Down in the gorge, Bea's sons do not agree with their ma that the falls was cruel to their father; they say his face did not collapse through worry of failing to support his family from the river, but through the energy he expended in the fantastic adventure of his life. Sure, he died with debts, but how can you put a price on carrying an injured swan out of the gorge, or James Harris's expression when Pa hauled him away in a rescue basket that harrowing night on the old scow? Theoretically, when Bill conquers or at least survives Niagara, the family IOUs will be cast to the wind and the souvenir shop will prosper once more. The last time Beatrice saw Bill was this morning at home, when he packed his good-luck charms: four silver dollars, a four-leaf clover, a chip from the Blarney Stone, some holy medals, a tiny doll, a wreath of heather, and his father's old rabbit's foot, given to him during the rescue of a daredevil. "He is in God's hands now, and it is up to Him whether he comes through," she says, trying to pace back and forth in the crowded gorge. When she turns to walk along the boat docks with Edith, Bea glances down with horror to realize she is still clutching the hymnal from this morning's service at All Saints. She wouldn't be surprised if the police are already on her trail.

Upriver in Chippawa, where the Niagara stays tame until it can't help it anymore, the man of the hour is ready to be sealed into *The Thing*. In a white shirt and slacks, he doesn't look like a rebel, but rather a tired man who has walked out of a factory during break to try to find a magic path out of town. Of the two dozen bystanders around the bridge, half look upon Red Hill Jr. as a god, the other half as a court jester putting his life in a vessel Eisenhower wouldn't get into. Hardly anyone says anything, except a whisper from his cousin, river man Ken Sloggett: "Not too late for me to drive you home. If the barrel hits just one rock, it's God bless America."

Bill smiles. "The river can get you any which way. Remember Lester." Three years ago, Bill pulled the lifeless body of Ken's brother, Lester Sloggett, out of Chippawa Creek, a tributary of Niagara also known as the Welland River. He had drowned in just four feet of water—strong weeds from the bottom binding and encircling his body as he struggled, gasped, and fell underwater.

"Lester we forget," Sloggett said. The men were not opposed to black humor, even about their family.

"If you're going to go out, better to do it on your terms." As the rumble of the falls talks louder to Bill, his heart beats as it did in his trips in a steel barrel down the lower rapids beneath the falls a few years ago. His brow doesn't show it, but he is excited and nervous at the same moment. This feels different than the time he rescued his sister Margaret from drowning or the time he pulled his father out of the Great Whirlpool as thousands chanted "hip, hip, hooray." He was excited then, as well, but too focused on getting them out of a pickle to feel it until afterward; now, while he's knocking on death's door seemingly for the sake of it, his mind releases something very stimulating into his system—a drug, a stimulant, a daring fluid. He's scared all right, especially of the rocks, but he's going through with it anyway, and his mind rewards him with this internal drug that slows the minutes and gives him a boost each time his memory plays the reel of his barrel shooting down the white rapids and approaching the brink. He has seen all of this since he was a lad, sitting at the base of the falls on a flat rock in the rumble, waiting for himself. Hill says he is confident of his vessel; its bantam weight should ensure that it will not get caught in schizophrenic eddies above the falls (he tested it in high tide at Sherkston Beach, and all he got was a thorough soaking and a lecture from lifeguards). Less is more. The bookies and the naysayers, including one of his brothers, non-stuntman Wesley, claim that the 100-pound barrel will spit out the 150-pound Bill into the upper rapids at the first sign of trouble, but Bill doesn't have time to wait for money to insert a steel lining; he is already past the Point of No Return in his life. Never has one man had so many reasons to challenge Big Nature *now*. Why shouldn't he survive? He's spent four years preparing for this, practically living down at Big Bass Eddy to record the habits and flaws of the mighty falls, to watch the huge downpour of water from the earth. He's been getting ready all his life. Now, by God, he's going to do it.

The last thing Bill does, after assuring Pal he will see him soon for treats, is to check the sky. Over the falls, he can see its spray rising into the blue yonder. His first wife, Franny, liked to read the skies above Niagara Falls; in its swirling plume of mist, forever changing form, she said she could sometimes recognize words and face profiles, including Winston Churchill, and sometimes wings of angels. Today, Red Hill Jr. apparently sees something in the mist and gets ready to meet it. Everything seems go, and he straps on a football helmet. In a few minutes, he will slip into the barrel, feetfirst, and stretch flat on a red air mattress like a kid on a hammock at summer camp, keeping a half bottle of Pepto-Bismol hidden underneath. He will touch the four-leaf clover, hopefully without knocking off a leaf, and immerse himself in the moment. To relax his hungry heart and claustrophobia of the small confines, he will take healthy breaths at first, then slow them into steady rhythm, and words will come back to him from his father's deathbed: "The falls will try to take your breath, son; don't take it from yourself. Save the drama for when they pull you out below at Big Bass Eddy. And do not listen to the queer voices inside your barrel. When you go against the falls, it will talk to you, try to trick you, exaggerate all the sounds and the creaks and the worries until your ears want to burst."

When the barrel is finally towed from under the bridge and ushered toward the Point of No Return, the river will pick up speed, and he will be in the gravity of destiny. It will take ten minutes, or, rather, six hundred seconds, and at times he will feel as though he is passing out from daring fluid. But at the end of the rainbow, everything will be fine—his estranged wife will return to him with open arms, and they will take Sally to see butterflies in the Niagara Glen; his bullshit criminal conviction will be forgotten; the reporters will fist fight to get a scoop; he will be on that new invention, television; *Time* will highlight his face across the globe; and all those who said he would never attempt this will eat crow. But first, he has to fall like an angel.

The winds have shifted into zephyrs, and the sun has turned the spray into gold dust. Soon it will be two thirty. The guys will push him out into the stream considered the river's friendly neighborhood, and for a while he will feel as though he is bobbing with the mallard ducks under a soft blanket of fog before anybody is up on a Tuesday or Wednesday morning, with one end of the barrel open so he can see what he is risking everything for. He will glance at the eagle's nest at the end of Navy Island, where he had watched a mother proudly hatch her eggs five years ago, where he had saved a deer from getting snared by the current. Then he will feel a slight tug under his vessel, the river will come alive beneath him . . . and when he is there, he'll know by the falls' wet breath on his nose just before he closes the rubber lid. Soon the gulls will start screaming.

CHAPTER TWO
MRS. TAYLOR AND A NEW DANCE

One afternoon in September of 1901, fifty years before Red Hill Jr. climbed into *The Thing*, his father, William "Red" Hill Sr., thought he could hear a school bell. From where he was standing in front of the Hotel Lafayette near the Upper Suspension Bridge at the river, the thirteen-year-old boy was perhaps one mile from school, but he thought he could make out its intimidating clang. He was playing hooky. He didn't particularly like school. At school, they called him William. Down here at the river, he was Red, and right now Red was loitering at the back of a substantial crowd surrounding newspaper reporters who were waiting on the steps of the Lafayette for a woman who claimed she was soon going to shoot over the Horseshoe fall in a barrel. Maybe that sound actually was bells going off in somebody's head—not only was she in need of mental examination, everybody said, she was a middle-aged schoolteacher—a woman! And yet the numerous reporters in front of the hotel, wearing suits and inquisitive expressions, were writing down practically every word uttered by Mrs. Annie Edson Taylor, and examining the odd barrel that she claimed would help her become the first person to go over the falls and tell about it. The air was stinging with cynical comments. *We believe you, Mrs. Taylor, seaweed for brains, but let's examine the cold facts: In thousands of years before you turned up, nobody had survived—not suicide victims, accident victims in stout boats, sacrificial Indian maidens in birch-bark canoes, nor that poor fellow last week from Raleigh, or somewhere, who was into the sauce, went over the railing, and got swallowed in one gulp by the falls. When their bodies come up, limbs are often are missing, sometimes heads. Beat Niagara Falls? Not a cat in hell's chance. What next—a telephone in every home, and perhaps one of those newfangled flying machines getting off the ground?* Oh, well, journalists were glad for something else to ramble about after the month-long discussion and updates on the assassination of President William McKinley, just up the road in Buffalo on September 6—not to mention the stock market crash of the spring and the rumors circulating among European governments that a great war was brewing between powers on that continent. The president had been visiting the American Exposition inside the Temple of Music, shaking hands with ordinary, hardworking citizens, when Leon Czolgosz, an unemployed factory worker whose name no one wanted to pronounce, jumped out of the crowd with a concealed revolver and fatally shot him because "I didn't believe one man should have so much service and another man should have none." Czolgosz was to be electrocuted in a few weeks, which meant he would still have more sunrises than Mrs. Taylor. Good God, no one had even *attempted* the falls, unless they were like sixty-year-old John Lazarus of Mount Carmel, Pennsylvania, who booked a one-way ticket to Niagara, hired a tour guide to show him the sights, and then jumped into the falls. As far as anyone knew, he was not resurrected.

Ducking and weaving through learned gentlemen, Red didn't know what to focus on—Mrs. Taylor's wooden whisky barrel or homely face and body, plump and bordering on corpulent. She wore pungent perfume, along with a hat (unless an exotic bird had landed on her head) and a long flowing dress with tightly corseted waist and gloves ladies with money wore when dining out. And everybody thought Queen Victoria had passed on! Mrs. Taylor was big chested and big hipped, resembling Red's mother, Mary Ann, but his mother was a housewife and nurse who would never put herself at center stage in such a calamity. Mrs. Taylor's face wasn't posh—she looked like she'd already gone over the falls—and some of Red's river-rat friends referred to her as an old battle-ax. She was, however, a lady of standing who spoke French, German, and Italian—or at least that's what she told the scribes, in a husky English voice. Put her in a police lineup for daredevils, and she would be the last one standing. Certainly, though, she nattered as impressive as any man; she told them she'd had the barrel designed at the West Bay City Cooperage Company, a supplier of kegs to a brewery, in her current home of Bay City, Michigan. The wooden thingamajig was constructed from oiled Kentucky oak, slightly tapered at one end, four and one-half feet tall, and approximately three feet in diameter. Not even the pocket-size Red would be able to stand up inside it, and to him it resembled an oversize bongo drum from a Caribbean postcard. At best, it was a container for spirits or beer, and you'd have to drink quite a bit from it before getting into the river. And with this she was going into battle against Niagara Falls?

Red wasn't surprised that another person, particularly a woman, had been drawn to the Niagara River; they were always coming by the hundreds and thousands—and some who originally came to see the sights on a Sunday afternoon were hypnotized and remained forever as victims of suicide or stunting. Perhaps, as some superstitious folk believed, Mrs. Taylor was just one in a long line of people lured by a siren song. "It may be Niagara casts a certain hypnotic spell over those who are susceptible to its fatal allure," opined a local daily newspaper, the *Suspension Bridge Journal*. "The Witch of the Lorelei continues to entice suicide victims, those who have every incentive to live as long as possible often feel an impulse to throw themselves into the maddening waters." The "Witch of the Lorelei" was taken from a legend about a witch in Germany who supposedly lured victims into the Rhine River from a cliff about the height of Niagara Falls. As the legend went, the witch had been a beautiful, enchanting woman with locks of gold who was betrayed by a sweetheart and threw herself off a cliff into the Rhine River, causing a fatal echo that some people had to obey by jumping into the water. An example, the newspaper wrote, was a young, beautiful, wealthy woman, Grace Vandyke, who, on a gray summer's morning, walked from her hotel at Table Rock and leaped over Horseshoe Falls, mere hours after she had been dancing, apparently gleeful and happy, in a ballroom. "What impelled her to destroy her life in the finest hour of her young womanhood?" the *Journal* asked.

> Was it a morbid desire for a dramatic ending? Whatever the prompting influence, the fact remains the [Niagara] cataract claims many victims each year, both the illustrious and the demented. Despite every effort of the Park Police, nothing seems to stop this Witch of the Lorelei, who continues to entice its victims.

A German gentleman of letters named Heinrich Heine (1797–1856) even had a poem published about it:

The mountain peaks still glisten
Where the evening sunbeams shine.
The fairest maid sits dreaming
In radiant beauty there.
Her gold and her jewels are gleaming.
She combeth her golden hair.
With a golden comb she is combing;
A wondrous song sings she.
The music quaint in the gleaming,
Hath a powerful melody.

Young Red felt the lure, as well. All of this brought to mind a day, not long before, when he had ventured down to the base of the Horseshoe fall for the first time without the chaperone of his father, Layfield, or anyone else, to collect driftwood and hopefully earn five cents for a Hershey's chocolate bar. Quite a journey it was, into a world where nothing liked to be touched, as he climbed among slimy rocks and jagged crevices yawning over spastic currents of water, then crept along a narrow ledge with his back to a huge granite wall—like a spy anticipating gunfire, or perhaps a Lorelei. At its climax, he entered a twi-light domain where hungry gulls fed and white swans nodded off and died in a ghostly mist coming off the huge falls. There, at the bottom, Down There, he stood steadfastly, all five feet of him, consumed by the thunderous voice, looking straight up at fourteen stories of cold, heavy water collapsing right in front of his eyes—according to the schoolbook under his bed, 150,000 gallons of water per second. It never stopped falling. With the hood of his autumn coat pulled completely over his ears and red hair to keep the wet and the roaring out, his breath was confiscated by gusts of wind, spray, and his own fancy.

The earth moved ever so slightly below his boots, shifting and playing with him, or was the vibration an emotional one? All of his senses were on guard, and it could be exhausting. His cheeks were apple rosy and his eyelashes glued with mist. His fingers shook. In his left pocket were a first aid kit and a rabbit's foot, from one of his father's kills in the Niagara Glen, which he would need as Jonah trying to get out of the whale. Most often, Red was not afraid of his own fear, having earned a lifesaving medal at age nine for dragging his sister Cora from a burning house, but the falls was something you could not afford to annoy. If you dared to look up, you were overwhelmed by a reverse fear of heights—a sky of water aimed at you in strict unison, controlled madness, driving down into a deep basin. If you survived that, there was the Underwater, another fourteen stories of liquid driven down and out of sight. You could toss anything you wanted in there—thick logs, buoys, rowboats—and it would disappear and die, reappearing as something less downstream. Death, taxes, and Niagara Falls, his father once told him, were the only three things in this world that were absolutely certain. These naive reporters should be asking Mrs. Taylor if she had ever been Down There. If you thought it was bad up top, at the brink, that was only concerning the fear of what *might* happen. Down There, it *happened*. The wonders of the continent—Niagara, Grand Canyon, Yellowstone—were beautiful, but you didn't dare get close to their beast.

The press gathering at the Lafayette was becoming as excited as twenty months earlier when church bells had sung for hours all over the twin cities to announce a new century. Two interested spectators were daredevils of legitimate ilk, Peter (Bowser) Nissen of Chicago and Carlisle Graham, a rugged cooper from Philadelphia and emigrant from England. The previous week, Nissen, a bookkeeper, had powered the world's smallest steamship, *The Fool Killer*—twenty feet long with an eight-horsepower motor—successfully and bumpily through the lower rapids below the falls, but he had to be rescued from the vortex of the Great Whirlpool when the boat up and sank while being filmed by lightbulb inventor Thomas Edison. Graham was just as triumphant, having constructed the first Niagara barrel in 1886—wooden and painted lavish red— and as the first to navigate the lower rapids without mishap the same year, he earned the title King of the Mad Torrents. Graham or Nissen should be making the maiden falls plunge—mustachioed men who could design boats and barrels and ride them into hell, who stood with feet planted firmly, their arms folded, when they weren't in action. In his tights and black mustache, Mr. Graham was right out of a Jules Verne dime novel. Red kept a close eye on the two men and tried to overhear what they were saying. What he didn't know was that twelve years earlier, Graham had pulled a hoax that fooled many newspapers, including the *New York Times*, claiming he had gone over the falls, complete with a description of the event: "I felt like a man who has passed into the painless portion of death by drowning . . . There was a terrible roar in my ears. I tried to speak aloud in the barrel to break it, but I couldn't . . . I felt a contented resignation." A few days later, investigative reporters from the *Buffalo Evening News* exposed Graham's story of cheating death as a pants-on-fire lie. Apparently, Graham had produced the hoax to beat New York bookie Steve Brodie, who had announced he would become the first person to go over the falls in a barrel, but Graham never made the attempt. Undaunted, if less credible, Graham made his fifth trip through the rapids later in 1889, and it was no hoax that he nearly suffocated as his barrel got trapped in the Whirlpool.

The air of skepticism around the falls had been growing for decades as men claiming they had gone over, or would go over, the cataract turned out to be all air. In 1886, Edwin R. Hatch of Conneaut, Ohio, a veteran sailor, arrived with plans to go over in a boat he invented—if kindly citizens would come forward with $20,000 so that he could "demonstrate the truths of science." The money was also to go toward his idea of building an aerial ship or propeller capable of flying. They didn't, and he didn't. A Buffalo printer, Fred T. Wood, in 1897 tossed around the wild idea of making barrel rides over the falls a tourist attraction. He claimed he had plans for an unusual machine, comprising a barrel, a boat, and a balloon. The egg-shaped barrel would have a rudder, a manhole, and small portholes at the sides for viewing. Protruding from underneath and at the end of the barrel would be a long flat plank designed to force the vessel well out over the brink of the falls to miss the weight of the falling torrents and rocks at the bottom. Attached to the top of the barrel would be a balloon that would supposedly drop it lightly into the lower river. Should the prototype be successful, he said he could make a larger device to carry six passengers "to become as popular as the *Maid of the Mist* [tourist boat]." Alas, he couldn't find a sugar daddy. Then, in the late 1800s, an unidentified man from Troy, New York, stated plans to go over in a barrel, to which the *Suspension Bridge Journal* said: "The champion idiot is an unknown man who proposes to outdo all the other idiots."

Little wonder, then, that Mrs. Taylor was met with eyebrows raised. She was one step ahead of other boasters, however, with her barrel in plain view. To Red, the only thing matching her importance was a horse-drawn cart beside the hotel, selling Polish sausage with sauerkraut with a luscious smell that, when breezes cooperated, eliminated her perfume. As she talked at length with journalists, Red sneaked through the crowd to get an intimate look at her curious barrel. Standing right next to it, he did not have to tippy-toe to rise above it. Up close, it looked sturdier, bound by ten strong metal hoops at regular intervals. He touched it softly with his fingertips, and it was hard. When he tapped a little firmer, he could hear an echo inside. On the bottom for ballast protruded a 175-pound anvil from George Hillman's blacksmith shop, with one, two, three, four . . . twelve strong bolts and three straps of iron holding it in place. The ballast, Mrs. Taylor explained, would keep her and the barrel upright during the wild ride down the Horseshoe Rapids and over the you-know-what. Discounting the ballast, the barrel weighed about 160 pounds—the same as her—so no wonder it cost four dollars to ship from Michigan.

When Red managed a peek inside, it revealed two pillows for padding; a leather harness; and a homemade breathing device of corks, a bicycle pump, and a rubber mouthpiece and three small air holes near the top. The barrel was crude and unpainted, the adult river rats sneered, and one of them noted that she ought to stencil *Amateur* on the sides. To these locals, it was just another crazy dame from the Midwest looking for attention, or hara-kiri. Men killed themselves in the brain with a shotgun, women threw themselves into fast rivers. Just a few weeks earlier, on September 7, Maud Willard, a singing actress from Canton, Ohio, had bumped and bounced through the Whirlpool Rapids, a fast, rock-strewn channel, in a barrel. The twenty-five-year-old Miss Willard had been working in a burlesque theatre in nearby Buffalo, New York, when she teamed up with her good friend Graham, who loaned her his honored barrel so that she might seek as much fame as he had been getting. The homemade barrel was crafted from Chinese locust wood, oval-shaped—except for its flat head—and was five feet long and nineteen inches in diameter at the foot and twenty-six inches at the head, weighing 165 pounds, including 100 pounds of ballast to keep it upright. According to Archer Butler Hulbert, professor of American history at Marietta College and author of *The Niagara Book* in 1908, there was some practical use to all this barrel action in the river, besides it being entertainment for spectators and an adrenaline release for the daredevils—it was also "proven to the observant that a particular shape of cask might, under certain conditions, be used to draw feeble or sickly passengers from a wrecked ship in bad weather, for a woman or a child could have lived in Graham's machine as well as the cooper himself."

Onstage, Miss Willard could play a feminine lady, and in real life, standing at attention next to Graham's barrel in a sailor's suit, her brunette hair parted in the middle, she often played a tomboy. The unique plan was for her to shoot both the Whirlpool and Devil's Hole Rapids with Graham swimming behind the barrel, all the way to Lewiston, New York. Miss Willard was hoping for a large crowd of people to come over from the Pan-American Buffalo Exposition in Buffalo, including, she hoped, President McKinley, who came from the same area in Ohio as she; of course, all that went out the window when McKinley was shot on September 6 (he died on the fourteenth). Sad but focused on her task, the day after the president was shot, she got into her barrel at four o'clock in the afternoon at the Maid of the Mist landing at the base of the American fall, along with her small fox terrier as a mascot. A cover was put on the hatch, and she was towed out into the river by a rowboat and released forty minutes later. Through the Whirlpool Rapids, the tough barrel resisted the tossing and turnings it received from the big, wild waves, and within five minutes she was in the Whirlpool, where her crew expected her to drift with the strong current to the Canadian shore, as Graham had done in the past in the same barrel. But, witnessed by hundreds of tourists, the barrel floated toward the center of the river and directly into the Whirlpool, where it was promptly seized by nature and held just before five o'clock, out of reach of rescuers on shore. For a brief time, the barrel sank in the deep vortex of the pool before popping up again a short distance away but unable to shake free of the maelstrom. An hour and then two went by and Graham became restless, waiting on shore in a life jacket and neck ring to complete the journey to Lewiston. Finally, a motion picture company filming the adventure could wait no longer, as sunset was approaching and light leaving the gorge, so Graham started swimming again, believing that Maud would in due course be set loose to join him. He made it to Lewiston without incident to become the first person to make that swim, then returned, shocked to find Miss Willard still trapped in the Whirlpool. Gallantly, he tried to swim into the vortex to get her, but the currents and eddies were too dismissive of his puny efforts, and he was pushed back. For a total of more than five hours, the barrel whirled around, while messengers were sent into town to have searchlights sent down into the gorge for a nighttime rescue. As they waited, huge bonfires were lit on the banks to warm spectators and illuminate the river right across from the Canadian to American shores. Gradually, the Whirlpool lost its grip and at first sent pieces of driftwood ashore, then the barrel came close enough that two men, Will and Charles Johnson, were able to swim out and bring it in at about ten o'clock. They cracked open the hatch with large stones, and to their surprise, the small dog leaped out of the barrel after apparently keeping its nose to the only air hole and denying its owner breath. Miss Willard was unconscious with "a remnant of life left in her," but she died before a doctor could be summoned.

Some of her friends came to bring her body up from the gorge. They had apparently been drinking heavily, perhaps celebrating the stunt prematurely, and what happened next was documented by the Toronto *Globe and Mail*:

> They half carried, half dragged the body of the woman up by her feet and hair. Some were carrying burning embers and torches to light their way. Others were falling off the rugged pathways in their drunken stupor as they climbed up the narrow pathway. The worst kind of blasphemy resounded through the glen at the pool and, with flying embers before the high wind, presented a weird sight not unlike Dante's Inferno.

With the stunt, Maud had hoped to win enough money to buy her elderly mother a nice home, but shortly after her daughter's terrible death, Mrs. Willard died, and they were buried together at Oakwood Cemetery in Niagara Falls, New York, in a section eventually devoted to daredevils. Young Red was at Miss Willard's stunt. He cringed to think about the chaotic, life-and-death struggle for that precious air in the tight quarters, with the dog yapping and Maud trying to scream. Nevertheless, he asked his mom if he could take the dog home (she said not this time).

In 1901, Graham had repeated his desire to go over the falls, if anyone would believe his guff anymore, but Miss Willard's death shook the stuffing out of him. He did, however, manage to make enemies with Mrs. Taylor, bad-mouthing her and her barrel in the press. "Let her die in the barrel," he said, which made her angry and even more determined to go through with her plans. For an instructor of waltz and music, and considering the plight of the brave woman who died just weeks before her, Mrs. Taylor seemed cocksure enough about the masculine stunt as she pored over details of her proposed trip with reporters. She told them that she had contracted one Mr. Frank M. Tussy Russell, a promoter of carnivals and high-diving acts in the Michigan area, as her business manager, and an attorney, Mr. James Donnelly, to represent her legal interests. "The barrel is good and strong and the inside will be cushioned so that the rolling movement will do me no harm," she said, walking around it to highlight its aspects, a twinkle in her eye. "Besides, I shall have straps to hold fast to. There will be a weight in one end of the barrel so that air can be admitted through a valve in the upper end where my head will be located." The straps were part of a harness rigging fashioned by a local harness maker, consisting of leather straps looped at the sides for her arms, and another for a strong girdle around her waist, which was fastened to the bottom of the barrel to keep her from pitching forward onto her head if she became unconscious.

Although Red was skeptical, and miffed that he had years of experience at the falls compared to scant for Mrs. Taylor, who admitted she could not even swim a stroke, he still absorbed every word, every idea. In fact, he jotted some things down with pencil and notepad, with designs of turning it in as a field trip for the teachers at school. Could this not be a firsthand account in the new age of education? Hey, locals rarely came to the falls, for whatever reason. "Of course, it will be necessary to place the barrel in the river more than a mile above the falls," Mrs. Taylor said. "It will naturally do considerable rolling on the way down and I expect to tell pretty close to when the great descent will take place. The [air] valve which will be kept open while going down the stream will then be closed. It is estimated that I will be able to live nearly an hour in the barrel after it has been made air tight, and if things turn out as I expect they will, the barrel will have come to the surface and right, long before that time. Then the valve can be reopened to let in more air. There will be straps fastened to the outside so that rescuers will have no trouble in towing it to a place of safety until I can be released."

Reporters did nothing to shut her up. When they inquired about her life experience, she enlightened them that she was born October 24, 1858, in Auburn, New York. Her father, Merrick Edson, owned a flour mill on the Owaco River, providing his family of eight children and wife, Lucretia, with comfortable days. Annie had five brothers and two sisters, and she was only twelve when her father passed away. "While this was an emotional loss for the family, the inheritance that he left behind was more than sufficient to offer them the lifestyle that the family had been accustomed to," a writer would later say. At school, Annie was an average student, but her love of reading gave flight to her dreams. With so many brothers, she became a tomboy and preferred outdoor sports to indoor gossip, and she also liked to read adventure stories until her brain was "teeming with romance." For her secondary education, she attended the Conference Seminary and Collegiate Institute in Charlottesville, New York, fifty miles from her home, and studied to become a teacher. At seventeen, she met Mr. David Taylor from Branchport, Yates County, New York, a few years older than her. Following a brief courtship, they married and had a son, who died within days of birth, and then David enlisted with the Union in the Civil War and was killed in battle in 1864, leaving Annie a sad widow who had lost the two most important men in her life, her father and husband, before their time.

At twenty-five, she moved to San Antonio, the home of one of her school friends, and took a job as a teacher at $300 per year, but in her apartment she was chloroformed by thieves and robbed of her savings of $3,000, so she returned to New York and learned to become a dance instructor. This became her nomadic life, and she traveled by train and stagecoach across the United States eight times, teaching dance in San Francisco; Chattanooga; Washington, DC; Chicago; Birmingham; Indianapolis; and Syracuse. Her upper-middle-class lifestyle started to wane, along with her family inheritance, and all the traditional jobs of schoolteacher, stenographer, and secretary were going to younger women. Finally, she settled in Bay City, which had been getting headlines as a place with jobs and money, thanks partly to the lumber industry. It was there she found her barrel and ambitions to go over a famous waterfall and hopefully make a mint, touring dime museums across the globe with stories of the first person, man or woman, to defeat Niagara. When she could find no work as an instructor in Bay City or realize her dream of marrying steel baron Andrew Carnegie, who announced he was retiring with a fortune of $300 million, she opened her own dance school and also taught lessons on how to charm. It worked for a short period as she managed a clientele of more than one hundred students; however, her steps were not as smooth in business, and she provided too-lavish accommodations for her students, eating into her profits. According to one historian, Annie became so financially desperate, she thought about hurling herself into the Saginaw River, but instead, in the summer of 1900 she moved to Sault Ste. Marie, Michigan, to teach music. More failed job searches in San Antonio and Mexico City brought her back to a small boardinghouse in Bay City in 1901, where she became depressed.

"For a woman who had money all her life and had been used to refined surroundings and the society of cultured people, it is horrible to be poor," wrote author David Whalen. Then Mrs. Taylor read an article in the *New York World* about the Pan-American Exposition in Buffalo, and how popular the nearby Niagara Falls was. "I laid the paper down, sat thinking, when the thought came to me like a flash of light—'Go over Niagara Falls in a barrel,'" she said. "No one had ever accomplished this feat." *No bloody kidding,* young Red thought. Any one of several demons could snatch your life at the falls, including the fifty-five-foot drop in wild rapids above the brink, with its uncompromising rocks, swift currents, and shallow reefs. And, of course, the lingering plunge at Horseshoe could induce a heart attack. If winds blew you off target, you could be smashed to matchsticks by murderous boulders hidden underwater Down There, or your barrel could get sucked behind the curtain of water at the base and you could suffocate, or the barrel could take on water and you could drown. In Bay City, Mrs. Taylor found opposition when she told people of her plans, but she was stubborn; in her apartment she got down on her hands and knees to make a large diagram of the barrel she wanted, then she called a local cooper, John Rozenski, to look at it and help her build the barrel. "*Mein Gott* [my God], woman!" he said. "You will be killed, and me to help; I cannot do such a thing!" However, she eventually talked him into it, then picked out the wooden staves for the barrel, oiled individually to shed water.

On the afternoon of October 12, Annie packed her bags and left Michigan for a three-hundred-mile trip to Niagara. On the way, she said, "I might as well be dead as to remain in my present [financial] condition." Over the next week, stories appeared in Niagara newspapers about her plans to go over the falls, leading authorities on both sides of the border to threaten her manager with a charge of manslaughter if she died. When the questions and the sauerkraut were all done at the Hotel Lafayette, Red Hill pedaled home on his bicycle, wobbling with excitement, to tell his father about what he had just seen with his own eyes, and show him what he had written down. His fifteen-year-old brother, Charlie, was more interested in model trains and the military than the falls.

On the eighteenth of October, Mrs. Taylor and her assistants launched her whisky barrel, containing only her kitten, Iagara (*Niagara* without an *n*), for a test spill over the Horseshoe fall. According to reports, it dropped down all the ledges and through the Horseshoe Rapids, reaching the brink of the falls and plunging downward feetfirst. It was one minute and a half from the brink when the barrel floated into view at the foot of the falls, then it passed down the river to an eddy and was picked up by the *Maid of the Mist* steamboat. When the lid was lifted, the cat sprang out with eight lives remaining, and the barrel received no major damage. Mrs. Taylor was delighted and said she would make the trip in the next few days, weather permitting.

She still had to worry about the coppers; for weeks, local police, given orders by Niagara coroner Dr. Hart Slocum, had talked about trying to stop Mrs. Taylor, but she warned through the newspapers: "If the authorities stop my attempt I will jump to my death over the falls . . ." Oh, well, Layfield and his son Red figured it would take a man to save her, in one way or another. At the turn of the century, men were supposed to be men and women women, a mind-set leading to the jailing in England of playwright Oscar Wilde for homosexuality. Over the next few days, Mrs. Taylor postponed her trip twice, blaming the rainy weather, until locals were sure she was just another fraud. During one of Mrs. Taylor's postponements, a rowboat towing her could not navigate strong winds that threatened to take it and the barrel past the Point of No Return. She tossed back some brandy during that aborted trip. (She was no Carrie Nation of the temperance movement, who was crusading across the United States against the evils of alcohol. Coincidentally, Mrs. Nation was giving lectures in Niagara Falls and spoke briefly with Mrs. Taylor.) Her postponements cast doubt on her credibility. "People will think I'm nothing but another faker," she said. "Now they'll laugh at me."

CHAPTER THREE
THE HORSESHOE FALL

Thursday afternoon, October 24, 1901, was cool and windswept, albeit pleasant enough for a day to meet your fate, and also the sixty-third birthday of one Annie Edson Taylor. Even if she didn't make it past this day, she had already exceeded the life expectancy of her era by a dozen years. Yes, journalists had discovered that Mrs. Taylor wasn't turning forty-three, as she had said, but was twenty years older. Oh, well, that meant she had one thing in common with many other women—she wasn't crazy about divulging her real age. Through her window that day, a slight breeze played on the few leaves still clinging to the autumn trees. Fearing she might get sick to her stomach during her adventure later in the day, she ate only a sparse breakfast at the Oxford House in Niagara Falls, New York—no birthday cake and no lunch. Down at the falls, tourist season was finished, and yet a crowd estimated at about two thousand—a sea of bowler hats—was on hand to watch the first challenge of the Horseshoe fall. First, man had tried to control the river with his hydroelectric diversions, and now this. Even the accomplished daredevils Nissen and Graham showed up for the madness.

In early afternoon, Mrs. Taylor met her manager, Russell, at Port Day, in Niagara Falls, New York, at the entrance to a hydraulic canal, where the barrel had been hidden on a sailboat overnight. It was a mere one mile from the brink of the falls, and a crowd of several hundred people assembled there, including reporters, river men, and two of her handlers, Fred Truesdale and his assistant, Billy Holleran, a smiling, round-raced youth—a handyman with a devil-may-care attitude. She had chosen them after talking with many locals on the American side of the river, an example of Mrs. Taylor dotting her i's and crossing her t's, although some people thought she might have been better served with Irish-Canadian river heroes McCloy and Conroy, favorites of Red's father. Another helper, Fred Robinson, had earlier chickened out when police warned him that anyone helping the daredevil would be charged with aiding and abetting a person with self-destruction if she broke her neck. "I don't want to get pinched . . . I wash my hands of the whole business," Robinson said. "I ain't going to be a party to the murder of any woman." The others called him lily-livered. The stage was set: Red Hill was at the brink of the falls with his father's field glasses, ready to rush down the Maid of the Mist incline once he saw the barrel plunge over the cataract. The woman of the hour appeared relatively calm as she got into a rowboat containing her barrel and manned by Truesdale and Holleran. There she was again—wearing that big fluffy hat and full-length black dress; in an hour or so she might look like she had been tarred and feathered. Before her boat was pushed off Port Day, she handed an envelope to a reporter, containing the address of her sister, Mrs. Jane M. Kendall, of Eddytown, New York. "In case of accident and I should not come back," Mrs. Taylor said, "would you kindly notify her?"

She then turned and said to several reporters, "I do not agree with Dante that who enters here leaves all hope behind. I know I'll survive, though it's possible I could suffer a horrible death within the next fifty minutes."

As people waved farewell, Mrs. Taylor stretched out her hand: "I won't say good-bye, it's just au revoir, you know. I will see you all again."

"We hope so," some in the crowd responded.

Just as the boat was leaving the basin toward the falls, a police officer ran to the edge of shore, blaspheming, waving a nightstick, and summoning them to come back. It was too late. The spectators at Port Day quickly dispersed to board trolleys and carriages for the Upper Steel Arch Bridge to the Canadian side and better viewing at the brink, or at the base of the falls. Then the boat was rowed to Grass Island, a small island on the American side, about one mile from the brink, for last-minute adjustments, where Mrs. Taylor was to get into the barrel for the launch of the new century. Four boats followed her, containing reporters and aides. On Grass Island, the barrel was kept in the water for some time, so that its wood might swell and make it tight and supposedly waterproof. As the moment approached, Mrs. Taylor seemed the coolest one in her entourage, focused and determined to go through with it, even though she was secretly terrified her barrel might elude rescuers at the base of the falls and shoot down the lower rapids to the Great Whirlpool, which she feared more than the falls because of Willard's horrible end.

As modest as the next woman, Mrs. Taylor then asked all the men to retire to another side of the island while she adjusted her clothes. With grasses and reeds forming a screen for her, she slipped off her hat, dress, and lacy cuffs to reappear in a blue-and-white blouse and skirt, her hair tied up in a bun. In this, and with a look of firm resolve, she finally squeezed into the barrel. She strapped herself in and was protected by two large cushions in the front and the back, from her shoulders down to above the knees. Connected to the walls and padded from breakage were a bottle of sherry wine, smelling salts, and a biscuit for a picnic in No Man's Land. After the manhole cover was applied, it took Holleran a full twenty minutes, using a bicycle pump, to fill the barrel with enough air to hopefully last at least an hour. A bicycle pump and a whisky barrel versus Niagara Falls? Next, the manhole fastener was screwed on, made from a heavy button of oak, twelve inches long and three inches both wide and thick, making it impossible for the barrel to be opened from the inside, which could be problematic if it got trapped behind the falls and Mrs. Taylor had to release herself. Inside the barrel, she placed a third cushion around her head and stuffed cotton into her ears to protect them from the compressed air. Meanwhile, restless photographers did their jobs and reporters' shorthand was tested; this could be some story.

From inside the barrel, snug as could be under the circumstances, Mrs. Taylor mumbled to her crew that she detected a faint shaft of sunlight. A small leak had developed in one of the seams in the barrel, presumably because it had been out of the water overnight and the wood had contracted. With caution and precision, Truesdale sealed it with caulking.

Finally, Mrs. Taylor announced, "I am all ready." It was 3:50 in the afternoon on the last day of Annie Taylor's life, or the greatest. From the tiny island, Truesdale and Holleran towed her whisky barrel far out into the Canadian current so that it would be assured of going over the Horseshoe fall and not the American fall, which, with its black boulders rising from the mist like fortifications of a witch's castle, could kill you twice over. A fairly strong wind from the south aided this goal by blowing toward the Canadian banks. Thankfully, the barrel remained upright in the water, with the heavy anvil doing its work, meaning that Mrs. Taylor was standing nicely in place, all strapped in; so far, so good. But then, just as in the aborted attempt of a few days prior, the boat started drifting too close to the falls, and the men decided it was time to cut her loose. Before that could happen, she gave a desperate rap from inside the barrel.

"What is it?" asked Truesdale.

"The barrel is leaking," she shouted.

"How much water is in it?"

"About a pail full."

"Well, that will not hurt you. You'll be over the falls and rescued in a few minutes and the water will help you to keep up. We're going to cast you off now. Good-bye!"

"Good-bye, boys," Mrs. Taylor said. Amazingly, incomprehensibly, she was going through with it. The other fears in her life apparently outweighed her fear of Niagara. All right, so women couldn't vote, own land, go into taverns, or work outside the home unless it was to serve others—but she'd be damned if they would stop her from going over Niagara Falls.

At five minutes past four, Truesdale knocked on the barrel with an oar, giving her "anchors aweigh," then let her loose. She was at the mercy of currents that had never spared a human life. For a few seconds longer, the rowboat continued toward the falls, faster than the barrel drifting beside and then behind it, until the men pulled strongly on the oars, and soon the boat was headed away from the falls and back to the American shore. "She's coming! She's coming!" shouted spectators on the Canadian banks closest to the departure.

At first, the barrel was a cradle rocking gently in manageable waters. Then as it proceeded toward the white line of breakers near the falls, the Point of No Return, it turned into a big cork, jumping up high walls of foam, disappearing briefly at times beneath the breakers; then, down the channel it scurried—ten, fifteen, twenty-five miles per hour into the Horseshoe Rapids, dancing and oftentimes bouncing reef over reef, caught in a flash flood of rapids and cascades nearly a mile long and on average forty feet deep. Spectators were everywhere—on Goat Island, Three Sisters Island, Terrapin Point—and teenager Red Hill at Table Rock on the Canadian brink; they had come by railroad or by ship through the Welland Canal, which bypassed the falls to connect Lakes Erie and Ontario. They stood two and three deep along parts of the riverbank, or watched from high in trees or buildings on either side of the river. Strangers became friends. Catholics crossed themselves. Red zoomed in on the barrel, ready to scurry down into the basin along his secret pathways as soon as it made the Plunge. He could not believe this was happening, and he pictured himself inside the vessel, shaking and breathing in fits and starts, trying to control himself for what was to come. The barrel was accelerating to thirty miles per hour, faster than any horseless carriage around these parts. At one point its heavy iron anvil briefly ground onto the shallow riverbed, but then the barrel made it to deeper water. Closing in, as anticipated, it was swept around a curve of green water heading toward the precipice. Inside her cramped quarters, it was dark, and Mrs. Taylor knew she was getting closer by the increasing roar of the falls, which at one time had sounded like applause but now like a big waterfall aimed on crushing her.

To spectators, just before the brink, three hundred feet out from the Canadian shore, the barrel seemed to rest on its side at a forty-five-degree angle. It was 4:23. For its grand finale, with all eyes taking their own pictures to remember, it stood at attention at the top of the world and gathered itself for a deep gasp. Over the centuries, many shapes and devices had made this divine fall—boats with stupid captains, uprooted trees from the Great Lakes, fractured docks from Cleveland cottages, wounded soldiers from 1812 to 1814, and, in some legends, maidens offered to the great Thunder God. But never in a month of Sundays had such a vessel been pointed deliberately and arrogantly at the cataract with a human inside. Although he was safely onshore, standing behind a man with a protruding belly, Red felt his stomach flutter and his fingers begin to tremble so that he had trouble focusing the binoculars. Long ago he had forgotten about putting pencil to paper about all of this; it was still in his pocket, along with the rabbit's foot his father had given him, many moons ago. For the last moment, as Mrs. Taylor tried to jump out of her old life into a new world, the barrel tipped slightly forward and slid into the long, long descent. *Good-bye, Madame—you'll need all your four languages to describe this.* True to her calculations, the anvil kept the barrel feetfirst, thank you, George Hillman. For a brief, anxious time, it could not be seen by spectators above or below the great cataract, and people fell worried and silent. Wrote the *Toronto Daily Star*: "People stood . . . with ashen faces, spellbound, watching the dark speck towards the center of the great horseshoe of water and with the awful exclamations of the people gathered mingled the roar of the tumbling water."

Down below, Carlisle Graham had his fingers crossed that he hadn't lost another female daredevil, that there was luck in the Horseshoe. Red was already on his way down the embankment when the barrel appeared directly below the falls in scum-covered water. "I see it—there it is!" he yelled. There it was, indeed, and in one piece! It was over too quickly for anyone to evaluate what had happened, or to appreciate the entire eighteen-minute journey. That was the disappointing part for Red. Was that all there was, three or four or five crummy seconds at the end? And yet, he found his heart pounding as never before. What must that have felt like? Was there blood in the barrel? Then the crazy craft was briefly sucked back behind the falls, but not for long, as it was spit out unceremoniously. By the time it worked its way clear of the white spray, into better view, crowds realized it was still in one piece, and they shouted, many tossing their hats into the air. Some people hugged. A boat and crew stood by, but the river had its way with the barrel for some time as it was swept downstream into Big Eddy, then a current carried it to another area called Black Bass Eddy, where it become stranded on rocks on the Canadian shore. "There it is!" people shouted. "Thar she blows!" Hill, Graham, and dozens of others scrambled over rocks and one another to get there. The *Maid of the Mist* boat, hovering just out of the falls' spitting range, saluted the occasion with several piercing blasts from its whistle. With Captain Richard Carter at the helm and many raincoated vacationists aboard at fifty cents apiece, the boat hoped to rescue the barrel, but it could not get close enough in the water's organized chaos. It was 4:40 when it was finally captured with pike poles and hooks by John Ross, an engineer, who pulled it close to shore. As Graham and other rescuers surrounded the barrel in knee-deep water, Red stayed back. He was only thirteen and not considered a real river man just yet, and he was supposed to be William in school. With Graham was his buddy Kid Brady, a noted featherweight boxer, and Harry Williams, proprietor of the Hotel Lafayette and a noted rescuer in his own right, who had won a Royal Canadian Humane Society medal for saving a clergyman and a woman from falling into the river. The valiant Brady stripped down to his swim trunks and grabbed onto the barrel as it passed through an eddy, and the crowd cheered as if it were at one of his Friday night matches. But no sound was coming from the cask, and the crowd went silent. Graham and Williams worked painstakingly to remove the lid, and when it was pried open, a feeble right hand, blue from the cold water, extended out of the manhole and waved.

"Good God, she's alive!" Graham exclaimed.

"Yes, she is," Taylor answered feebly from inside the barrel with what was left of her husky voice.

In a way, it was eating his own crow for Graham, who had previously belittled her in the papers and was quoted as saying, "Let her die in the barrel." He said a lot of things. Now he was overcome by the moment, the courage of a woman.

Graham shouted again, and soon the Niagara Gorge echoed over and over: "She's alive!" People could not believe it, and Red let go of his rabbit's foot to start clapping. A teacher had made a field trip, after all, and Red would have to alter his image of a hero. But Mrs. Taylor was weak and could not pull herself through the barrel's small opening, even with the muscle of the men outside, so it was enlarged with the use of a saw. Crowds up and down both sides of the border continued to cheer and applaud until it became an international event. The barrel was half filled with water and some blood. Finally, Mrs. Taylor emerged, soaked, groggy, and bleeding from wounds to the scalp and jaw. Her flesh was showing, never mind her knees and ankles through disheveled clothes, and Red had never seen the river do that to somebody still alive—the suicides were always so pale and bloated, they weren't real. The way she came out of the barrel, teetering and blabbering, not to mention staggering, some people thought she was blind drunk. "Have I gone over the falls yet?" she said. It took her some time to adjust to being on land. As she tried to stand on rocks, a delegation of helping hands emerged; suddenly, everyone wanted to touch Annie Edson Taylor. However, as she staggered, she was not in a mood to celebrate or to give lengthy interviews, although she did have the presence of mind to tell river men to please save her barrel. At various moments, she gasped or blurted out:

> If it was my dying breath, I would caution anyone against attempting the feat . . . I prayed every second, except for a few moments after the fall, when I was unconscious . . . I was whirled about like a top. I felt that all Nature was being annihilated. When I went over the fall, I fancy I lost my senses for a minute . . . I would not go over the fall again for a million dollars. I would sooner walk up to the mouth of a loaded cannon, knowing I was about to be blown to pieces, than make that trip again.

It certainly wasn't like the Loop-the-Loop at Coney Island, as she had imagined.

People started making their way home, believing anything was possible. Get that flying machine off the ground! Overcoats were thrown around Mrs. Taylor's shoulders, but the way to the shore was hazardous, and at one point she had to crawl on her hands and knees to a boat. Eventually, she was taken to the Maid of the Mist docks, put into a carriage, and driven to a boardinghouse in Niagara Falls, New York, where she was warmed with a blazing coal fire and hot water bottles while three doctors administered to her for shock and a three-inch cut in her scalp behind her right ear, as curiosity seekers who had followed her from the falls peered through the window. Her arms were black-and-blue, and she complained of pain between her shoulders, which the doctors attributed to her being knocked backward during the plunge. The physicians expected her to recover within a week.

Later, she gave a full account of her trip to reporters.

On her sendoff:

> "As I faced the inevitable, life or a horrible death in fifty minutes, my courage rose. Thus, as the rap came on the barrel, which told me I was cut loose and no human power could avail me, for I was started on a trip no traveler had ever taken. My heart swelled and for some moments I felt as though I were being suffocated, but I determined to be brave. By a supreme effort of will, I calmed myself at once and began earnestly to pray—if it was God's will to spare my life, if not to give me an easy death."

In the rapids above the falls:

> I could feel the barrel toss and often turning partly over, until I came to the first drop over a reef, when the bottom caught for a moment. The barrel swerved and for a moment I thought I would go head first, but with a jerk it loosened, turned foot down, and plunged to the bottom. I felt the water close over my head, but was not hurt. The barrel rose to the surface instantly, and pursued its course.

If it hadn't been for the straps for my arms, I know I would have been killed. I hung onto them tightly with my forearms bent and so managed to keep to the bottom of the barrel and avoid having my brains beaten out . . . but, oh, the water leaking in on me was so cold. It was terrible . . . I was tossed and pitched about most terrible in the rapids.

Again the barrel swerved to the left, and I knew instinctively that should it pursue its course it would be dashed to atoms on the giant rocks near the Canadian shore. But God was good. The barrel paused, raised slowly on its head, then turned over on a rock and pursued its course down to the brink of the Precipice. I tore the cushion from my head, placed it quickly under my knees, and dropped to the bottom of the barrel.

At the brink:

As I reached the brink, the barrel did what I predicted it would do, paused for a moment and then made the awful plunge of 158 feet to the boiling cauldron below. I thought for a moment my senses were lost. The feeling was one of absolute horror, but still I knew when I struck the water of the lower river. The shock was not so great, but I went down, down until the momentum had spent itself . . . I struck on some rocks, I believe, and was hurled about and knocked frightfully. I could tell when the descent began by feeling that something had given out from under me. Ugh! It's a terrible nightmare. I don't want to experience it again.

Below the falls:

Below the surface all was still. Not a sound reached me. Slowly I arose, but unfortunately on coming to the surface I came under the falling of water and was carried back of the sheet that tumbles over the precipice. It was then I began to suffer. The barrel was whirled like a dasher in a churn; lifted, I should think, four or five feet clear of the water and thrown violently about, at the same time turned around and around at the greatest velocity, struck on the rocks, and each moment water was forcing itself in at the point where the anvil at the bottom had been imperfectly put on. As the barrel turned around and around, the sensation was terrible . . . The barrel then shot out from the Cataract like an arrow from a bow, giving me a frightful lurch. After a short time, I felt the barrel being drawn up to a rock. It was none too soon, however, as my strength was spent. When I realized I had been rescued, my senses immediately left me . . . I became unconscious.

Mrs. Taylor added that she often closed her eyes during the trip and "prayed to God Almighty to protect me. I owe a debt of great gratitude to Him." Meanwhile, coroner Slocum came to scold her for making such an irresponsible trip, but she assured him that if she had not been permitted to do it, she would have jumped off one of the Niagara bridges or sought suicide in some other way. That night her barrel was taken back to the city, but not before souvenir poachers carried off the hatch and the harness straps; the saw that had cut off the top was black-marketed for five bucks. The press had a field day; telegraphs relayed the news across the globe, albeit some editors did not believe it at first, and the New York papers went to deadline with only part of the story, choosing other headlines about the Boer War, new president Teddy Roosevelt entertaining at the White House, and Scottish immigrant Alexander Winton in his automobile roaring around a ten-mile motor track in Detroit in an unbelievable eleven minutes.

Eventually, though, Annie got her due:

"The Climax of Niagara Wonders," proclaimed the *Buffalo Courier-Express*.

Penned Vince H. Hickox, columnist for the *Niagara (New York) Gazette*: "It will go down in the history of Niagara Falls as the most wonderful undertaking on record. What makes it all the more wonderful is that a woman should be the first person to perform this great feat."

The *New York Times*: "It was beyond any conception but her own that she would live to tell the story, but she is alive to-night, and the doctors say as soon as she gets over the shock, she will be all right." The *Times* added, "Everybody was agreed that it was a foolhardy trip . . . [but] she has impressed everybody . . . with her wonderful nerve."

Some of the coverage revealed the sensationalism and even macabre sensibility of some newspapers. The *Welland (Ontario) Tribune*: "This has been a year of wonderful things at Niagara Falls and on the Niagara Frontier. A great world exposition has been opened and carried on for six months, a president of the United States has been assassinated; the Whirlpool Rapids have been navigated, but now comes the event, which in many respects overshadows all—for the first time in history, a human being has passed over the great cataract and lived to tell the tale. The feat is all the more remarkable from the fact of its having been performed by a woman."

Mrs. Taylor couldn't have received more attention had she been a suffragette chained to the Empire State Building. She basked in it triumphantly, looking forward to once again enjoying the finer amenities of life that her fame was sure to bring, especially a ranch in the West with a bathtub. "I have given freely to charity all my life, and now the world will do something for me," she told journalists. And yet, in the next breath, she added, "The greater part of my life that remains to me will be devoted to doing good for others, for a woman, be she a true woman, can bless and glorify the lowest grade of humanity."

If police had been vigilant about the barrel trip, elected officials and tourism operators on both sides of the border were not. Mayor Mighells B. Butler of Niagara Falls, New York, gave Mrs. Taylor a letter of reference:

> *To Whom it may Concern:*
> *This is to certify that on October 24, 1901, Mrs. Annie Edson*
> *Taylor went over the Horseshoe Falls at Niagara Falls in a barrel*
> *and survived.*
>   *Mighells B. Butler, Mayor.*

For the next few nights at Kick's Tavern, river rats and journalists ate crow and downed a few ales for Annie. She was not there. Women, of course, were not allowed in saloons. At home, Red told his father everything until they were both sick of it. His writing pad was damp and blank, but his mind and imagination were not. Within two months of her feat, the widow Taylor said she had 162 proposals of marriage from men all over the country. "They wired. They wrote letters. They telegraphed. They stood out in the rain," she said. "They sleuthed me around in buggies and followed me to church telling me how much they owned, and what a queen I was." One persistent lawyer from Knoxville,

Tennessee, said he would get a divorce from his wife and leave his children if Annie would marry him, she said. Then there was a man worth $100,000 who asked her to marry him. "Some inquisitive woman asked me if I ever would have gone over the falls in a barrel if I had had a husband," she said. "I told her, 'No, I probably wouldn't have . . . I probably would have gone over *without* a barrel.'" Mrs. Taylor married none of them. "I have battled with life alone for many years and now I am in a better position than ever to care for my own needs."

And yet, she quoted a segment of the book *Parted by Fate: A Novel*, by Laura Jean Libbey, which seemed to somewhat contradict that:

> If love is a crime—a sinful passion,
> Why, then, should a God so good and so wise
> Have molded our hearts in such wondrous fashion—
> That nothing but love e'er satisfies?

CHAPTER FOUR
EARLY DAYS

I was born upon thy bank, river,
My blood flows in thy stream,
And thou meanderest forever
At the bottom of my dream.

—Henry David Thoreau, 1817–1862

The first Hills to take a big chance were Mike, a farmer, and his wife, Elizabeth, who sailed from Yorkshire, England, to the Canadian colony of Niagara in 1851 and established a home at Ussher's Creek in Chippawa, where Red Hill Jr. launched *The Thing* one hundred years later. The Hills were Anglican and staunch political Conservatives. They grew to love their Canada and the bordering United States, but remained loyal to Britain through the Orange Order, a Protestant fraternal society formed in Ireland to commemorate the 1690 victory of King William III of England, a Protestant also known as King Billy, at the Battle of the Boyne over the forces of James II, a Catholic. In Niagara Falls, the Hills became members of the Orange Lodge, and they were thrilled to discover that Canada's first prime minister, John A. MacDonald, was an Orangeman. Indeed, the Orange became a force in Canadian politics. The aims of the Order included the unity of the British Commonwealth, maintenance and upholding of the Protestant faith, and practicing benevolence among all men—and that meant trying to stifle any tension there might be with Catholics. Religion and structure were solid foundations of everyday life. In 1856, Mike and Elizabeth Hill had a son, Layfield, taken from his mother's maiden name. As a lad, Lafe was small, quiet, and fond of gardening, hunting, and fishing. The Niagara Peninsula in Ontario and the Niagara Frontier in western New York were a boon for outdoorsmen, with game-filled woods, fertile soil, a moderate climate, and waterways teeming with a generous assortment of bass, pike, and rainbow trout. As he grew into a man, Layfield honored God and country, becoming a charter member of Local 13 of Noble 998 Lodge. In a ceremony at the King Edward Hotel in downtown Niagara Falls, Layfield pledged to keep loyalty to the Crown and the British flag and to uphold the motto "Fear God, honor the Queen, love the brotherhood, and maintain the law." That oath was tested on May 24, 1870, when, as a pimply teenager and a volunteer member of the local militia—the Lincoln and Welland Regiment—Layfield was called out of his warm covers in the middle of the night to shed blood. A warring Irish American group, the Fenians, was planning a takeover of Canada, and they invaded Ontario. But Hill and his fellow militiamen pushed them back across the Niagara River to the United States with bayonets and musket fire. "Here we were from England, fighting the Irish," Layfield would laugh. As a reward for his service, he received a silver medal from the Canadian government and a free block of property in northern Ontario. If the Hills had developed that land and moved north, this book might have been about lake men.

Shortly after the Fenian kerfuffle, Layfield married Mary Ann Neal, who had come to Canada in 1873 at age eight and remained a proud Brit, her London accent eventually mellowing, if not her sarcasm. They attended Holy Trinity Church, whose worshippers included singer Jenny Lind, War of 1812 heroine Laura Secord, and Edward, Prince of Wales. Established in 1820, it was one of North America's oldest churches, and had been burned by rebel William Lyon Mackenzie in 1839. Then the Hills moved their worshipping to All Saints, also steeped in tradition. Mary Ann was an official with the local Orange Lodge. Her favorite day of the year was July 12, Orangeman's Day, the anniversary of King Billy's glorious triumph. In the annual parade up Victoria Avenue, she would march up and down the street behind a policeman riding a white horse, her big bosom dripping with medals, her sarcasm directed at the rival St. Patrick's Roman Catholic Church (especially when Catholics showed up at the

Orange parade to toss cabbages and tomatoes at the Protestants). Mary Ann was a bespectacled, stay-at-home mum who loved teatime and treating her family and friends to jam tarts and phonograph music. She also worked as a nurse and helped out in a flu epidemic in Niagara Falls at the turn of the century. Her husband, Layfield, was a working-class bloke, a full-time gardener with the Queen Victoria Park Commission, tending to the lovely grounds around the falls. Like his father, Mike, Lafe was content with growing things. He purchased his own house, and yet he had a weakness for the Niagara River and its famous waterfall. He couldn't put his finger on what he liked about it, but he knew it was an unusual place, attracting people from thousands of miles away.

On October 27, 1887, Mary Ann gave birth to William Thomas Hill, her third son, in their home at 144 Stanley Avenue. At first, no one noticed his fiery red hair. The parents and his two young brothers were distracted by something else covering the crying baby's head—a membrane, or type of veil. A midwife told everyone not to panic, that it was a caul, an inner fetal membrane sought by sea captains to protect them on long voyages. Some people believed it blessed its owner with second sight, or a charmed life. For a while, Red's gift from heaven was kept in a bottle. To the children, this caul seemed like a prank by adults four days before Halloween, but they dared not say anything. Children were at the mercy of their parents; everything adults did, even if oftentimes cruel, was the law in 1887. And so the children played along—in true British fashion, they were to be seen and not heard. But when a baby like William Thomas Hill was born with a caul and within the roar of the great falls at Niagara, who knew what the future held? Layfield, not a man prone to superstition, didn't know quite what to think. As William sprouted into a skinny kid, he took him down to the river, along with his older happy-go-lucky brother, Charlie, teaching them about the strengths, weaknesses, and joys of the river and, especially, about the incredible Horseshoe fall and the American fall. When they each reached five, he tossed them, fully clothed, into the turbulent waters below the falls and instructed them in the sink-or-swim method; on one occasion, Layfield swam out into the maelstrom with William on his back. Although in some ways they were traditional, the Hill men were occasionally prone to such impulsive acts, particularly when they were away from the women, or sometimes to impress the gals.

William had two brothers and five sisters, but three of those siblings died young. Even before he set foot in a school to become educated about life, he had seen death up close—the body of a suicide victim, a Boston woman who had carefully paid all the family debts and quietly taken the train to give her cancer to the great falls. And William had been there when his brother Michael died before his fourth birthday. Grandmother Elizabeth died when William was four, and then his little sister Edith perished before her third birthday. Of the eight children born to Layfield and Mary Ann, three would die young, two from black diphtheria. Onion poultices were applied to the children's skins as often as shirts and trousers. Young William often sought refuge from this pain and suffering by going down to the Horseshoe fall—always full of life, of fish, fowl, and adventure, of torrents of water that kept coming and coming, never ending, always there as a trusted teacher and friend.

William was said by some relatives to grow up with a type of clairvoyance; although they had neglected to keep his magical caul in a glass bottle for long, its legacy was reportedly at work when he was seven. William awoke one night at three o'clock from a dream that reportedly told him that a family property several miles away was in flames. Ma and Pa pacified the boy and tucked him back in bed, away from the monsters of the night, but when dawn came, they found that the house had indeed burned to the ground. Red couldn't explain his occasional gift, except to say that when it happened, he felt something in the wind. The next event occurred in their house on October 24, 1896. The restless boy could not sleep, when suddenly, a fire broke out and Mary Ann shouted for everyone to clear out of the house. The small but quick William dashed out first, but when his four-year-old sister Cora was nowhere to be seen, he scrambled barefoot back inside. Through smoke and heat, he quickly got through the parlor and past the picture of King Billy, but had trouble negotiating the smoke in the back bedroom, where he found Cora crying in the thick blackness. She was coughing and choking, and he picked her up in his skinny arms, tightly wrapped her in bedclothes, and whisked her out, stumbling but not falling. Firefighters who had just arrived looked on in amazement, hardly believing that a child—a kid who was afraid of cough syrup and going to the dentist—had done it on impulse to win the night. A few weeks later, a Royal Canadian Humane Society medal for bravery hung high on William's shirt. The next day, Ma got her own Orange Lodge medals out of a padded box and let William play with them, although she told him not to take his medal to school. To her, he was a hero. It was the beginning of a glorious—and sometimes painful—career for William Red Hill.

In everyday life, his parents were relatively strict and supported William's teachers when they sold the idea that the turn of the century was a new age of education and civilization, an age of study. But at Buchanan Street School, and to the dismay of his parents and the vice principal, the strong-willed lad with protruding ears and red hair parted straight down the middle actually kept his own strict educational schedule from eight thirty in the morning to four in the afternoon—down at the banks of the falls. He became intrigued by the individual currents and mannerisms of the entire river, from the calm waters of Lake Erie to the Horseshoe Rapids above the falls to the Great Whirlpool and out to Lake Ontario, and its moods seemed to fit his occasional desire for drama. Every day, twice a day, he tossed bits of driftwood into the water and charted their course over the falls and through the Whirlpool Rapids. One day, when his parents started to scold him, he pulled a dead mallard from behind his back and plunked it onto the supper table. Red's three *R*s were readin', 'ritin', and river. Anyway, few young men graduated high school in 1900; rather, they went to work in factories.

His siblings did not share his love for the river. Older brother Charlie went down to the falls once in a while, but what gave Charlie more of a kick were trains that chugged through the city and brought sightseers from Chicago, New York, and Montreal. A relative once handcrafted a rocking chair and a horse for William, but he rarely bothered with them. Those were for ordinary children.

CHAPTER FIVE
FIRST RIVALRY

If the Horseshoe fall was the teeth of the Niagara River, the Great Whirlpool beneath it was its hungry throat, and just as carnivorous. Anything tumbling over the cataract had to eventually deal with the Whirlpool, a slippery mile downriver, if it hoped to escape out to Lake Ontario in the enormous Great Lakes organism. Around and around in a sorcerer's recipe of green pea soup drifted boats, bodies, logs, and a spinster's mattress from the beach, and then down, down, and all the way down—at their unluckiest 125 feet to the bottom-most center of the vortex, its spiraling, counterclockwise eye of the storm. By 1910, the Whirlpool had been a boiling cauldron for more than four thousand years since being formed by the retreat upstream of the falls, a freak of nature in a river teeming with freakish things. Four stuntmen and -women died while daring to swim or barrel the rapids between the falls and the Great Whirlpool, not to mention many mishaps, such as the deaths of two young boys when their boat capsized near a dock. In 1901, Miss Martha Wagenfurher got so dazed, twirling in her barrel until after nightfall, that when they rescued her with searchlights and opened the hatch, she fainted cold. The fast Whirlpool Rapids leading into the Whirlpool had magnetism of its own, even to the pathological; in 1900, Miss Gertrude Roth of Allentown, Pennsylvania, killed herself moments after commenting to a tourist that "it was wonderful more people did not commit suicide at the Falls, because the rapids were so fascinating."

By 1910, the rapids and whirlpool were having a chill on stunt making at Niagara. When the dust had settled from Annie Taylor's unprecedented feat over the falls in a barrel in 1901, it became clear that the age of daredevils had struck a big boulder and stopped dead. From 1902 to 1910, no one dared enter the turbulent Niagara River. One would think Mrs. Taylor's heroics would inspire others, but actually the earlier stunt of another woman—Miss Maud Willard—helped douse that enthusiasm. Mrs. Taylor had not talked about it much before her brave falls endeavor, but she had been petrified of her barrel eluding rescuers at the base of the falls and drifting downstream into the rapids and being deposited in the Whirlpool, where Miss Willard had died just a few weeks earlier in what was supposedly a safe barrel. After 1901, only one stunt was attempted for nine years; Swedish sailor Klaus Larsen, living in Cleveland, beat the Whirlpool Rapids in a specially constructed eighteen-foot, eight-horsepower motorboat, *The Ferro*. In contrast, in the year prior to Maud's death, there had been five stunts in the lower river. Annie went through with her stunt only because she was desperate and apparently ready to kill herself anyway, and so her feat was looked upon by many as a one-shot deal. Meanwhile, accidents continued along the river; in 1903, the body of all-star baseball player Big Ed Delehanty of the Philadelphia Phillies, who thrice hit for more than a .400 batting average in the major leagues, was found below the falls, his leg chewed by something with teeth, likely the propeller of the *Maid of the Mist*. He had been inebriated and ejected from a train by the conductor upriver in Fort Erie and presumably fell off a bridge and was swept far down the river and over the falls.

The area immediately around the Whirlpool was said to be snakebitten, even haunted. Local residents occasionally reported screams coming from Devil's Hole in the gorge, just downriver from the Whirlpool, where eighty-one British soldiers were slaughtered in an ambush by four hundred Seneca warriors in the Massacre of 1763. Many of their bodies ended up in the rapids, which turned red. Twenty-two-year-old William Red Hill didn't believe in ghosts. The adventures of Mrs. Taylor and Miss Willard inspired him, more than anything, but they also kept him respectful of the river as he grew into a young bloke with the nine lives of the curious. For a trip over the falls, it would just take the true barrel, and he wanted to ponder it. Initially, he wasn't sold on the wooden drums of the two women. Another issue was Red's new rival, Mr. Bobby Leach, originally of England and more recently of Watertown, New York. Leach was not a river man in the usual sense; for one thing, he had a foreign accent, and his joy was parachuting out of hot-air balloons and off bridges; he claimed fifteen hundred balloon ascensions. Little was known about Leach's background or upbringing or why he constantly put his life on the line, except that it was reported he was at one time a professional stuntman. By the late 1800s, he had become enough of a local personage that the Niagara Falls (Ontario) *Daily Record* described him in one of its editions:

> [P]hilosopher, pool shark, partial to perils by land and sea, pilot of peculiar craft in the air and in the water, professor of aeronautics, author, frankfurter merchant, a dozen times hero, capitalist and restaurateur. He has produced proof that he is all this and some more. All of his American friends back up his claim that he is Niagara's hero.

Niagara's hero? In 1888 and 1889, Leach had barreled through the treacherous lower rapids and talked of going over the Horseshoe fall in a barrel with his Saint Bernard dog, Gomez. In 1907, in none other than Madison Square Garden in New York, Leach dove 154 feet (nearly the height of the falls) into a five-foot tank of water—after Captain Paul Donaldson had perished in the same trick just a few minutes earlier. In 1908, Leach parachuted 208 feet off the Upper Steel Arch Bridge, which connected the twin cities. But at first glance, if you saw him sitting with his feet up in Kick's Tavern, the diminutive, sprightly forty-eight-year-old Leach did not resemble the aforementioned portrait in the newspaper clipping; the only color seemed to come from his bow tie, diamond-studded tie clip, bowler hat, and smoky cigar. Posing with one of his barrels, sometimes with crossed elastic bands keeping the cuffs on his white shirt in place and showing only the start of a smile, he offered the expression of a banker, and yet his trousers were sometimes striped. His face didn't give away much; if men, as well as women, could be frumpy, he was. However, when suddenly surrounded by two dozen pairs of ears and a table littered with draught mugs, a giant came out of Bobby Leach, and you could plainly see how he had at one time paraded his talents for the Barnum & Bailey Circus. The giant bellowed about the little man, and he referred to himself as "Perfesser" Leach, albeit he never produced academic credentials. And now, he told the patrons at Kick's while tossing back one lathered mug after another, "I'm going over the falls in a special boat." Apparently, this was part of Leach's master plan to win something he called the "Triple Challenge" of three separate feats—going through the lower rapids, parachuting off the steel bridge, and plunging over the falls (he had already attained the first two).

First, a little trumpet music. It was believed that Leach was born in Lancashire, England, in 1862 (not Cornwall, England, as widely reported) and had four sisters. As a youngster, he developed into a swimmer of merit by working in bathing establishments to the point that he immigrated to Canada in 1887 at age fifteen as a trick swimmer. After that, he returned to England to live in Bolton, but in 1900 returned to the New World on the passenger ship *Umbria*, arriving at Ellis Island from Liverpool at thirty-eight. He became a pool hall manager in Watertown and then a lunch wagon owner in Plainfield, New Jersey, before moving to Niagara Falls, Ontario, in about 1908, where he and his wife, Sarah, had a daughter, Viola Pearl, and opened a restaurant a stone's throw from the Whirlpool Rapids. From the beginning, Red Hill was skeptical of "Perfesser" Leach, but didn't say as much; he was modest about his rescues and body recoveries at the falls. In his photographs, Hill was deadpan, with just enough of a smile. He didn't like to be out of control. According to a pamphlet later written about Hill: "He is not the frothy, mouthy, erratic type, who came to Niagara to belittle the power of the river torrent . . . He has a home and a family, and he loves them both." In fact, the newspapers were brimming with news about the river in 1910, and Niagara was becoming more famous around the world than ever before, drawing crowds many times the local population. Red authorized his headlines to talk for him. His father, Layfield, was not a public windbag, either; however, behind closed doors, Red did enjoy flapping his gums with family and buddies, especially those from the local militia group, the Lincoln and Welland Regiment, Second Dragoons Cavalry, which included his pal Ed "Mousie" Sloggett and cousin Charles "Sheep" Hill (nicknames were aplenty). Sheep was somewhat of a recluse who lived in a cave on the side of the gorge, whereas Mousie was articulate—one of the few young bucks to finish high school—yet deep down they were all river men, river rats. Sometimes on horseback, they stopped at Kick's for a pint or two before heading on to Niagara-on-the-Lake for militia training exercises. "Are the old nags tied up outside today?" Leach would say, widening his dull gray eyes, then Hill would come back with something like "Careful, you meet the same people on the way up as you do on the way down." That maxim became a standing joke between the two men bent on falling down Horseshoe.

One of Leach's pastimes was to light a fire under Hill: "I'll beat you and anybody else over the falls. And I can beat you down the rapids in a barrel." When he talked like that, Leach would smoke his cigar like he was chewing on somebody's neck. Until 1909, there had been a third serious contender at the Horseshoe fall, but Carlisle Graham, the first man to dream of going over the falls, had died from the effects, of all things, of a common cold. It was a sad but brilliant example to the river rats that you could croak from practically anything, so ladies, don't go lecturing them about risking their lives when you couldn't save them at home. In 1910, Leach announced he intended to go over Horseshoe in a big boat—twenty-five feet long, shaped like a submarine or one of his Havanas, and reportedly able to withstand a tumble into deep, rough water. Built from wood and steel, it was entirely enclosed and copper covered, with a porthole and two sliding hatches for entry and exit. It had wooden staves, surrounded by hoops and strengthened by stout ribs. A boat tempting the rapids was one thing, but the Big Splash? It would certainly be one-upmanship over Mrs. Taylor's whisky barrel, and then some. The unique vessel had a name, the *Mitchell Lifeboat*, after its inventor, James Mitchell of Arrow River, Manitoba. Mitchell got the idea while reading a newspaper account of a sailor found frozen to death, tied to the mast of a ship that had grounded on the English coast. Besides a lifeboat, barrels such as Mrs. Taylor's could be brilliantly stored on ships in case of trouble, Mitchell said. "I arrived at the conclusion that if a man had a barrel [on the boat], he could have easily escaped. If planks would wash to shore, why would a barrel not do the same?" In early 1910, a prototype of the boat was built in England, soon to be shipped to Niagara so that Leach could test it and become the first man over the cataract in what he termed the Dip of Death.

Hill was not fazed; with the chase to the falls usually carried out on page one, he intimated to reporters that he would take the plunge in a giant rubber ball in the summer of 1911 "if sufficient inducement is offered." Daredevils were always looking for sponsors, hard to find because of the potential liability in case of death. But a rubber ball? That got the boys at Kick's chortling, but Hill wouldn't back down and started saying things unlike him: "I'll beat him to [the falls] yet . . . the only way they could get Bobby to go over in a barrel would be to chloroform him first." Ouch. Since he was old enough to walk, Red had spent day after day down at the river, swimming, hunting, fishing, and studying its behaviors, but it didn't totally consume him; he also acquired somewhat of a social life in the community, becoming the manager of a roller-skating rink and planning on finding a wife to have children. Societal changes at the turn of the century were so frequent, one had to pay attention to keep pace. In 1903, the Wright brothers had sparked a call to arms for all daredevils by making the world's first flight in a heavier-than-air machine—it got off the ground!—and now anything was possible. In many ways, things seemed to be moving indoors, even on the road, where in horseless carriages you were surrounded by doors and wheels and windows and soft seats; they were called automobiles. Other things, however, were coming out into the open. By 1910, people did not have to cover up their knees or their legs while playing the piano, unless they felt the urge, and it became morally acceptable to leave the wooden legs of a piano uncovered in the middle of a parlor.

Teenager Beatrice Victoria Clark was not so sure about all these changes. Named after British royalty Queen Victoria and Princess Beatrice, she liked to tinkle the piano and sing in her mother's home, but she kept the legs covered whenever company came; she didn't want it said that another tradition was out the window. She tried other things to express herself, dabbling in softball with the lads and smoking one cigarette after a game, but she knew her place as an attractive brunette, a devout Anglican chambermaid who scrubbed bathrooms and carpets at city hotels. Bea's father died young, and her mother was sickly; they owned a bakery and had five other children, two boys and three girls. To her, a woman going over Niagara in a whisky barrel nine years hence had not been a groundbreaking feat, but something in a circus program. During this time, most of the fairer set were still not allowed to vote or go to Kick's (the reasoning: drunken men were more likely for fisticuffs with the gals around). Up to six nights a week, Beatrice took the streetcar to the Olympia Rollerdrome on Ferry Street, a captivating place of music and dancing on skates and fine-looking lads, where she could let her imagination run away on wheels. One particular young man caught her eye; she liked his long, confident strides and sometimes risky turns and maneuvers, but he did not cut corners, and made sure that he finished each step. Quite sure of himself, he flowed well with the music, she thought. In fact, there *was* a kind of music about Red Hill, even though he was diminutive of stature and often didn't have time to change his shirt, which was frequently splattered with red and blue from his day job painting barns and bridges. Besides being a painter, Red had an additional job that bordered on bizarre—he fished floaters (bloated bodies of suicides and accidents that rise to the surface) out of the Niagara River at five bucks a stiff. Beatrice didn't have to take anyone's word for it—it was in all the newspapers about River Man. He was active in the community, too, as a volunteer firefighter and an athlete; he and his brother Charlie once challenged Indian runner Tom Longboat (*the* Tom Longboat) in a marathon race; they lost, of course, but received local recognition for even trying against the world champion, who had won the Boston Marathon.

Soon after he met Bea Clark, Red dropped some of his handyman jobs and became the twenty-three-year-old manager of the Rollerdrome. He moved out of his parents' house to live in an apartment with construction worker Ed Sloggett, a small man with big ears, four years older than Red, who was dating Red's sister Cora, a plumpish, loveable woman. Unemployment was relatively low, less than 6 percent, and the average annual household income was about $750. Pretty soon, Beatrice and Red were getting along romantically, and they liked roller dancing to "While Strolling through the Park One Day." There was only one thing out of place—she sometimes wore a red dress, and he thought that color branded a woman as a prostitute; most of the time, though, she wore brown clothes of the day and rimless glasses. Bea and Red enjoyed the waltz the most, whether it was roller-skating or dancing at one of the local clubs, one-two-three, one-two-three; they got so good at it, others stopped and watched, and soon they were teaching it in their spare time (Red could be competitive, but he also liked to pass his skills along to others). Beatrice was small of bosom and wiry—a strong, healthy skater who glided across the glossy floor. To them, skating was ten times better than walking or dancing. Everybody walked or danced. You could let yourself go, lose most of your inhibitions, at the Rollerdrome. One night, Beatrice even allowed her hair out of its bun, and Red admitted some personal stuff that Leach and his rivals would love to know; for example, he was scared stiff of the dentist. If Beatrice was in love with William Hill, however, she did not show it. If she loved a lot and laughed a lot, it was mostly inside.

Whenever Red talked of doing the Big Splash, Beatrice reminded him even a woman could do it. However, nine years after her splash heard around the world, Mrs. Taylor had not earned the money she had so desperately sought during her vaudeville-type tour around the United States, lecturing about her feat and signing her John Hancock on postcards and shirts (she talked of going over the falls again in 1906, but nothing came of it). Her personality didn't have the power to bring her accomplishment back to life, and now the self-anointed Queen of the Mist seemed headed for the poorhouse, as her dreams of socialite friends and a Western ranch faded. She was not exactly the kind of hero the public wanted to hear about. Worse, acidic rumors were circulating that the widow was operating a whorehouse in Niagara Falls, New York, arranging for painted girls to travel by carriage to a train depot for potential customers interested in more than the sights.

In 1910, both Hill and Leach grudgingly admitted that their falls barrels were not quite up to snuff, so they agreed to settle things for now in the daunting Whirlpool Rapids. However, they were disappointingly not invited to enter in September of that year a boat race through the rapids, sponsored by the Niagara International Carnival Committee with a whopping $1,300 as first prize. While police and authorities discouraged such races and stunts, they were silenced by city officials and tourism operators on both sides of the border, who were looking for the international publicity that daredevil acts had brought to the twin cities before the quiet period of 1902 to 1910. The seven-mile course for the John A. Penton Cup was to start at the Maid of the Mist docks, through the Great Whirlpool, and on to the villages of Queenston, Ontario, and Lewiston, New York, near Lake Ontario. The committee was so fearful of accidents in the rapids and especially the Whirlpool, they would not allow boats with open cockpits in the race. Unfortunately, the only boater to show up was Captain Larsen, in *The Ferro*, and so the rule was changed. From a distance, *The Ferro* looked like a smart whaleboat with an open cockpit, and Larsen claimed he would stand up during the entire trip, with his head and shoulders protruding, giving him a better chance to control the boat (so much for the rules). Hungry for action, a crowd estimated at forty thousand showed up for the race. Smoking a cigar, and with *The Ferro*'s flag flapping in the wind, Larsen triumphantly rode his boat through the rapids and, unbelievably, the side of the Whirlpool, then he went through the Devil's Hole Rapids all the way to Queenston. The admirable stunt garnered attention across the globe. "That the daredevil navigator should live to tell the tale astounds everybody who has seen the maddening swirl of waters through which he passed," said a story in the *Wairarapa Daily Times* in New Zealand. "At one place, the terrific force of the current lifted [the boat] clear of the water and it took a flying leap of twenty feet and then skidded after the fashion of a flat stone. The spectators had a continuous thrill from start to finish." However, just before Queenston, *The Ferro* got swamped with water, and the captain had to unceremoniously ditch his cigar and bail out. Red Hill was waiting for him—he waded into the water and tossed Larsen a rope. Because the event was universally acclaimed, Leach took this personally, as he was supposed to be Niagara's hero. Red did not. He enjoyed being a rescuer as much as, if not more than, the one who would be saved.

Not long after, on the afternoon of September 24, 1910, as early autumn rain donated sprinkles to the river, Bobby Leach made a daredevil out of Red Hill. The Englishman didn't need a boat to snatch the headlines away from Hill; he simply got his old steel barrel out of a garage to challenge the Whirlpool Rapids as a tune-up for going over the falls, upgrading it with an anchor as ballast so the barrel would maintain a steady path through the rapids. Of no surprise, Hill dismissed the barrel as inadequate. What else could it be used for, a septic tank? "I'm confident of success," Leach said. "I've been through those boiling waters before and I know I can do it twice again. I hope to make the trip so successfully that I will be able to repeat the performance [the following day] at three o'clock. Watch me go through and see if I'm not game. Bobby Leach has nerve, all right." He also relished competition; in 1898, Leach had developed a friendly rivalry in his rapids barreling with the St. Regis Mohawk Indians, who canoed down the Devil's Hole Rapids each Sunday, from the Whirlpool to Lewiston, offering to take passengers on the ride of their lives for a fee. They had few takers, although the rapids were considered by many not quite as fierce as the more southerly rapids closer to the falls, which ran headfirst into the Whirlpool. For the barrel ride, Leach hired several men to help him, including Hill, believe it or not; his mind-set obviously was to keep his friends close and his enemies even closer, especially if they had their doctorate in the river. In fact, there became a sort of fraternity among river men; so many outsiders laughed at their lifestyle, they might as well be bedfellows. Wearing a business suit and bow tie, Leach climbed into the barrel below the falls, laughing nervously as aides strapped him into a canvas hammock to prevent him from cracking his noggin against the vessel's walls.

Indeed, the Niagara rapids, one of the world's most dangerous white waters, one and a half miles of disagreeable foam, had been the graveyard for many, but Leach couldn't allow Larsen, Hill, or anybody else to steal his thunder. The initial part of the trip from the Maid of the Mist docks was tedious, albeit anxious, but soon the red barrel picked up pace under the Michigan Central Railroad Bridge, which spanned the two countries, in a current known as Swift Drift. Eventually, it passed under the Lower Bridge, then with increasing acceleration plowed along the rapids and through the gorge, which was dense along the banks with trees and studded with craggy underwater rocks. The barrel was traveling so fast at twenty-five miles per hour, it was difficult for automobiles on the Canadian shore to keep up with him; J. K. Dunham, a hotel owner in Niagara Falls, New York, wrecked his auto and was later fined fifty dollars and costs by a magistrate for speeding. As his barrel tossed and turned, the sprightly leprechaun Leach was giddy, a child again. Onshore, his wife held their four-year-old daughter away from the peril and withheld her breath whenever the barrel vanished under waves. As the river's teeth bit into Leach, its haystack waves hurled the speeding steel projectile into the air. At one juncture, it came down on rocks, and its anchor was knocked off, adding more unpredictability to the wild ride. Halfway home, Leach encountered a series of high, choppy waves known as the Himalayas, featuring for its peak a huge white-topped flood that flipped the barrel twenty feet into the air, then crashed it underwater for a good five seconds.

Hill and Mousie were eagerly waiting and watching with hundreds of others on the banks of the Niagara Glen near Driftwood Point, where flotsam was wont to hide. Though he watched Leach with a certain amount of envy, Hill had seen such adventures before and was not astonished by the arrogant attitude of the rapids, which were pale with excitement and sometimes fury. Out in the water, nature's energy surrounded Leach, who was caught in the middle of a storm on high seas. Bobby Leach helpless! The barrel disappeared underwater again, then was spit out by The Great Wave, the watery red carpet to the Whirlpool. Suddenly, the barrel's four-minute, one-and-a-half-mile journey ended when it entered the Whirlpool in the glen, a huge semicircular part of the gorge, seventeen hundred feet long by twelve hundred wide, where the river paused before making a hairpin right turn toward the lake, trying to gain some control of the geography, but succeeding only in spinning itself and everything in its grip quite dizzy. For viewing purposes for several thousand people, being in the glen felt as though you were at the U-shaped Harvard Stadium for college football or the Coliseum in Rome; there were no lions or gladiators romping out of a tunnel, just a man-eating river, gushing and roaring with arrogance, smashing and crashing into itself, a loud, lonely voice looking for company. If so many people were not sitting and kneeling in its nooks and crannies, the setting would have seemed like a lost world of primordial trees and unique fauna that smelled like a rich man's greenhouse, but if you weren't careful, sleeping under a rock here and there were timber rattlesnakes. One had to keep one's ears perked.

Around and around the steel barrel rocked and rolled for ten minutes in the Whirlpool, then fifteen, thirty, and forty-five. Inside, Leach was hot and sticky with sweat and nerves. For a while, the revolving took him to disorientation and sometimes inebriation, three sheets to the wind from wooziness. It was kind of restful, kind of spooky, with not much to do except sit there, bide his time, and hope to hell that Hill wasn't so jealous that he'd toss his rope over his shoulder and go home. As time passed, the crowd increased in size along the American and Canadian shores, and when the coroner showed up, they began experiencing déjà vu—was this Maud Willard all over again? Even after fifty minutes, no one could reach the barrel to pull Leach to safety and find out if he had finally been humbled, or if he was suffocated or otherwise dead. Meanwhile, Hill was becoming restless and had to be talked out of trying to swim into the maelstrom or take a rowboat out to the barrel. It wasn't until a full hour later that the Whirlpool lost its command, or motivation, and the barrel floated near Thompson's Point on the north shore of the basin. Hill was tired of doing nothing—he removed his heaviest clothes and fourth cigarette, tied the rope around his waist, and put his most confident dive into the water. Immediately, the swimming was demanding, stroking through wet cement, but his adrenaline was flowing, and he didn't need to get close to the deadly vortex. Before long, he developed a rhythm of strokes and felt as though he was part of the mad current; he'd been a fierce swimmer ever since that breathtaking ride on his pa's back seventeen years earlier. To resounding cheers, Hill made it to Leach's barrel on the edge of the Whirlpool, tied the rope around its handle, and slowly swam it ashore. When Hill, Mousie, and others popped open the hatch, a jubilant and relatively uninjured Leach declared: "Now don't get excited, boys. Take your time. I guess I have made good." But his jaw dropped a little when it dawned on him what rescuer he would have to share the headlines with. Eventually, friends helped a tired Leach, in his wrinkled suit, up the gorge bank, into a streetcar, and off to a celebration at his restaurant, where strong men carried him around on their shoulders. He planned on completing the trip the following day down the Devil's Hole Rapids, and with a swagger offered Hill fifteen dollars to go back to the glen and secure his barrel for the night. Bad decision; Leach should have had the instinct to realize that it was a major mistake to put the ball in his rival's court. Of course, Hill hustled down to the river before it got dark.

As Hill was tying the barrel to a tree, a bystander commented, "Bill, I'll bet you twenty-five bones [dollars] that you can't go through the lower rapids to Lewiston tonight."

"You're on," Hill said, climbing into the red barrel. Three men by the names of George and William Donald and Percy Chamberlain pushed him out into the river. As it was getting dark, Hill was in haste to make the four-and-a-half-mile trip and didn't put on the safety straps, choosing just to lie on the canvas hammock. He hadn't finished closing the manhole cover when the first wave struck, and he was drenched with buckets of water. Almost at once, the barrel became trapped in an eddy and was held for twenty-five minutes, just south of the Whirlpool, until twilight shadows sneaked into the canyon. But then the main current plucked it out, and Hill could feel the river start to seethe again, then to boil as the barrel avoided the Whirlpool and took a direct path through the glen past Wintergreen Terrace and a dry gorge abandoned by the river eight thousand years earlier. Then the barrel went past Foster's Flats, where a hermit had lived for years, past Erie Gorge, and finally to Roy Terrace, where, according to geologist Roy Spencer, the falls had been born in 10,000 BC, if anyone cared. Boulders broke the surface near the end of the journey; the barrel struck three of them, and suddenly the world went helter-skelter. Hill took a battering as the river kicked up a stink, and he was also feeling fatigue from the earlier rescue swim. After the barrel flipped twice into the air, its manhole cover popped off and water surged in again; little wonder the St. Regis tribe got few takers for their Sunday trips. At this point, Hill was not too proud to shout for help. It was not the way he wanted his first stunt to end, but he was relieved when the river suddenly became cooperative and he finished the journey to Queenston, across the river from Lewiston. A man in a motorboat, James Humphrey, had trouble finding the barrel in the dark, but when he did, Hill was standing erect out of the open hatch, his face and hands bleeding. It had taken a full hour and seven minutes to make the trip. Sadly, it was too dark for Hill to have his photograph taken for his scrapbook—with a copy for the newspapers—but at least Leach could not repeat the performance the next day without the lost hatch cover. It had been the first barrel to defeat the lower rapids; Hill was proud, and from then on he went around town with an impish smile. Later, a river historian pointed out to Hill that this was the first rapids trip for such a small stake, "although twenty-five dollars isn't bad for a bridge painter." Hill also pocketed fifteen bucks from Leach, and gave an interview to the *Niagara (New York) Gazette*: "When I was offered a bet to go through the lower rapids, I wanted to show I was game. On the trip, I struck three rocks and was badly shaken up. Near Queenston, I lost the top of the manhole after shipping about a foot and a half of water." When he discovered what had transpired, "Perfesser" Leach was incensed that Hill had upstaged him and lost his manhole cover. Leach's words during an interview with the *Daily Record* "would have melted the type if we had attempted to print them." Hill did not apologize. Instead, he minimized Leach's achievement and built up his own: "I'd sooner take the trip through the upper [Whirlpool] rapids than the lower [Devil's Hole]," he said. "There are not so many rocks in the upper rapids and for this reason they are easier to navigate than the lower . . . at no time during my trip did I lose my nerve. I know the river as well as the next man, if not better, and knew I was perfectly safe." However, he had received a number of bumps and bruises during the ride and said he'd never do such a thing again without strapping himself in. Exhausted but satisfied, Hill spent the rest of the night thinking about what he had done. Suddenly, he started talking about performing more of his own stunts of derring-do, beginning with the Horseshoe fall.

By autumn of 1910, Hill and Leach were back into a spat in the press about who would be the first man for the Big Splash. Leach seemed to be ahead; the twenty-five-foot *Mitchell Lifeboat* was apparently ready in England. With its unique design, Mitchell said, the boat when launched from the deck of a ship "goes under water and glides under the surface for several hundred feet before coming up." He added that this concept should work at the falls:

> The higher the drop is, the better the boat will work, and the great drop over the brink of the falls will give the boat enough momentum to carry it beyond the treacherous currents directly below the falls. The boat has got to come up and I have every confidence in its ability to make the trip safely.

Mitchell hoped to sign a contract with a steamship line for lifeboats made from this prototype. At eighty, the octogenarian was too old to make the incredible trip himself, so he invited Leach to be its star. Although Mitchell owned the boat and its patent, he asked Leach to pay its freight from Liverpool, England, because he was short of funds, which Leach did. When it arrived, Leach made some modifications to the boat, including caulking to make it waterproof, and showed it to Hill. River Man declared it too fragile to go over the falls and said he'd rather risk his life in a barrel several times rather than go over the brink once in that thing. The *Daily Record* called the boat frail, but added, "Bobby is a fearless person and may essay the plunge . . . he is professor in the gentle art of going where the angels would fear to tread." Leach's wife and daughter were dead against it; nevertheless, the boat created much excitement and made page one of local papers a half-dozen times, and a motion picture company signed to film Leach in the boat. As the claims and counterclaims of the two rivals dragged into December, some local residents believed Leach was more talk than action when it came to the falls. They had heard tall boasts from others who never tried it, and of course, Carlisle Graham and Steve Brodie had faked trips over Horseshoe. The skeptics did accept that Leach had defeated the rapids earlier in the year, but they didn't buy his claims that he had beaten the same rapids twice in 1898, and so he had police officers, politicians, river men, and distinguished local residents who had all seen the two barrel trips sign a document that they had actually happened.

Leach and Mitchell decided to send the boat over the falls for a test run— empty—on December 13, 1910, an unusual time of year for such an event in the northeast, and Leach hoped the ice floes in the river would not be too heavy. On that day, looking for the biggest publicity bang, Leach invited his new rival, Hill, as a witness. Also showing up, along with many tourists, was Leach's wife, Sarah, to make sure her husband didn't get into the boat. On that day, the empty boat was set adrift in the upper river off Hogg Island, a small man-made island where the Chippawa Creek dumped into the Niagara River in Canada, a mile above the falls. Initially, the boat cruised, then bumped along the rapids to the Three Sisters Islands just above the brink, where it grounded on a reef for more than twenty minutes. Finally, the beefy currents rocked the boat off, and it soared spectacularly over the brink of the falls and down into the maelstrom closer to the American side than the Canadian . . . emerging in the lower river ass-up, badly splintered, with its nose and part of its top ripped off. The only good news was that it didn't sink. "I believe that had a man been inside the boat at the time, his chances of escape would have been good," said Sydney Thomas, who was Mitchell's son-in-law and one of the promoters of the event. Hill disagreed and believed Leach would have met his end, because it appeared the boat had struck rocks. The *Geneva (New York) Daily Times* agreed with Hill: "It was clear to all observers that had Leach had been a passenger, he would have lost his life." A downcast Leach blamed the starting point and a stiff west wind for the failure: "If the boat had not been set adrift so far out in the river, it would have come closer to the Canadian shore and in the deepest water, where there are no rocks." Leach announced he was postponing his Dip of Death, scheduled for the following day, because of "adverse winds and water currents." Bobby said a stunt was possible the following spring, when another boat could be built "with additional ribs and braces." Mitchell agreed: "It could stand at least fifty per cent more bracing." In his heart of hearts, Leach wasn't certain he could wait that long, and, indeed, the lifeboat never went over the falls again, much to the relief of Leach's wife and daughter. And so Annie Taylor remained champion of the falls, for now. Surely, his fans thought, Bobby must have a backup plan, and he did—a cylindrical barrel of steel with tapered wooden ends to act as shock absorbers. Inside would be a canvas hammock and a pipe leading outside as an air vent. It would be dunked in paint bright, like his personality, partly to infuriate Red Hill.

Seven months after the Leach affair, Hill would take an even bigger gamble; Valentine's Day in a blizzard was as good a time as any for a river man to get married. Red and Beatrice Clark could have been doing any one of many romantic things on Tuesday, February 14, 1911. If the weather had been more copacetic, they could have gone one-two-three skating or waltzing, or perhaps to the River Road Rink for twenty-five cents to watch ice hockey—the Tecumsehs versus the West Ends. Then, over at the Princess Family Theatre, for ten cents, there were high-class comedians Berley and Mercer under the floodlights in a singing, talking, and dancing act with up-to-date and clever sayings, followed by a moving picture, *Patricia of the Plains*. Beatrice was fond of singing to herself and once considered taking private lessons in "Voice Culture and the Art of Singing" from Dr. Alfred Wooler, winner of an international anthem competition. Or they could have gone to visit newlyweds Mousie and Red's sister Cora, who had tied the knot the previous fall, leaving Red to live alone in his apartment. But on this snowy day, Red and Beatrice found themselves stuck in Lockport, New York, where Bea was visiting her grandmother and Red was working on a hydro project. He'd been doing a variety of odd jobs on hydro tension work and painting flagpoles, showing nerve and a direct approach by going up poles in his sock feet, then sliding down. He had such fearlessness of elevation, some people thought he must have Indian blood in him (he didn't). Anyway, there was a terrific storm in Lockport, and a stiff northeast wind piled snow into huge drifts, blocking roads and sidewalks, halting trains, and trapping students in their schools until midnight. Worried mothers flipped through newspaper advertisements to find the latest price to "Cure a Cold in One Day with Laxative Bromo Quinine Tablets." Laid up in Lockport, Red and Bea must have been feeling a romantic fever, or perhaps they were just impulsive. In any event, they dug a justice of the peace out of a snowbank and had a simple one-ring ceremony, both promising "with all my heart." When they returned home to Canada, they were Mr. and Mrs. William Hill.

"Anything to declare?" the customs officer asked at the bridge.

"Oh, we have something to declare." Beatrice smiled. "I declare this gentleman as my husband."

On their wedding night, she found out something: he snored. They eventually got their own house, and soon enough Red got fond of being catered to with Post Toasties cereal and Bea's hot and sweet chili sauce, which he lapped up in a big bowl like a happy retriever. For dessert, there was always her priceless chocolate cake from a secret recipe garnered at her parents' bakery in nearby St. Catharines, Ontario. The sweetness did not last forever; later that year, Beatrice lost her first child. She wept and confessed to Red that, as a child, she had accidentally swallowed drain cleaner, which had burned her throat and stomach lining. After consulting with doctors, she was afraid it would affect her ability to bear children. They were both sad and tried not to think about it.

***

When the good weather of 1911 moved in, newlywed Red was not ready with a barrel for the Big Splash, but Bobby Leach was. "It has been my ambition for the last sixteen years to go over Niagara Falls in a barrel, but up to the present, circumstances have never been favorable," Leach said during an interview the week of July 17, 1911, in the office of the *Daily Record* in Niagara Falls, Ontario. "Now, however, everything is arranged and you can tell the public that I shall do the trick on Monday, July twenty-fourth between one and three p.m." Unlike Mrs. Taylor, Leach was not looking to jump out of his old life into a new one, but to progress professionally and increase his viability as a daredevil while occasionally feeding his self-image a three-course meal.

The cask to carry Leach to fame or foible was a cylindrical old boiler made watertight—eleven feet long, fashioned from sheet steel three-eighths of an inch thick, painted black and red with ends of wooden planks bolted to the steel shell—a vessel one might see in *Twenty Thousand Leagues under the Sea*. Leach paid the Dobbie Foundry and Machine Company of Niagara Falls, New York, $275 to make it. Inside the barrel were pillows at one end to protect his brain and a harness of three-inch webbing to strap around him so he would be suspended away from the sides of the barrel. Canadian customs made Leach pay duty on the barrel when he brought it over a bridge, after which he secluded it on Navy Island in the Niagara River, a small tree- and deer-filled deserted island rarely patrolled by the coppers, located in the neutral part of the river, one mile from the falls, between Canada and the United States. In June, Leach experimented with an old barrel he had used for a rapids trip, but after he sent it careening empty over the falls, it got lost in an eddy and unceremoniously sank. Leach's wife and friends pleaded with him to postpone the trip, but he said he had to go through with it, even if he died in the attempt.

When Monday, July 24, came, an estimated ten thousand tourists and other spectators surrounded the falls and waited. As moviemakers stationed cinematographic cameras at all angles, Leach took a horseless carriage along the Canadian shore, toward the boat to take him to Navy Island, but he was intercepted on the road by the Ontario Provincial Police, who presented him with a letter proclaiming, "No matter how artistic a suicide was contemplated, it could not start from any part of the King's domain" (Canada was still considered a British colony). On the same day, Leach managed to get his boat and take it to the American side, where he was again detained by authorities. On shore, as a test, he launched three wooden soap cartons, which were carried off course by high winds and went over the American fall, rather than Horseshoe. If he had launched his barrel, he would likely have been crushed by boulders, so he postponed the trip. Some people, including Taylor, thought it was fear and not high winds that caused the postponement. She was not a fan of Leach and saw the little blowhard as a threat to her Niagara Falls crown; whenever possible, she asked the press not to associate her name with his. Interviewed in the parlor of her modest home on First Street in Niagara Falls, New York, Mrs. Taylor was asked by a *Cataract Journal* reporter if she thought Leach would ultimately go through with it. "I certainly do not. I have no faith in Leach or his assertions. He is a man in whom I never placed any dependence. Still, I wish him every success and have no hard feelings for him in any way. If he makes the trip, rest assured that I would be the first to congratulate him if he came out successfully, but he will never do it." Mrs. Taylor knew, though, or should have known, that the wrong winds could certainly tip the scales between life and death. Hill called challenging the falls a fool's game because of all the fickle factors beyond one's control—a shifting wind that could blow you over an undesirable section of the brink where boulders conspired below; erosion that could put boulders in places they'd never been; currents in the Whirlpool Rapids altered by hydro companies; and, of course, interference from police before you even got into the moody river. Some of this information Leach had garnered from standing at the back of several of Mrs. Taylor's postplunge lectures, which did not sit well with the Queen of the Mist.

On Tuesday, July 25, despite more high and cool winds, Leach's barrel was towed behind the launch of river man Al Mang and friend Bill Perry to Navy Island, but the wind kept pushing the boat around, and it took more than an hour to get there. Along the way, Leach was worried that authorities would corral him again or the boat would be carried over the falls. "Stop a bit," he told the men. "It's too risky riding in this launch. Suppose something should happen. I'll have a try at the barrel." The American authorities, he said, "thought I was attempting suicide." The men towed the barrel to nearby Hogg Island, where Leach climbed into his vessel—the wheels were in motion to make him the first man to go over the falls. With the deliberate theatre of a professional stuntman, which he claimed to be, Leach closed the hatch, a type of manhole cover, which was bolted shut by his helpers. The handle was on the inside, in case he needed to get out before men could reach him below the falls. Next, Leach fastened his harness around him and lay on the canvas hammock that stretched from one end of the barrel to the other. Mang and Perry rapped three times on the outside to indicate they were ready to cut him loose in the river, and Leach kicked the interior three times in response. He could have stayed on shore and led a good life as a manager of restaurants and bars. People stopped eating when he started talking. But he needed things to talk about. Mang and Perry left him in the hands of Niagara at 2:55.

"The condition of the water and weather were adverse to the trip but he went ahead anyway," later wrote the *Newark (Ohio) Advocate*. As tourists and other spectators lined up along both banks and stuck their noses out of tents they had slept in overnight at Table Rock, an automobile sped along the Niagara Parkway, announcing that the barrel was heading toward the falls, as dozens of motorists followed the barrel along the road. The steel vessel started slowly, unsurely, before it was scolded by the rush of the Horseshoe Rapids. Across from the Electrical Development Company, the last of the upper river plants on the Canadian side, half a mile from the falls, it was met by obstacles as a big wave tossed it onto a rock, and some water was forced into the barrel before it reached a deeper part of the channel. Two hundred yards from the brink, the barrel struck another rock very hard, and a large section of one of the wooden ends broke off. Finally, it reached the precipice of the Horseshoe fall, where dreams and nightmares always met, about one hundred feet from the Canadian shore. Red Hill watched the scene from below.

Ladies and gentlemen, boys and girls, presenting for your afternoon pleasure at the Niagara Palladium, Mr. Robert Leach, latterly of England.

At the brink, the damaged ballast could not keep the barrel upright as it plunged on its long axis, headfirst, into the chasm. It was 3:13. In the initial part of the plunge, the barrel stayed visible, resembling a submarine out of its ocean, then it vanished under a torrent. According to a witness, Cleveland Moffett of *American Magazine*, whose colleagues were filming the stunt:

> There were thousands watching along the banks and we had to be overlastingly quick to catch the barrel as it came over the falls. We didn't know exactly which way to aim our camera . . . I was stationed on the bank at the bottom of the falls with my motion picture machine ready, and I don't mind saying I never expected to see Bobby Leach again. I saw this black shape of a barrel with its wooden nose pointed at the brink. It hung there a few seconds before it went down one hundred and sixty-five feet below.

According to the *Advocate*, "There was a great splash in the lower river." The crowd all around the brink and below in the Waiting Room fell prayer silent. The only sound was the roar of the great falls. "A minute passed, two minutes and we searched the smooth black surface where the *Maid of the Mist* was lying ready to help," Moffett said. "Nothing! Three minutes! It seemed like hours and then a little distance off the shore, we made out the black shape of the barrel sweeping on toward the rapids." It was badly dented, yet still riding fairly high in the water.

"There he is!" shouted a number of spectators.

A powerful wake from the falls sent the barrel shakily toward the rapids and, in the distance, the Great Whirlpool. With its second wooden end also destroyed, it swept past the Ontario Power Company, but luckily caught in an eddy to swirl around and around, but not close enough for those on shore to grab it. A young employee of the power company, Frank Bender, was nearer to the barrel than Hill and took control. "Here, give me a line and I'll show you how to get him out," Bender said. Without removing his clothes, Bender tied a rope around his waist and jumped into the turbulent water. After a few strong strokes, he reached the barrel and attached the rope to one of its handles, then bellowed to those on shore to pull him and the barrel in. "Everybody yelled and a big strapping fellow [Bender] leaped into the river and struck out bravely," Moffett said. "We saw him swim up to the barrel, throwing one arm over it and turn struggling toward the shore. Then two other young fellows rushed in and, among them, they brought the barrel to the bank." It had been in the lower river twenty uneasy minutes. Hill was among the group to secure the dented barrel, along with Harry Williams, owner of the Hotel Lafayette, which had helped sponsor Mrs. Taylor's plunge. Williams, with a reputation as a daredevil and rescuer, knocked hard on the outside of the barrel and listened. A knock was returned. The spectators immediately around the barrel "let forth a mighty cheer, and was immediately answered by one of greater volume from the masses assembled above, when they understood that Bobby was alive," according to the *Daily Record*.

"Get me out of here!" Leach yelled from inside. But it was another twenty minutes until he was released. With the motion picture cameras whirring all the while, the barrel's manhole cover was unscrewed, and there he was—the braggart Brit, seemingly in one piece, albeit bleeding from a deep gash on the side of his face and with a right leg so sore, he believed it to be broken. Leach tried to extricate himself from the barrel, but his pain was too great; instead, he thrust his arm up through the hatch, and the crowd cheered tremendously. He had also injured his jaw against the inside handle of the manhole, and both knees were sore. When aides helped him out, Leach waved to the crowd. "Somebody send for and tell my wife I'm all right," he said. "Who's for a sip o' gin . . . I want no more of [the falls]. But they [the competitors] have got nothing on me." Hill and other aides carried Leach to the gatehouse of the Ontario Power Company and tried to fill him with whisky, but the company's works manager, H. H. Wilson, took the whisky away and replaced it with a tank of oxygen. "They worked over Bobby with stimulants . . . and got him out on a stretcher," Moffett said.

Hill said little, but Leach was healthy enough to give interviews. "I always keep my word, even though it hurts a little sometimes," he said. He had worried that he might die in the upper rapids: "I minded the tumbling about the falls more than the big drop . . . the further down the river I came, the more the barrel rolled. Once I struck a great wave, my barrel was tossed upon a rock, I thought it was *stove in* [a vessel incapacitated]. About two quarts of water rushed in." He added that about 150 feet from the brink, "there was a huge rock over which the water rushes over. The barrel struck the rock, rose into the air on end until two-thirds of it was visible. One of the ends was torn off down to the planks which were bolted to the steel case." Of the tumble over the falls, Leach said, "I felt the water rushing along outside. I was going head first but I says to myself, 'God save the King and the Devil take the hindermost' and away I goes . . . it seemed a long way to the bottom, but I knew what was going on and held my breath. I could tell when we went under water. Way down under, we seemed to stop. Then up she came, like an express train. I felt the barrel shoot out of the water and then fall back and then I kind of lost interest for I knew the lads would get me out. It seemed an hour before they had me ashore and a bit of comfort between my teeth."

Added witness Moffett: "After the first crash at the bottom of the falls, Bobby says the barrel stayed on end for over a half minute and he thought it was wedged in rocks at the bottom of the river and would stay there. This is when he fainted." Leach felt that only the tough shell of his barrel saved him from serious injury or death. Dr. F. W. E. Wilson arrived at the power company to find Leach with numerous bruises and minor cuts, a nasty contusion on the left knee, and perhaps a fractured right leg. The only consolation for Hill was that he was counted among the rescuers allowed in the official photograph with Leach, Bender, and others, smiling around the beached barrel for posterity. In his gut, though, Hill was steaming, and now lagging behind Leach in daredevil stunts. The "perfesser's" feats had finally caught up with his mouth, and he had completed his "Triple Challenge" of going through the rapids, parachuting from the Upper Steel Arch Bridge, and going over the falls, in the center ring in his own performance. Meanwhile, Moffett and his crew got their footage, and "then we packed up our apparatus and made a hasty departure for the authorities were after us." Leach was taken to his home, where he was expected to be confined for several days.

Next morning, Williams supervised the removal of the barrel from the lower river and hauled it to the Lafayette, where it was put on full exhibit. Leach, whose leg turned out to be not fractured but just sprained, inspected the dented barrel, then he went to his little restaurant near the Lower Bridge to give interviews.

> Now you'll have to speak to me nice and call me "Perfesser" and maybe pay a bob or two to hear me tell about it . . . when I left home yesterday I told my wife I'd never again put my foot on Canadian soil unless I came over in my barrel. I made good. I want to say right here that I'm through with taking chances in my life. I've done a good many things that make insurance companies unwilling to take me as a risk. When I came here fourteen years ago, I made up my mind to go over the falls some time. I realized my ambition today.

Immediately, offers came in from amusement hall proprietors for Leach to go on tour with his moving pictures, but his honeymoon lasted not much longer than one of his cigars. Two days after his falls debut, on July 27, 1911, a man in a flying machine soared over Niagara Falls at the height of twenty feet, then, incredibly, ducked under the Upper Steel Arch Bridge. The plane was a box-kite Curtiss biplane and the pilot was Lincoln Beachey, who closed his eyes from the stinging spray as he flew dangerously low. Airplanes had been in existence for just eight years, and no one had flown *under* anything before. Beachey was paid $1,000 and bumped Leach off page one. To make matters worse for Bobby, a few days later he discovered thieves had entered the barrel on display and cut away most of the harness. In ensuing weeks, he received numerous offers from museums and amusement hall proprietors to go on tour with his stories, which he did, selling postcards of himself posing with his barrel, on which was painted "The Only Man in the World Who Has Performed This Feat." Of course, that neatly sidestepped the issue of Mrs. Taylor being the first *person*. While he remained relatively chipper, Leach complained of insomnia and stomach problems for a few weeks. "I was not only a nervous wreck, but my stomach was in bad shape," he said. "I could barely eat anything and my strength left me. I couldn't sleep and every night I lay in bed and repeated my trip [over the falls]." And yet, he continued to proclaim that his falls feat was "the greatest trip of my life."

It stung Hill's eyes to see Leach's name and quotes in the papers. Oh, well, Leach was the second person over the falls, and first British dwarf. In a funny way, however, he felt a sense of relief; the river and the falls did not belong to him and his father Layfield, after all, and the pressure to be Everything Niagara was eased. For his part, Leach knew he couldn't live in that moment forever and needed to produce something more soon. Meanwhile, Hill never went through with his own barrel plans that year. He had a feeling they would meet again on the watery battlefield.

CHAPTER SIX
KILLER AND RESCUER

Winter at Niagara Falls could be ridiculous, a river of never-ending motion seemingly frozen solid in its lower basin. Tourists came by train from hundreds of miles away to frolic on horse-drawn sleighs at the base of the usually terrifying falls; to dine on sandwiches and whisky at wooden shanties in the middle of a frozen, cavernous gorge; and to toboggan down glaciers with little worry for the power of Providence beneath. And any attempt to get a daredevil barrel over the brink would result in a cement landing. They called it the Ice Bridge, on which people in dandy hats and soft mittens played leapfrog in a blizzard. From street level, those way down below in the gorge were black ants provoking grizzly. You didn't need a Hill or a Leach—everybody was a daredevil. Railway excursions boomed with a special Sabbath run, and by 1912, there were an estimated thirty thousand visitors each winter. Rather than a bridge formed by ice freezing on the surface, it was actually a conglomeration of mammoth blocks of ice crashing over the American and Canadian falls and piling up end over end in the channel of the lower river. Most people considered the Ice Bridge as safe as the unsinkable passenger steamship *Titanic*, set to sail on its maiden voyage from England. In winter, they called the base of the falls No Man's Land, where bubbling water, invisible under the ice, could discreetly gouge holes in the bridge, pop up, and suck a two-hundred-pound man to his end—in theory.

On Sunday, February 4, 1912, following a late breakfast, a Toronto couple, Eldridge Stanton, thirty-six, and his twenty-eight-year-old wife, Clara, left their room at the Allen Block Hotel in Niagara Falls, New York, and proceeded to Prospect Point to cross the river and visit Canadian friends. Their spirits were high. Eldridge had a respectable job as secretary-treasurer of a stationery company, while Mrs. Stanton was a pretty housewife, and soon perhaps they would produce their first child (Niagara visits had that effect on people). Meanwhile, two seventeen-year-old boys had taken the red-eye train from Cleveland; Burrell Hecock and his friend, Ignatius Roth, were chucking ice balls at one another, ducking in and around the charming shanties, including one in which Red Hill sold hard liquor and cigarettes. At 11:30, about twenty-five people were on the ice, braving a stiff downriver wind. The temperature was zero, but it was sunny and worth it. Back in Cleveland, hundreds of miles away, Mrs. and Mrs. H. L. Hecock sat down to Sunday lunch. Burrell was their only child. As family was later told, suddenly, to the horror of everyone at the table, Mrs. Hecock grabbed a glass of water. "See!" she shouted, looking strangely into the glass. "There's ice floating there! And people running! I see my boy. He is in danger!" Mrs. Hecock became hysterical and had to be calmed. Winter and cabin fever could make one hysterical.

For one moment on the Ice Bridge, Eldridge and Clara Stanton bumped into Burrell and Ignatius. They exchanged small talk, and Mrs. Stanton snapped a photograph of the two boys, promising to send copies along to Cleveland. Without warning, a titanic grinding sound seized the gorge. Hill felt a tremor beneath his shanty. He scurried out and scanned the Ice Bridge. Good God, it was coming apart at the seams! Keeping his cool, Hill shouted for people to follow him to the Canadian shore and led about twenty people safely to the Maid of the Mist boat docks. The Stantons, though, left in the other direction, toward the American shore. With a primordial growling, the Ice Bridge shattered into two chunks the size of small villages. Another loud report echoed the length of the gorge, as though some deity was belching and cared little about the company at the table. The Stantons ran fast toward the United States, then stopped cold. Their big ice floe had become separated from the shore, which was now twenty feet away, separated by a freshly created channel of black open water—on its way to the deadly Whirlpool Rapids. They had company—Hecock and Roth were scurrying around at the other side of the floe. From shore, several hundred feet away, Hill recognized the dilemma. All around him, people were yelling and crying, but he stayed focused. With strong legs overcoming his heavy boots, he jumped from ice floe to ice floe, bounding crags and crevices and tripping over ice mounds. Nearly breathless, he got to within thirty feet of the Stantons and bellowed: "You can still make it! To the shore! Back to the Canadian side! Don't panic! Follow me!" It was something his father had instilled in him—never fluster. The large, runaway ice cake proceeded under the first of three bridges across the gorge. When Clara became frantic, her husband grabbed her hand and they stumbled toward Hill. Remarkably, Hill managed to get onto the Stantons' ice floe and convinced Mrs. Stanton to sit down while he removed her rubber overshoes and ice cleats. As spectators watched from both shores, the wayward floe entered a channel of slush ice, and Red announced it was thick enough for all three of them to wade ashore, but Mrs. Stanton was still in a panic mode and refused to chance it. Hill pleaded with her, but instead the couple moved toward the New York shore again. At the other end of the floe, Hecock and Roth either did not heed Hill's advice, or they were too upwind to hear. Hill could wait no longer and plunged into the slush, plowing again toward the Canadian bank. He could only do so much for them, he thought, remembering his father's advice about such occurrences. He told himself he could get a clearer mind from the bank and perhaps analyze another way out for the Stantons and the two teenagers. Meanwhile, Hecock and Roth met up with the Stantons again. Now the gorge walls were moving—hotels, houses, boat docks, and billboards were starting to pass quickly. By this time, police, firefighters, customs officials, reporters, railway workers, and volunteers had wailed to the scene in motorized and horse-drawn vehicles. Ropes were dropped from cliffs and the bridges. Hill ran along the Canadian bank, keeping pace with the runaway ice block. Mrs. Stanton collapsed. "Oh, let me alone!" she moaned. "Let me die now!"

Unable to contain her, Eldridge shouted once more for help, and Hecock joined them. Several hundred yards from the next bridge, a shore party of rescuers tossed a thick rope over the slush ice to Roth. He clutched it and called to the other three people to follow him. Hill splish-splashed into the ice and pulled Roth, half-conscious, ashore. Stanton and his wife and Hecock were now alone on the death trap, staring point-blank into the dreaded rapids. As he passed under the bridge, Hecock grabbed a trainman's rope, but his frozen hands went limp and he fell back into the water, vanishing under crashing waves. Sighed police officer Pat Kelly from above, "We'll never see a braver lad." Another line, which Eldridge grabbed, snapped. He raised his wife to her feet, kissed her, and clasped her in his arms. They dropped gently to their knees before three large waves broke over them, and they were swallowed by spume. Swallowed by Niagara. Crowds stood on the banks and the bridges, frozen with shock and pity. The couple's bodies were never found. A lot of people in Niagara and Cleveland cried the night away.

Not long after the tragedy, Hill received a God-bless-you letter from Roth, recommending he get a bravery medal. Two months later, when the *Titanic* stole the headlines by striking an iceberg and going down off Newfoundland, Hill remained upset about the three deaths. But his medal gave Hill's reputation a foothold in Niagara. He wanted to make the river his job, his calling. Sure, Niagara had humbled him—it humbled everyone—but somebody had to stand watch. That summer, he stood solemnly as a memorial tablet to Burrell Hecock was blessed in Queen Victoria Park.

***

Another February, five years later in 1917, was spent in a far different land. For more than two years, the most powerful armies in history had struggled for supremacy along the Western Front. The Germans kept the Allies at bay at Vimy Ridge, a strategic German fortress on a limestone ridge seven kilometers long near a French town. It was the First World War, the Great War, and when you were in the middle of it, things that happened back in Niagara Falls, such as Hill's old rivalry with Bobby Leach, seemed dwarfed. The Canadian Army's Fourth Division came from a volunteer stock of farmers, trappers, cowboys, and militia river men—as in the case of Private Red Hill, who spent much of his days lying on his stomach in the middle of yet another No Man's Land, the two-hundred-yard buffer zone between the Allied and German lines. Even though everyone tried to be camouflaged, each movement was conservative and well conceived. You stayed alive for your next swig of rum, which took the edge off one of the coldest European winters in years. With all the snow, sleet, and frozen mud, Hill thought he was back home, and yet how did they expect him to be a sniper, a sharpshooter with a Lee-Enfield rifle, in a goddam winter coat? In the Niagara Gorge, the ducks never shot back. Also bothering Hill was the fact that his role in life had suddenly changed; for saving the tourists on the Ice Bridge, he had been officially presented his second lifesaving medal, and now the army was telling him to remove life. One day, Hill's unit spotted the Red

Baron, Manfred von Richtofen, above Vimy, tossing bombs from his airplane at the Allies. Whenever he felt threatened, Red glanced at Bea's latest postcard: "I understand you've lost your fear of the trenches . . . perhaps you will one day lose your fear of the dentist's chair!" Back in Canada, a depression had hit, and she had to generate a few dollars by sewing, and rounding up bedbugs at tourist hotels. They had a family now, and besides a son they had adopted, Harry Boltz, two little miracles came into their lives (there was nothing wrong, after all, with her reproductive organs):

- William Guy Hill Jr., on September 8, 1913. He did not have a caul, or magic membrane, over his head like his father had, but he did have sandy, almost red hair and, like Pa, blue eyes.
- Edith Adeline Hill, on October 26, 1915, named after an aunt who died young.

In her letters, Beatrice gave Red updates on the children, and wrote about how seventeen tourists had been hurled from a gorge railway in Niagara Falls, New York, to their deaths in the rapids. He felt he should have been there to help, and he worried that he would be a different man if he ever got home, a killer. At the least, he was becoming a heavy smoker and cusser. In his return letters, Red never told his wife the truth about bloody Vimy Ridge, where the Germans had superior weapons, rocking the earth with deadly short-range projectiles known as Moaning Minnies, which were lobbed in a high arc over the battlefield, leaving a trail of hot sparks and sulfur stench. Through all of this, it was rough enough having to look out for yourself, never mind having two brothers-in-law on your flanks, as Hill did in Privates Mousie Sloggett and Lawrence Young. Of course, Mousie could take care of his own skin, having saved Hill from the Niagara River on more than one occasion. The Canadians' boldest raid was on March 1, 1917, to try and take a hill nearly five hundred feet high. There was no artillery bombardment, but rather the cover for the advancing troops would be the newest ultimate weapon—poisonous phosgene gas known as White Star, an unholy union of carbon monoxide and chlorine, without color or noise and promising to creep into enemy lines and render everything helpless—troops, rifles, even field guns. With Hill and his infantry mounting a charge in heavy fog, they had to remove their gas masks to see where they were charging. When the wind suddenly changed direction, Hill and many others were overcome by their own poisonous gas. He was also shot in the hand and fell into a foxhole. Red barely survived and spent the next eighteen months in twelve different hospitals in France and England, suffering from the gunshot wound, gas inhalation, and tuberculosis in his lungs. His brothers-in-law also inhaled gas, but they recovered to fight again as the Allies finally did take Vimy Ridge. At one point, Hill was so sick, a doctor estimated he might have only six months to live, and so he sent him home on a boat. The doctor advised that a warm, dry climate was best for his health; Hill informed him he was from cool, damp Niagara.

***

When she had her Will back, Beatrice knew he had censored his Dearest Family letters; he had one lung remaining at best, the spirit in his soul seemed asleep, and he couldn't talk without a rat-rat-rat cough, as though the Germans had followed him across the Atlantic. He was such a mess, she couldn't properly care for him, and he was shipped to the hospital in Hamilton, Ontario, fifty miles from his beloved Niagara Falls, for six long months. Following that, Red was allowed to earn a little money painting bridges and gardening for the rich Langmuir family, which had one of the first automobiles in town, yet he saved much of his energy for hugging his wife and three children—eight-year-old Harry, William Jr., almost five, and Edith, almost three—and for Bea's chili sauce. It was wonderful having Father home, and Beatrice learned to laugh again, opened her face up for one of the first times Red had ever seen. Will's hair wasn't as fiery as it was before the war, more of a sandy brown, and his skin was ghostly. She kept her arms around him, and he resisted some of it, which was partly the war talking and partly the way Red Hill was; they had never been lovey-dovey, and Bea wanted him to put some of his handyman verve into his relationships. In the summer of 1918, she had an announcement—she was two and one-half months pregnant, but before she could choose another baby name and arrange Will's military medals in the china cabinet, a hot summer's day sneaked up and grabbed her man. On August 6, she was just about to lay out a nice tea of shrimps and olives when the telephone started shrieking. In fact, telephones all over the city were ringing, and men with eager faces were thumping on Hill's door.

"In the river!"

"At the falls! A canal barge!"

"At the brink!"

It wasn't Annie Taylor or Bobby Leach in a barrel. Apparently, a big steel barge had somehow become marooned near the top of the Horseshoe fall. Beatrice practically got down on her knees: "You can't go, Will. Heavens to Betsy, you're just back from the war. Somebody else can do it—the military, the firemen, the people who get paid to do these things—remember what the doctors told you. Next thing, you'll be talking about going over the falls again."

"They say the barge is still moving, Bea, it's goin' over!" he protested.

"Daddy! Daddy!" William Jr. shouted, as much from excitement as from fear.

He had to go—other people were moving in on his territory. Down near the brink of the falls, even Red Hill could not believe his eyes: an enormous steel scow, eighty feet long with a thirty-foot beam, was sitting nervously in the rushing water just off Gull Island, one-half mile above the brink. It seemed to be lodged on rocks, 850 feet out from the huge Electrical Development Company, an elongated six-story building on the Canadian shore. His first reaction was to comprehend what a fantastic thing this would be to plummet over the falls, and he felt ashamed to be thinking this first and foremost, before considering the plight of the two poor gents in harm's way, who were peering just above the high sides of the scow like schoolchildren separated from their parents. But just imagine! Mrs. Taylor's whisky barrel and Leach's steel cigar were pip-squeaks next to this juggernaut; what a sight it would be to behold many tons of steel crashing 165 feet into the depths, and what a feeling to be aboard! It would not plunge over the cataract, it would somersault, perhaps right down to the uttermost depths of the river, another 165 feet below the river's surface. Nothing this humongous had challenged Niagara since the *Caroline*, a seventy-one-foot side-wheel steamer, was set afire by a raiding party in 1837 and allowed to smash to bits over the falls. But no one had been aboard that craft.

Masquerading as seagulls, vultures coasted in lazy but inevitable circles over the two men in the scow, who were waving their arms and barking for help. Would-be rescuers stood on the banks with good intentions; they came with alarm bells and bicycles and horse-drawn carriages—men in suspenders and constables with their hands on their hips and hydro workers with empty lunch buckets on their way home—but to a man they all stopped cold at the water's edge. The fire department was here, with bells a-ringing—not one but three companies—and the parks police and the city police and a fire rig pulled by the horses Beach and York. There were soldiers on horseback, and even Niagara Falls, Ontario, mayor Harry P. Stephens came on his day off. And now other Yanks were on their way with fire and police departments. Little wonder no one was ready to venture into the fierce water, a series of rapids and whitecaps, traveling at a sneaky-fast fifteen miles per hour at the scow and alive with undercurrents—about twenty-five hundred feet from the brink of the fully awake Horseshoe fall. Hill was given a lowdown on what had transpired: the Niagara Power Company had been enlarging its facilities and deepening a hydraulic canal near Port Day, New York, less than two miles from the falls, when the scow broke loose from a tugboat and was swept downriver with its freight of two men, Swedish sailor Gustav Lofberg, fifty-one, and James Harris, fifty-three, of Buffalo, employees of the Great Lakes Dredge and Dock Company. Like a dinosaur doing the polka, the barge had bounced up and down in the rapids, and Harris called out: "Look, we're going over the falls! We're lost!"

"We can only die once," said the cooler Lofberg, a veteran of the seven seas since he was fifteen.

The brave men employed a variety of methods to slow the drunken dino, such as dropping a six-ton concrete anchor into the relentless water, but its chain broke. Then the men opened up the seacocks—hatches in the flat bottom of the barge used for unloading—and the scow took on enough water for it to ground to a halt on a rocky ledge. Meanwhile, an impromptu rescue command post was set up at the Electrical Development Company, a beautifully designed, imposing structure with heavy pillars, a monument to man's growing attempts to harness the power of the Niagara River (good luck with that one). The heads of the various emergency services agencies huddled on the roof of the building, but nobody knew what in the hell to do. By this time, the largest crowd of spectators at the falls in several years was lining the banks on the Canadian shore and over on Goat Island in the United States. Tourism had been down lately, partly because police had outlawed stunting on the river and partly because the Niagara Parks had come under military control during the war, with some tourist attractions boarded up. In fact, all major hydro installations were under military guard, and bayoneted soldiers and coils of barbed wire were everywhere.

Finally, the United States Coast Guard set up a lifeline cannon on shore, a brass gun that fired a line of strong hempen rope over the water and successfully across the deck of the barge, three football fields away. Geronimo! After they poked their heads above the side, Lofberg and Harris enthusiastically grabbed the line and pulled in a heavier line, which was attached to the hemp. On shore, the heavy line was secured to a streetcar railing behind the electrical building, and more lines, including a block and tackle—a set of ropes and pulleys—were fired out to the helpless barge. One hundred and fifty men on shore took deep breaths and pulled the heavy line to take up the slack. By then it was dark, but the air was still wringing from the one-hundred-degree temperatures of the afternoon. A breeches buoy, containing a rescue basket big enough for one man, was sent along the rope toward the scow. The plan was for the stranded men to clamber inside the basket and be hauled ashore, one at a time, but the operation dragged on for hours; by two in the morning, the breeches buoy still had not reached the barge. The Coast Guard could not get the rope high enough to keep it out of the rushing water, and the lines were all fouled up and drifting toward the falls. Someone would have to go out and free them, sober or otherwise. In the dark and damp, it was a job for a one-in-a-lifetime, albeit wounded, man—William Red Hill. "I'm willing to take the risk," he said. "It's certainly not impossible."

Hill took off his peaked cap, climbed into the breeches buoy, and slowly but surely, the hydro boss riggers pulled him out over the angry waters, his legs dangling not far above the rapids. With powerful searchlights and the crowd's best wishes and prayers intensely upon him, Hill sped up. The rapids growled as he rode out just above the water, his feet sometimes nipped by the dancing currents. A log swept under his feet, and Red watched it carried toward the falls, and over. He wondered if he could survive going over the falls without a barrel or life jacket, which he had considered wearing but discarded in the oppressive heat. At the halfway point, the block and tackle became jammed, so he climbed out of the basket and pulled himself by hand and foot along the main rope toward the crippled scow. Aboard the barge, Lofberg and Harris were working their end of the ropes in teamwork with the men on shore, who instructed them by holding aloft large cardboard signs, illuminated by searchlights:

PULL IN ON THE SMALL LINE.

REST.

LET GO.

Hold Tight.

Line Is Fouled.

One instruction the men need not be given was to check if the scow was moving; they did it instinctively every few minutes and sometimes overreacted to slight movements of the vessel from wind and waves. Neither man would dare look toward the grumbling, impending falls.

In the middle of the night, Beatrice and her three children, their lips black from gumballs to keep them quiet, arrived by horse and buggy and were ushered to the front of the big crowd. For the past few years, while her man had been fighting overseas, Bea had tried not to think about the river too much, avoiding it like a woman might avoid a blonde who batted eyelashes at her husband. She did not like the water, and she couldn't even swim, but she was tired of worrying at home while Red was in crisis. Watching him, he could have been anybody—slightly below average height and weight, an even demeanor, a cap sometimes, and a cigarette; a common man doing uncommon things. There he was, the bloke next door going up against a global wonder. At this point, the main rope was too low in the water, and the current seized Hill's backside and spun him around 360 degrees until he swallowed a pintful and held on for dear life. Suddenly, Red Hill was shaken by the river; he had been away for too long, he thought; power companies had been monkeying with the currents, and he couldn't quite figure them out. Still, he managed to untangle the ropes and the block and tackle, removing the obstruction that prevented the breeches buoy from reaching the stranded men. The only time Hill slipped out of concentration was to glance back to shore to Bea and the young ones. He hadn't seen them much, and there was the possibility he never would again. William Jr. was not loud, but eager, and Bea was having difficulty keeping him behind the railing; just like his father, he was wondering what it would be like to see a barge go head over heels into the gorge. He would be ready for his first swimming lesson soon—Pa chucking him into the lower river. Meanwhile, his sister, Edith, was keeping her hand firmly planted on whatever was the closest of her mother's limbs, and eight-year-old Harry couldn't wait to tell his friends in the morning that he'd been up and dressed at this ungodly hour.

But Harry was worried about something else lately. He'd been hearing disturbing rumors in the neighborhood that the stork really had not brought him to the Hill house, that he was adopted from German parents. He wondered about the people who came to the house from Waterloo, Ontario, from time to time. If he didn't know better, he would have thought they were checking up on him. Although rescuers were shouting and scurrying all around her, Beatrice remained calm and recited psalms under her breath, trying to keep her children in a tight circle. When she took a long breath, she explained it was for the new baby in her belly. As her husband inched closer to the big black barge, shadows increased like ghouls on the river, and the searchlights were not showing him enough detail in the knots he was trying to untangle. With his soaked undershirt melted to his body, Hill started to lose some steam. Until now, spectators had cheered Hill's efforts—there hadn't been this much ballyhoo since he and Leach had been on the warpath—but as the night and the lack of success wore on, they became disappointed, particularly when an exhausted Hill motioned that he was returning to shore. Slowly, he straightened himself into his army posture and retraced his movements along the lines, telling himself that he would return to the scow in a while, even though he felt like quitting. Two more lives lost? Did it really matter? How many were still dying on the Western Front? On shore, Red was not too tired to hug his children, and Beatrice let him have a smoke in front of them. Then he caught forty winks beneath the gently swaying willows of Queen Victoria Park as great waves of hot air poured up through the ventilators of the electric company from the generators below. Out on the barge, Lofberg and Harris shuffled about, avoiding waves that occasionally crashed over the side. With no guarantee Hill would return, the two men considered swimming to Gull Island, about fifty feet away, but that would require the freestyle of an Olympic medalist. The other option, swimming to shore, would mean battling a downhill current that would likely carry them to the hungry falls before they reached the outstretched arms of rescuers. And so, both men fastened themselves down and tried to sleep in the unsafest bed in the free world; Lofberg crawled into a bulkhead compartment, half hitching himself to a pipe, gambling he could survive the long plummet over the falls, which might make him more famous than Leach or Taylor.

This disaster was serving as a wake-up call for all the men who thought they had the Niagara River tethered; they were not cocksure of the river and the falls anymore, albeit mankind had made great progress—since before the turn of the twentieth century, they had been harnessing the river's fury for commercial use, specifically hydroelectricity to launch the age of electrical power. Five companies on both sides of the border were generating more than four hundred thousand horsepower from turbines operated by the swift fall in water, which provided lighting and energy for the industries, homes, heaters, and electric irons of more than two hundred municipalities in the province of Ontario and the state of New York. No more coal and no more candles at five o'clock on a winter's eve! Someone had even penned a catchy tune that was becoming popular, "Oh, What a Difference since the Hydro Came." But this luxury was creating more demand, and so more and more power companies were springing up, and the world's largest hydroelectric plant was under construction—a twelve-mile tunnel under the city of Niagara Falls, Ontario, from Chippawa in the upper river to Queenston, well below the falls. Some famous physicists, like William Thomson, Baron Kelvin, wanted to shut down Niagara Falls entirely as a sightseeing mecca in order to use all of its water for the world's electricity.

When a hot, robust sun awoke on August 7, the rescuers feared that a high west wind would swell the water level and shake the scow loose from its perch. Hill awoke to sore muscles, but he wolfed down a cold egg sandwich somebody handed him, then climbed back onto the breeches buoy. He knew he had to get at least two-thirds of the way to the barge to untangle the lines. Suddenly, Hill was sweating again, and it was only partly about the heat—his adrenaline was flowing. He had forgotten what this had been like, to rescue rather than to shoot between the eyes. The adrenaline and the endorphins also killed the pain from his stomach and his lungs. As he went into his arduous hand-and-leg act again, feeling like actor Elmo Lincoln in the silent film *Tarzan of the Apes*, power plants on both sides of the border worked their turbines at maximum levels to try and keep the river flow down.

As Hill got closer to the barge, the long rope sagged and dunked him into the fast waves. Squeezing the line, he swallowed water and felt a sharp, hot pain in the back of his head. Scrambling, he tried to get back in sync with the river; you could never fight Niagara, only try to work with it, so Hill took long, meaningful breaths from the abdomen and tried to relax and focus at the same time. Soaked to the skin, he righted himself on the cable and made it to within 120 feet of the scow, so close he could see the victims' fluctuating expressions of anticipation and dread. To his left, the Horseshoe fall was near enough to see its crest twinkle and start to tumble in the otherwise beautiful morning haze. There was still a problem—one of the small coils of rope on the barge was wrapped around the big rope from the breeches buoy, preventing it from getting closer to the scow. Hill shouted directions toward the barge, but the two men had become so weak, they had trouble untangling the ropes or getting the main rope high enough out of the water. Other secondary lines were caught in the rocks.

For two more painstaking hours, Hill worked at loosening ropes and wires from the main line, half of the time while he was being battered by the unsympathetic current. Whenever he felt drained, he listened for the crowd on shore, and then he grew in size. The river was throwing its best at him, but he was still here, writhing and kicking on the line, beginning to smell victory. For two years, he'd been living in an inch-by-inch world—on the battlefield and in the hospital—and he knew that patience sometimes wins, when you outlast demons—because even they get tired. He tried to keep Harris and Lofberg motivated with reports of his experiences in the war in Europe. Up close, Lofberg had small sharp eyes and a weather-roasted face. Lofberg could not get the image of the *Titanic* out of his mind—this was the second catastrophe in recent times off Canada. Was Providence sending humanity to hell in a handbasket for the Great War or for letting women have the vote and the option of their knees showing or for men drinking more and going to church less? Harris talked a little, too, whenever he could drum up the strength, about his wife and five children. Meanwhile, the crowd was becoming more optimistic, sustained by hawkers of hamburgers and sodas. Some old Brits and soldiers started singing "It's a Long Way to Tipperary," which deteriorated into "That's the Wrong Way to Tickle Mary." People were saying that Hill was blessed, that he had someone or something watching over him. His mother, Mary Ann, had always said, perhaps tongue in cheek and perhaps not, that the caul she had given him at birth was protecting him on his voyages, like the old sea captains had said it would. And yet Hill's cough was making a comeback. "You got a cold?" Harris shouted to him as Hill was getting the last knots out of the lines.

"Something I picked up in Europe."

One moment the men were cheerful, and the next their expressions were forbidding because it was hot again, and with the whitecaps bubbling around them, it felt as though they were in a giant pan of popping corn. "It's out of our hands now," one of the men said. Red Hill did not and could not think the same way, and so far history had been on his side. Finally, he got all the lines untangled so that the two men would have a safe passage back to shore. It had taken Hill seven hours, and he returned to the powerhouse alone on the rescue basket to the roar of the crowd. By 9:00 a.m., the breeches buoy was working well, and it was sent all the way back to the barge. Lofberg helped Harris, who was weak from hunger and exposure, over the side of the scow and into the basket. "You go ahead, James," Lofberg said. "I'll stay behind for the next run. I know how to handle the ropes better than you do."

From the top of the powerhouse, one hundred muscular men strained to yank Harris to safety over the turbulent waters, one body length at a time. On several spurts, the basket dipped down to hit waves, and he became submerged in the rapids, one time for nearly a minute, but Harris clung bravely. He was safe at 9:45 a.m., by Lofberg's waterlogged pocket watch. On top of the electrical building, Hill's happy brain was jumping from one thing to another, and he suddenly recalled the nice words of that letter from Ignatius Roth, one of the chaps he had saved from the Ice Bridge. Hill owned two lifesaving medals already; if a third resulted from this, he would not turn it down. You didn't think of such accolades during a time like this, of course . . . but, dammit, of course you did! He didn't make many bones off the river—who wouldn't want a medal? He'd killed enough men in France and wondered if he was still in God's good graces with the head count (not that he was religious), with the rescues and medals hopefully outnumbering his kills. As the crowd hailed, Harris smiled sheepishly while being helped out of the basket. "I'm going away back on land somewhere and lash myself to a tree, then I'll know I'm safe," he said to laughter all around. While being examined by a doctor, Harris peered across the water to Gus on the barge. "Hustle, please, boys, and get poor Gus. He's a brick. He made me go first."

The now-confident rescuers methodically sent the breeches buoy back to the barge as the spectators buzzed. Mayor Stephens commented about Lofberg: "The man's as game as he could be." Once inside the rescue contraption, Lofberg held himself high so that he would not get a drowning, and he clung to a rope support, his chin locked with determination. As Lofberg approached the roof of the powerhouse, Hill grabbed one of his feet and pulled him in, home free, while both men laughed nervously. Lofberg had just enough strength to check his watch. It was 10:25. Unbelievably, he was concerned that his boss was going to dock him a day's pay. The people on shore—adults as well as children, William Jr. and Edith among them—began screaming and crying unashamedly and running around in happy circles, bumping into one another and falling over. They had just seen something to last their lifetime. As he was lowered to the ground on a rickety ladder, Lofberg asked for a chaw of tobacco. He and Harris were treated for heat exhaustion and patched up with dry clothes and a hearty break-fast. As journalists rushed off to meet four o'clock editions, Beatrice was back at the powerhouse and embraced her husband like never before as their three chil-dren attached themselves gleefully to his legs and hundreds of people sang "For He's a Jolly Good Fellow." Firefighters picked him up and tossed him playfully into the air and he felt no pain from his war wounds, only the battle between his exhaustion and exhilaration. He did not feel even close to death anymore. He was back, and everybody knew it. Somewhere on his world tour, Bobby Leach was growling; and soon there would probably be a clash over squatter's rights for the $35,000 scow. It would take city bureaucrats more than two years to officially recognize Hill's rescue with a medal, as historians debated whether to name the scow *Lofberg* or *Red Hill*, but that wouldn't matter. Nobody forgot. It continued to sit there on a reef above the falls, waiting for an adventurous soul to climb in and hold on forever. It was never named.

CHAPTER SEVEN
RED AND THE DEMON BARBER

By 1920, it had been nine years since the second Big Splash at Niagara, and people wondered if a third would ever occur or if locals had come to their senses or just become terrifically boring. Bobby Leach hadn't exactly encouraged other stuntmen and -women, thanks to the embellishment of his 1911 victory over the falls—on a subsequent tour of England and North America, he told audiences he'd been hospitalized for twenty-three weeks after his encounter, when, in fact, he had suffered only minor injuries and never saw a hospital bed, although his nerves apparently did suffer for a spell. He must have contracted the habit of hyperbole from his travels with Ringling Bros. and Barnum & Bailey Circus. ("Come to City Varieties and see a full account of his death-defying fight with the falls and the Whirlpool of Niagara, illustrated by motion pictures. Come see the original barrel!") In any event, newspapers occasionally published rants and ravings and promises from would-be showmen, yet summer holidays of peering over the railing came and went with no stunting.

Behind the scenes, however, Hill, Leach, and others were in serious planning. One night in the spring of 1920, the two rivals were invited to a dimly lit warehouse on the outskirts of Niagara Falls, Ontario, to view the newest barrel. Its owner was a complete stranger, one Charles George Stephens, who had just had it shipped by ocean liner from his native Brighton, England. The fifty-eight-year-old Stephens quickly found the best locals to advise him—Leach, the second and last person to go over the falls, in 1911, now operating a pool hall in town; and Hill, who had attended or helped in most every stunt in the river since the turn of the century. With the long, grueling war to end all wars finally at an end, people were looking to get back to their lives, which meant the occasional spectating of damn fools throwing caution to the wind. Hill was hungry for something, as well. He and Stephens were joined at the warehouse viewing by Captain Richard F. Carter of the *Maid of the Mist*, who was also interested in daredevil feats, and young reporter Miss Winnifred Stokes of the *Niagara Falls Evening Review* (if women could barrel over the falls, surely they could write about it). As soon as the four laid eyes on Stephens's wooden barrel, there was serious issue about it. There was always an issue about a barrel challenging Niagara Falls or the Great Whirlpool. Hey, if we could put a man in the air, why couldn't we come up with a better barrel?

Mrs. Taylor's vessel of 1901, according to the pessimists—which was pretty much everybody before her shocking triumph—had been far too much of a whisky container, and Leach's steel cylinder ten years later was supposedly too rigid, a septic tank waiting to fill up with more than his BS. And so, when Stephens pulled a canvas tarp off his barrel, it was difficult to withhold judgment; to the naked eye, it seemed hardy enough, fashioned from Russian oak two inches thick, standing six feet two inches high (four inches longer than Stephens), and weighing six hundred pounds. Ten steel hoops encircling the barrel were reputed to provide added strength. The heavily padded interior was lined with horsehair, with a harness for the occupant, and it also contained battery-powered lights and a breathing apparatus, consisting of an oxygen tank and mask, built by a professor from London and providing enough air for three full hours. At the top of the barrel was a safety valve that Stephens could open if he ever wanted to see what was coming. It was hard for anyone to disparage the barrel when Stephens kept gazing upon it, as Leach said, like it was the "Queen goddam Mary." He'd had the barrel made to his own specifications in London for a whopping $250, and before it was shipped to Niagara Falls, it had proudly been on display at the Empire Theatre in Bristol.

However, Hill, Leach, and Carter had been exposed to too much reality and mayhem to beat around the bush with the barber: to a man, they were not quite sold on it, particularly Leach and Carter. They said it did not look much sturdier than Dame Taylor's barrel, and that had been knocked around pretty good by the falls in an era when the falls was perhaps more predictable and easier to deal with. The barrel was too light, according to Stephens's fellow Englishman, Leach, who added that the falls was now more of a crapshoot than it had been nine years earlier, when he'd made his trip, because boulders unseen to tourists' eyes at the sightseeing railings had eroded at the base of the cataract and, in spots, acted as jagged death catchers. For her part, the wide-eyed Stokes said little, except to ask questions. Stephens thankfully and respectfully heard out all the guidance, even taking notes, but dismissed Leach's warning as largely jealousy and scoffed when he called himself a "perfesser" (Stephens should talk: he referred to himself as Professor Stephens, although neither he nor Leach had the academic credentials for such privilege). Meanwhile, Carter turned down Stephens's request to be his manager because he didn't want to be involved in a suicide mission. Stephens understood that Carter and his steamboat company had lots to lose professionally if he backed an amateur who drowned in his river. Of course, Hill added his two cents' worth—he agreed that the falls was riskier than it had been for Leach's stunt because of the boulders and because the Horseshoe Rapids were now shallower and more erratic—in recent years water levels were lower in the river, somewhat because more of it was now being diverted for hydropower.

Just a few weeks before, a mud scow from the United States had drifted to within 150 feet of the brink of Horseshoe Falls before getting briefly stuck, and a man on board jumped into the river and was swept over the cascade. Yes, times were a-changin'—many people didn't even refer to it as the *Horseshoe fall* anymore, but *Horseshoe Falls* (the American fall was now most often referred to as the American Falls). Still, Hill agreed to assist Stephens, as long as he was allowed to make some modifications to strengthen the barrel, which he did, and he convinced the barber that his barrel had no chance of flying over the falls and crashing into a *Maid of the Mist* boat in the lower river, as Stephens had fretted. Hill noted that the boats usually didn't get closer to the cataract than one thousand feet and the barrel would go over the falls at a maximum of twenty feet from the brink. Hill took a shine to Stephens, who reminded him of his father, Layfield, with his stretched mustache and bold blue eyes. With those eyes, you could go into any darkness. Anyway, with the misery of the war still in the air, who couldn't use a rousing event? Hill even introduced Stephens to his wife, Beatrice, who invited him over anytime for tea and biscuits to talk about his large family back home—a wife and eleven children. She still couldn't believe he was taking "this gigantic risk . . . with his wife and himself, he had a baker's dozen. Am I missing something?" In a way, it helped Bea understand her own eccentric husband. She also noticed that Stephens had on his right forearm a tattoo of a garland of flowers and two clasped hands with a motto beneath: *Forget me not, Annie.* He explained it referred to his loving wife in England, although some believed it was about Annie Taylor.

Before he'd left England, Stephens had been a stuntman of some renown, a jumper off bridges, a parachutist, a carnie; goodness, before packed audiences in music halls he allowed marksmen and knife throwers to fire projectiles at things on his head. Like Hill, there was a people's champion in Stephens; he once whisked a woman bent on suicide away from a speeding train just as her upmarket skirt was being ripped away. In the war, like Hill, he had won a trio of decorations from three years of dodging bullets in the mucky trenches of France with the British Army. For some ungodly reason, though, his lifelong dream was to shoot over a waterfall in a town on the American-Canadian border while crouching in a barrel. Newspaper stories and newsreels from abroad had told him of such incredible acts by Mrs. Taylor and the cocky Leach, and that the future of daredevils was in America, but Charles Stephens had never ventured to the New World, hardly surprising since he and his wife, Annie, had spent much of their adult lives with all those kids. He carried photographs of them in his wallet, making it bulge. His wife, a bit of a madcap herself, having earned a certificate for going up five thousand feet in a hot-air balloon, had expressed some interest in going to Niagara with her husband, but could not on account of her asthma.

The daring barber arrived in Niagara on July 6, 1920. "I'm not the kind of bloke you'd expected to see, am I?" he said to a reporter, knowing the value of quickly cultivating relationships with local journalists. And yet he described himself as "a man who just doesn't seem to have been born with the power to become frightened." Nicely into his middle age, with a bushy mustache, witty charm, and soft-spoken tongue, Professor Stephens seemed anything but a man bent on giving it all away on chance, and yet he had already cheated death at least twice, not counting run-ins with the enemy jackasses in Europe. At age five, suffering from an unknown illness, little Charlie had slipped into an apparent coma and was thought to be dead to the world before he had a chance to test it. He was placed gently into a coffin as a puzzled physician examined him one more time before grudgingly issuing a death certificate. Anyone would give a farthing to have seen the look on the doc's face when the corpse sat up and spoke cordially to him. Then, at age sixteen, while Stephens was hauling sludge in a Welsh mine, a runaway coal car bore down on him and another miner at the end of a tunnel, when it suddenly changed its mind and derailed, just short of crushing them. "My companion was driven crazy with fright," Stephens later laughed. Soon after, he clipped out a newspaper advertisement seeking "a man of nerve to take parachute jumps." That's when he started referring to himself as Professor Stephens, launching a would-be career as a "tempter of fate." When he settled for barbering as a full-time job, one of his sidelights was to shave a man in three seconds flat (presumably, the customer got that one gratis).

In the Bristol Coliseum in 1912, Stephens earned the nickname the Demon Barber when he shaved a man in a lion's cage, of all places, with the beast licking its chops nearby (careful, Leo, you're next). In the papers, Stephens crowed, "Will a man who had bearded the lion in his den balk at the puny currents of Niagara?" Still, he hoped the falls stunt would pay for his children's education. "I want the money. I have a [four-chair] barber shop in Bristol and a good business, but I don't like barbering," he said. "When I have completed the Niagara Falls feat, I can go back to English music halls and lecture and show my barrel." He also hoped to cash in through a movie he was having made of his plunge by the Canadian Aero Film Company, and he had a deal to write a first-person account of his plunge with a Massachusetts newspaper, the *Lowell Sun*. Following her victory over the falls nineteen years earlier, Mrs. Taylor had not attracted the wealth she had craved, but she was not the self-promoting showman that Stephens was, and she didn't have an exotic accent like Stephens and Leach. He had heard that Taylor had fallen ill in recent times, and he was sad because she had given him a unique respect for women, for another Annie. Beatrice told him she had stumbled across Mrs. Taylor on a recent shopping spree in Niagara Falls, New York, where, near the falls, she was sitting at a table, trying to sell signed postcards of herself and displaying a barrel that did not seem to be her original one. "She looked like an old, sad woman, trying to get people's attention," Beatrice said.

***

When he arrived in the falls and saw the twenty-five-hundred-foot crest line and heart-stopping gulf of the Canadian falls, Stephens refused to be swept away. "If I thought there was a chance I would be killed, I wouldn't attempt to shoot Niagara Falls in a barrel," he said. "But there isn't a chance. I will be as safe in the 'Thundering Waters,' as the Indians call the Falls, as I would be at home. I don't expect to be as seasick as I was coming from England on the boat."

"But suppose you don't come back?" a reporter queried.

"No use supposin'," Stephens shot back. "You does it, or you doesn't. I bets I does." Stephens denied he was doing this to appease a big ego. "You might think I have what you Americans call a swelled head, but I haven't," he said. His plans were grandiose; he announced that after he had beaten the falls, he would immediately continue downstream through the Whirlpool Rapids and the Great Whirlpool. The barber's biggest concern was the police; he was so worried they would try to stop him, he kept secret the details of the plunge and the day it would be held, except from Hill and a few others who were helping him. On July 10, 1920, the night before his stunt, Stephens checked into a hotel with his film crew in Hamilton, Ontario, an hour's automobile ride from the falls, registering under an alias, W. J. London. The next morning, he awoke before dawn and read selected Bible passages, then wrote a letter to his family: "I am not wishing you goodbye but only so long . . . until we meet again. What a day that will be." Stephens also wrote out two cables, one of which would be sent to England after the plunge. One read: "Feat Accomplished, Tell Dan" (referring to his manager in England). The other covered his bets with: "Professor Stephens Lost in the Attempt."

Then Stephens went to an all-night diner for breakfast with the cameramen. "Coffee and sinkers [doughnuts]," ordered W. T. Brown, one of the film crew.

Stephens corrected him, chuckling. "Take something else—we don't want any sinkers today." Brown changed his order to toast and coffee, and everybody got the tension out of their shoulders with giggles. It was the last laugh for some time. Then they drove to Snyder's Point on the upper Niagara River, two miles above the falls on the Canadian side. As the sun peeked over the watery horizon, Stephens suddenly blinked. The river above the falls could be ominous when you knew your heart was going to sink at the end. Waiting for him at the point with smiles and wide eyes were Leach and Hill. Red was typically at the falls after his first black coffee of the day.

If he had his way, it would be *his* barrel pointed at the brink on this midsummer's day, but he wasn't in soldier's shape, mentally or physically. It was, after all, just two years after the horrors of Vimy Ridge, wound after wound, hospital after hospital, and Red was still not in the pink, coughing and wheezing at inappropriate times. A doctor had given him one year to live in 1918, and now, in his early thirties going on fifty, he was playing with house money. Ironically, Beatrice had recently received a nicely signed letter from one of his old regiment buddies, expressing condolences about her husband. "I haven't heard from dear old Ready since we all left Vimy, and I heard through the grapevine that he had gone to his Great Maker," the soldier penned. On the battlefields of Europe, Hill got the nickname Ready for his pluck in the face of cutting danger, and, of course, it was an offshoot from his original nickname. Another letter from a sergeant who *did* know that Ready was alive and kicking made mention of the fact he thought Hill had killed more men with his rifle than any of his fellow Allies (Hill never talked of that, and when the subject came up, he never got past a deep sigh). The sergeant wondered if Ready had now destroyed more chaps than he'd saved from death (soldiers could be cruel in the way they talked; it was one of the ways they stayed alive).

Ready was having problems sleeping at night; he'd often awake with a Jerry (German) on top of his position behind the charred elm tree in No Man's Land, bayonet drawn at his throat. He liked cold sweats a little more at the falls. In his daily ventures to the river, some days Hill didn't have the required pep and vigor, but if another scow got stranded above the falls, he was Ready (believe it or not, by 1920 the heavy scow was still grounded above the falls). Some strength he had to save for his wife, who put up with his escapades as long as they went waltzing every couple of weeks at the Emporium (somebody spread the rumor that singer Al Jolson, *the* Al Jolson, was coming to town soon!). His children once went to a dance and thought it odd to see their parents holding one another. Of course, Red was still healthy enough to father children—the fourth child of Red and Beatrice, counting adopted Harry, was born Major Lloyd Hill on March 12, 1919, with a hint of the old man's reddish hair. Harry was nine, William Jr. seven, and Edith five. Niagara Falls was being dubbed as Baby Town for the thousands of children being conceived here each year, mostly by honeymooners wonderfully losing their virginity to the orchestral music of the rushing waterway. Others, like Stephens, came to conceive other things.

At Snyder's Point on the day of the plunge, there was another discussion about the viability of Stephens's wooden barrel, now painted zebra in black and white stripes to make it easier for the camera to focus on it in a fast river with a mind of its own. Looking around on the edge of the shore, Stephens entertained about fifteen people at his bon voyage, although many more were at the traditional tourist spots closer to the falls, even at eight in the morning. Usually daredevil crowds were in the hundreds, even thousands, but if the numbers didn't reach that, it was quite all right because, with the police in mind, he had kept mum about his schedule. "Small crowd to see a man perform a feat like this, but wait until I have gone through with it," he said. "Crowds will greet me everywhere." Stephens certainly looked the part for the center ring, with his gray tweed coat and a plush red vest clanging with medals and ribbons he had accumulated for various acts of daredeviling through the years. Although the sun was still low in the sky, he was sweating and sticky and about to take the world's biggest shower. Among the helpers and onlookers were Leach, Red, and Beatrice, who had presented Stephens with two pillows, stitched by herself and daughter Edith, so he could rest his head in the barrel.

Harry and William Jr. were here, as well, digesting every moment and every souvenir, every glimpse they could get of Mr. Stephens's medals, to see if they were as shiny or relevant as their father's; in the morning freshness, they looked more colorful. The boys had already learned some things along the river, including how to occasionally blurt out filthy words when no adults other than Dad were around (Red was quiet and hardly swore, although he'd been doing more of that since Vimy). Much of the time, they bragged about the bass they caught—Harry's was two pounds, William's three, Harry's four, and so on. Their mother grew weary of it, especially when she knew darned well that the boys overstated to win attention, but Red reminded her that the Wright brothers had been sibling rivals. Even Edith, a sometimes tomboy, caught a five-pounder. In the end, Beatrice sided with all of them; Red was beginning to worry she was spoiling them. On this day, the kids were more interested in Mr. Stephens's zebra barrel and how the river might deal with it. William tossed a willow twig into the current and made note of the way it fussed. Nearby, Harry had the gumption to tell his mother and another woman not to get too close to the water's edge. They looked daggers at him, but excused it for today because of the circumstances.

Suddenly, a cloud appeared on the horizon—Mayor Harry P. Stephens (no relation) pulled up to the launch site in a new automobile. The rogue barber was sure his jig was up and that the bobbies would be next in line. "Now they'll stop me," he said grimly to Hill, but his apprehension was unfounded as the mayor had simply come to wish him a harmless trip with, naturally, plenty of publicity for the city. A relieved Stephens posed for the movie camera, handed his jacket, vest, medals, and four hundred pounds sterling to Hill for safekeeping, then put on a life jacket, a woolly cap over his iron-gray hair, and a specially padded suit. "Don't worry," he said. "I'll be back in a short time." People trusted Red Hill and felt securer in his presence. Next, Stephens slithered into the barrel, securing himself with straps attached to the 110-pound ballast at the bottom of the barrel, which would hopefully keep him upright when the going got rough.

Shuffling his feet, a still-skeptical Leach had more trouble getting a "good luck" out of his mouth than he did his cigar. The mayor reached into the craft and shook the barber's hand.

"I'll see you below the falls," Stephens said before putting on an oxygen mask. "I'll not say good-bye, only so long." What else was he supposed to do—stand in a barbershop while hair piled up on the floor?

"Don't lose your nerve, old man," an unidentified bystander chortled.

"Good luck, Charlie," Hill said. "I'll be waiting down below for you with a doctor and an undertaker." So much for the sense of security with Hill around.

Mrs. Hill leaned forward and said to Stephens, "Are you sure?" He didn't respond, but she recalled what he had told her the previous night: "Don't fuss, Ma'am, it will just be a hop, a step, and a jump, and then Bob's your uncle." Beatrice had gotten to know Charlie in the few days he had been in Niagara, and he'd gone out of his way to compliment a duck dinner she had made him.

A soggy cigarette dangling from his mouth, Red kept his peaked cap out of his eyes and intensely screwed the lid of the barrel shut. Lastly, he got into a boat with a tiny gas motor to tow it out into the river. Red didn't make a big deal about being Stephens's aide. The time was ten past eight. Almost right away in the water, one of the steel hoops appeared to snap off the barrel as it was being towed. Hill stopped the boat, examined the barrel, and decided to continue without the hoop. On shore, Beatrice waved and started crying a little, dabbing her face with her apron. She thought of all his children in a land far away, agonizing about their father. They should have been here when he was on the edge of his life. In a brown paper bag in Mrs. Hill's purse was a pocket Testament from which Stephens had earlier read: "Cast thy bread upon the waters; for thou shalt find it after many days." Red rarely quoted the Bible; he did the type of things that happened in the Bible. Beatrice opened the purse, touched the book, and felt safer.

Time to go. The electric crowd hustled to cars and drove to the brink of the falls to find the premier spots. In the river, with a mile left, Hill thumped on the barrel three times to signal Stephens that he was cutting the tow rope from the boat. The mad barber and his barrel were alone, and his internal clock was ticking. What else was he supposed to do with his life at nearly sixty years old, sign up for another war? He'd already lied about his age to get into the last one. As a camera atop one of the cars on the roadway filmed the action, the barrel entered the Whirlpool Rapids of fierce water and started to spin and bounce at fifteen miles per hour, and twenty, then twenty-five, sometimes airborne. At first it spun head forward, then feet forward, then sidelong, then in almost every direction at once, bumping from small reef to small reef when it got jolted by a big rock and was diverted toward the American side. There was no chance, however, that it would go over the American Falls, which would be fatal with its wall-to-wall boulders.

Leach decided not to drive all the way to the falls. He stopped to watch at the Electrical Development Company and was skeptical Stephens would survive. Before the barrel could finish its journey, Leach got in his car and went home (he now lived in Niagara Falls, Ontario). Perhaps he didn't want to watch the macabre along with the several hundred people gathered near the brink, or perhaps he was resentful that his nine-year reign as king of the cataract was about to crash. Completely oblivious to what was to come, the barrel shone brightly in the early morning light, gracefully approached the brink, stopped to take a glance, then was carried straight down by the oceanlike torrent. Hill, who had raced by car from Snyder's Point, and others witnessed what they did not expect to see—the barrel plunged facedown, 165 feet, and disappeared in the thick, wet noise of Down There. Headfirst it went into the maelstrom, despite the fact all that heavy ballast at the bottom was supposed to keep it upright. The time was fifty minutes past eight. *Good God*, Hill thought, *what's that feeling like?* He and other Niagara watchers were starting to realize that watching a barrel go down the falls was a fleeting, almost disappointing thing, that you don't see much of it, that seeing it on top, ready to plunge, and then finding it in the lower river were better experiences, almost as good as the anticipation of excitement and dread.

The only class remaining for Professor Stephens was a waiting game. On rocks beneath and beside the falls, as close as they could get without decapitation, Hill and other stout river men lingered with grappling hooks and field glasses to capture the barrel. They watched and waited until the cows came home, dragging Lucky Strikes, squinting into the spray, and wiping their faces. Five minutes passed by, ten. Was it entombed behind the raucous wall of water? From where they stood, they could see how erosion had pulled away the rock face and left big boulders littered in the path of a barrel, and they shuddered at the thought of anything meeting up with them. Some of the boulders were round from the constant pounding.

Up on safe ground, a large crowd had gathered at the Table Rock railing above the falls as well as on Terrapin Point on the US side and the Upper Steel Arch Bridge. Word had spread on both sides of the border that Stephens's barrel had been launched. Tourists were frantically scanning all parts of the river, and the "Did you see that?" from Table Rock became "A man is in the river!" from the bridge and finally grew on Terrapin Point into "A cabin cruiser just went over the falls, all hands on deck!" Sunday church services hadn't started, but the praying had. With the war still in everybody's soul, there was soft sentiment among Americans and Canadians toward the English, their allies, especially the Canadians who remained British subjects and raised Stephens's Union Jack as one of their proud flags. Down below, the river men were plugging for Stephens, as well, but that didn't mean there weren't the usual pokes at black humor:

"Well, Mr. Demon Barber, this looks like a close shave."

And, "Did you hear the funny one about the Limey [Brit] who jumped over the falls and missed?"

"D'ya think ya can just show up in town and perform a miracle in a few days?"

Beneath the wisecracks, something was wrong. In the two previous plunges by Mrs. Taylor and Leach, their barrels had come up for air in the plunge pool within ten minutes of the big drop, but now it was up to fifteen, and twenty. Hill worried that the backwash of the falls might not release Stephens before his three hours of oxygen ran out. If he didn't put in an appearance by noon, he might never. The strong words of Stephens about the surety of his stunt were taking on the sound of a whistle past a graveyard: "Will a man who had bearded the lion in his den balk at the puny currents of Niagara?" Until twelve o'clock high the vigil continued, when a dark object popped to the surface in an eddy near the Maid of the Mist landing.

"There he is!" a spectator shouted. After circling several times in the eddy, the object bobbed into the docks and turned out to be not the barrel, just a little chunk of it, a broken black stave. Hill had a vial of smelling salts in his pocket, but it was starting to look as though Stephens would need more than that. River Man turned sick and coughed up cigarette smoke. Why hadn't he more closely checked the barrel in the upper river when the steel hoop had come off? Throughout the afternoon, more debris washed ashore until it was abundantly clear that the fears of Hill, Leach, and Captain Carter had been realized—the barrel simply had not been up to the ultimate challenge in the unforgiving waters.

Mr. Charles G. Stephens had gone into the lion's den once too often, and who was going to tell all of those kids across the big pond? Hill and others combed the shores into the evening, when the new searchlights of one billion candlepower were shone from the Ontario Power Company at the base of the falls to illuminate the area, but all that the men could find was Stephens's life jacket, and he wasn't in it. By this time, police were on the case and quite perturbed that this calamity had occurred under their noses. An officer sent a telegram to Stephens's family in England: "Professor Stephens lost his life in an attempt to go over the falls in a barrel." It wasn't until morning that a more definitive clue surfaced—somebody's right arm, torn from a shoulder, at the Maid of the Mist. Tattooed on the victim's forearm were two clasped hands, a wreath, and the legend "Forget me not, Annie." The Big Splash had claimed a life. Beatrice Hill cringed when Red told her. A second telegram was sent with that description, and Stephens's distraught wife identified the arm as belonging to her husband from its markings. Hill theorized that after going over the falls, the barrel had rotated into a feet-first position and got smashed to smithereens by boulders at the base of the falls and that Stephens was pulled by the heavy anvil he was strapped to through the bottom of the barrel and into the river's neurosis. Also found in the water was a rib, apparently from the barber, but all that was left of the barrel popped up from time to time in the form of wooden splints and staves; a pity, because Red wanted to recover the barrel and claim it. Stephens's arm and rib were buried in an unmarked grave at Drummond Hill Cemetery in Niagara Falls, Ontario. The fifty-dollar funeral was covered by the film company, reportedly the only money they paid to his family. At least the family got back Stephens's pocket Testament—mailed to them first class by Mrs. Hill.

"In another contest between man and the mighty Niagara, the latter won," wrote the *Border Cities Star* in Windsor, Ontario.

Leach was hardly surprised. "I told him that his barrel was not strong enough. The hoops were too light. You know how the hoops on my barrel were bent, and they were twice as thick. He may be caught behind the falls' curtain. I was in there for ten to fifteen minutes."

The political fallout from the tragedy was horrid. Mayor Stephens was criticized for giving his blessing to a daredevil act, as an "official approval of suicide." Many people aimed angry letters at Ontario's attorney general, some saying that the brazen, doomed feat desecrated the Sabbath. Toronto mayor Thomas Langton Church said that police should find and punish those responsible for helping Stephens kill himself. Even some newspapers suddenly wrote sourly of misadventures at Niagara. Opined the *New York Tribune*:

> The great cataracts are something to be enjoyed in a scenic way . . . hundreds of thousands of people see them every year, stroll along the banks of the rushing waters, explore the parks on both sides, as well as Goat Island in the center of the river, enter the Cave of the Winds, ride on the *Maid of the Mist*, spend honeymoons and holidays communing with nature in its majestic splendor . . . but to be sure, Niagara has taken a heavy toll on human life, mostly through suicide.

And yet, within a month of Stephens's demise, requests had poured in from nineteen people wanting to barrel over the falls. Just two days after the fatal plunge, a twenty-four-year-old woman from Detroit, Vernia Morrison, wrote to Niagara Falls, New York, mayor Maxwell M. Thompson, requesting permission to go over the falls in a barrel. In one breath, she wrote she was "crazy to do it," and in the other she asked if citizens of Niagara would take up a collection to pay her costs. He sent her a copy of the *Niagara Gazette*, carrying a full account of Stephens's grisly death. Another would-be stuntman, Frank Lazar of Buffalo, called himself "as game as they make them" and asked the mayor for suggestions on how to beat the falls. Charles Ensign of Medina, New York, had apparently been planning his own plunge for a long time and was miffed that Stephens had beaten him to it. A railway fireman from Cleveland, Thomas Whitford Jr., said he had been a sailor and was not afraid of the water, and Dudley Peterson of Minneapolis thought the falls could be beaten in a "blown out rubber suit."

After huddling with his lawyers, Mayor Thompson drafted a response to answer these people:

> I beg to advise it is the opinion of the Deputy Corporation Counsel that any person attempting such a feat as going over Niagara Falls

would be clearly a disorderly person. In view of the above, the official granting such a permit, as well as the person performing the feat, would be violating the law.

Some of the daredevils contacted Hill, but the political pressure was too great to go into those waters; in fact, Hill, supposedly the keeper of the Niagara River, had been embarrassed about his role in the Stephens tragedy and, worried about the cops, lay low for a time, refusing interviews. The attorney general promised an official investigation, but it was never conducted, and no charges were laid. A few morbid people wondered if Stephens had actually survived the plunge and vanished to set up a barbering shop in New York with his one remaining arm so that he wouldn't have to return to England to feed his large family.

The Stephens plunge received considerable media coverage. Editorial writers at the *Des Moines (Iowa) Daily News* conjectured on July 13, 1920, that three out of five of their readers had read the story of the plunge before any other in the paper. "Why? We all like thrills. We like adventure . . . it was the spectacular nature of Charles Stephens' gamble with death in attempting to go over Niagara Falls in a barrel that interested every man, woman and child that read about it . . . Stephens' fate again reminds us that man is a puny weakling when he attempts to overcome the forces [of nature]."

And thus, in a way, the Roaring Twenties had come in at Niagara "not with a bang, but a whimper," as poet T. S. Eliot would write five years later. But Hill was glad for himself and his four children that he had not gone through with his own plans at Horseshoe Falls. Meanwhile, one night not long after Stephens met his fate, Bobby Leach in his still-strong English accent told anyone who would listen at the Cliff House that the only way to beat the leviathan was in a series of gigantic rubber balls. Wooden barrels hadn't worked—Stephens was in his watery grave, Mrs. Taylor was one lucky lady, and Leach's old steel barrels, resembling hot water heaters and septic tanks, were retired. A series of rubber balls might work, one within the other, making it more resilient on the rocks than a steel or wooden barrel and giving it a better chance of being tossed clear at the base of the falls. Leach and Hill agreed on something.

CHAPTER EIGHT
RUM-RUNNING SWIMMER

As the 1920s roared, Hill and Leach remained off-and-on rivals, although Hill spent some of his time helping his wife, Bea, raise their five children, including the newest, Helen. He was still a hero, though; at a medal presentation in 1920, honoring the scow rescue, an official praised him: "I consider Red Hill a true hero, in that with him, soul triumphed over self. He is entitled to all the honor we can give him." By this time, Hill looked like he had worked for the praise: hardly forty, he was hard-boiled, with an old, sea-worn expression, even in a tie and white shirt with sleeves rolled up to the elbows. Did he have daring left for the devil? "Perfesser" hoped not. Approaching sixty, Leach didn't allow his age to shrink him or his personality; in 1920, attired in a bathing suit, he parachuted two thousand feet out of a plane to land in the Niagara River, but, as several thousand spectators watched, the wind blew him off course into a hayfield in Niagara Falls, Ontario. Hill got a wry chuckle, yet he was there to help, as usual.

Despite Stephens's death, Leach talked about going over the falls for a second time if he could get backing of $2,500 from a railroad company, the city of Niagara Falls, or a steel firm. "The lure of notoriety and fortune is stronger than caution to the recklessly adventuresome," said the *Montreal Gazette* in an editorial. When Leach couldn't get his sponsorship, he sold his billiard parlor and took off for a tour of England, with future plans for South Africa, Australia, and New Zealand. "I'm through with making money for the railroads and resorts around here," he said. "I've been diving off suspension bridges, shooting the rapids, and going over the falls for years. I'm through risking my life for the love of adventure. I'm out for the money now." When the English tour did not make him a millionaire, restless Leach was back in Niagara by 1924 and getting more serious about a second crack at the falls in what he called a big rubber football—seven feet four inches end to end with a width of four feet at the center, made from the same stuff as balloon tires, and costing him $3,400. The ball weighed 280 pounds without a passenger. Its interior was a compact, oblong space, just large enough for a man of Leach's small dimensions.

For the trip, Leach would lay on a hammock suspended at each end by swivel fixtures to keep him upright, no matter which way the ball turned. Air compartments were at each end. "It'll be a lead pipe cinch to do it now in my rubber football," he said. "I'll ride the big plunge like a bubble and I won't even get a jar." He was concerned that authorities would try to stop him, "but I've outsmarted them every time before and I'll do it again." As an added feature, Leach said an airplane would drop him into the rapids above the falls, and he described it: "Now here's the way it's going to work: at the head end of the ball is a big ring to which it will be attached to the bottom of the airplane by a rope. A cutter, operated from the pilot's seat by a lever, will release the ball at the right place. I'll tell them to drop me in the rapids near the Toronto power house [Electrical Development Company] . . . There'll be enough air inside the ball to keep me alive for an hour. But if I am not picked up below the falls within twelve minutes, I'll never be."

However, Leach had trouble finding a pilot willing to take the chance. "You'd think they was being asked to be a party to a murder plot," he said. "Well, we drew up my death warrant. I signed my own name, Bobby Leach, and they signed John Doe from China, and I hand 'em one thousand dollars in cold cash when I get sewed up in my rubber ball. And that's that." Leach, of course, was talking more hope than reality, because he couldn't get a plane in 1924. His wife, Sarah, suggested he wouldn't be welcome back to his home—which they shared with their fifteen-year-old daughter, Viola Pearl, who boasted black locks like movie star Mary Pickford—if he dared the falls again. "If he hadn't already done it once I wouldn't say anything," his wife said. "Let someone else do something he hasn't done and let him do that."

No stunts occurred in 1924, except a lot of Charleston dancing and action at the local speakeasies, one operated by Leach in Youngstown, New York (he was fined \$150 for illegally possessing liquor). Besides lecturing in Australia, Leach hoped to barrel over a lost waterfall there, apparently higher than Niagara. Looking older than in his sixties, he leaned heavy on a cane, although his eyes remained clear, his demeanor still defiant. "If [a man] has the right stuff in him, he never is too old to find it," he said with a grim face and stern jaw. Finally, in 1925, he announced he would swim across the treacherous river just below the falls from the American to Canadian shores, and asked his rival Hill to assist. Beatrice protested because she'd finally had her man home and away from danger for seven years. It was by far the longest stretch he had looked into Bea's brown eyes. Although they still weren't touchy-feely with one another on the dance floor, they had six kids: the adopted Harry (fifteen) and five natural children, William Jr., nearly twelve; Edith, nine; Major, six; Helen, three; and Norman (Corky), one. The boys loved the falls and the river; William's highest mark in school lately was an A for his drawing of Charles Stephens's barrel going over the falls. Major got a note sent home by his teacher, however, for his "grotesque" drawing of what was left of Stephens's arm. Beatrice went to the teacher's house to apologize and explain that Major was just trying to outshine his older brother. Otherwise, they acted like many other kids; in fact, Red and his kids would roller-skate up and down the street in front of their house, the boys copying their father's long strides and pirouettes, up on his front wheels and going like mad. In winter, there was ice-skating in Queen Victoria Park, a winter wonderland, carving figure eights around frozen trees. Red was not a strict disciplinarian, and rarely did he take off his belt. They never took a vacation. The Niagara was their vacation. William was becoming quite the little river man, ahead of his father at the same age in adoring the falls and learning its manners. Harry was not quite as daring in the gorge, but was becoming an excellent swimmer. Red also taught his boys fishing, skeet and trap shooting, and hunting, and they fought to be the best at those pursuits, as well, or at least to be the one to keep Dad's consideration.

Nineteen twenty-five was also the year of the ringing telephone in the Hill household at 1499 Robinson Street. The family now had their own taxicab company, Red Hill Taxi Service, along with several other small businesses on the side, most of them legal. Automobiles were no longer a rich man's sport, and roads were being built all over the twin cities, inhabited by noisy black Tin Lizzies (Model T Fords), which could go thirty miles per hour, with room in the back for women and children. That summer, a group of river rats would gather regularly at the Hill home, including Leach, Mousie Sloggett, and Hank Stewart Jr., for tall tales over beer and whisky in a back room while Beatrice and daughter Edith prepared dinner. Stewart was a character out of a dime novel, a thirty-five-year-old one-armed marvel. Whenever the overgrown boys went pheasant hunting, Stewart would steal the show by flipping his 16-gauge shotgun onto the stump of his right arm, taking keen sight, and unloading both barrels before a bird could take wing (too bad some of the others were not so accurate—in 1910, one of his friends had accidentally blown off Stewart's arm). The door to the Hill homestead was never bolted, allowing a variety of people in and out, including many after hours for booze-ups and rum-running across the river to the United States. Everybody in town knew their telephone number, 717, but not every call was for a cab; on a typical night, there would be at least one call that Red would identify as a "trip to Cuba," and everybody would laugh. That was the code for an illegal liquor trip by motorboat to the United States in which Red and some of his pals would load the boat with liquor or beer near a pump house on Chippawa Creek or down toward Queenston, and make a short trip of only several minutes to the dry Lewiston, New York. Prohibition in the United States lasted from 1920 to 1933, and liquor produced in Canada was exported to Lewiston or Niagara Falls, New York. The Canadian government did not object, but the US customs agents did—to the point of sometimes firing bullets from steel boats in the river. But the agents usually waited upriver from Niagara Falls in the Fort Erie–to–Buffalo route, so Red and the boys were often able to slip quietly across the border under cover of dark. Besides the border business, Red hosted businessmen, big shots, and even tourists late at night after the bars had closed, for drinking and chain smoking at his house. The children were puzzled when police showed up on several occasions, although no one was ever charged; in fact, the coppers sometimes had a beer along with the river men.

Drinking was a lifestyle that seemed to touch everybody; in the summer of 1925, the gang got a chuckle from the sports pages—baseball slugger Babe Ruth, the Sultan of Swat, was fined five grand and suspended for the season following a drinking binge. During these *men things*, the Hill women tried to look the other way; Beatrice played the sewing machine, and little Edith would listen to Bessie Smith's jazz tunes on the Victrola phonograph or the wireless box (radio), then she would play "Sunrise and You" on the player piano with her fast fingers. Sometimes when Edith got up in the middle of the night to pee, she saw the visitors drinking out of bottles with no labels on them and didn't know what to make of it; she also listened with interest as Leach, in his thick English accent, and her father talked of swimming the river. For nine years old, Edith was a heckuva swimmer, but she didn't particularly like Niagara, which she and her friends at school were calling the River of Dead Bodies, and her father was always Down There, retrieving accident and suicide victims. She was a good girl and helped with the dishes and kept Pa's clothes dry with a sharp crease in the trousers. Once she helped Ma make a beautiful white nightgown for him, and he used it in the winter, all right, but for camouflaging himself to sneak up and save limping swans on the Ice Bridge (tourists were no longer allowed on the Ice Bridge, but who was going to stop Red Hill?). Edith looked up to her father; when she was six, she got too close to a bonfire while helping clean the yard, and Pa saved her by grabbing a blanket from the clothesline and tossing it over her.

The most celebrated person to walk through Hill's door was Harry Houdini, escape artist extraordinaire, magician, filmmaker, and the world's greatest show-man when Bobby Leach wasn't in the room. Houdini was in the falls in May 1921, to film and produce a silent movie, *The Man from Beyond*, a melodrama featuring the mesmerizing Harry rescuing a damsel in a canoe in distress above Horseshoe Falls. Red Hill wanted to be part of the film, or at least its safety adviser, but Houdini liked to control things as the film's director and to keep the secret of his stunts. While he was staying at the Prospect House in Niagara Falls, New York, rumors circulated that the forty-seven-year-old Houdini was planning on shooting over the falls in a spectacular stunt, but he denied it to the local papers:

> They say that I am here to go over the falls, swim the rapids and dozens of other foolhardy exploits, which can be performed only at the risk of one's life . . . I have taken great risks, but that was earlier in my stage career. I am long past that.

His petite and charming wife, Bess, backed him up: "Why of course he will not risk his life in any exploit here, going over the falls or otherwise. I wouldn't let him." Houdini claimed he was earning $200,000 a year making movies and that his escape artist days were over. What wasn't publicized was the fact that Houdini, accompanied by his wife, went to Hill's home and picked his brain about the possibility of one day going over the falls in a barrel or other type of vessel, and he was fascinated by Hill's stories of the three people who had gone over the cataract. For the film, Houdini shot a harrowing scene, swimming in the rapids above the falls with a hidden cable tied around his waist. He also escaped from a straitjacket while suspended from a crane with the falls in the background. In another scene, two canoes manned by dummies were sent over the American Falls and smashed to bits by the rocks below.

Houdini filmed his rapids sequences the same day as the funeral of Annie Edson Taylor, who had died a pauper at age eighty-two and was buried next to her hated rival, King of the Mad Torrents, Carlisle Graham, at Oakwood Cemetery in Niagara Falls, New York. Long live the Queen of the Mist. The *Niagara Gazette* was not impressed with the timing of Houdini's film. It reported on the events of May 6, 1921: "These pictures will form the climax of a picture romance of Niagara that will probably make thousands of dollars for its producers, while Mrs. Taylor, the only woman who ever made the Falls trip and survived, was unable to derive a fortune from the feat and was buried through the generosity of friends."

Houdini told Hill that he would return to the falls, and for several years after he reportedly contemplated a barrel stunt, but concluded it would be a grave threat, possibly because of the warnings Hill had heaped upon him about the unpredictable river. The falls offered no abracadabra, no trapdoors, no second takes. But Houdini never returned to the falls as a daredevil; in a stunning development, he died of a ruptured appendix in 1926. Later a museum honoring him was built in Niagara Falls, Ontario, and held periodic séances to try to reach the spirit of Houdini, who had said he would try to return after death.

Between fielding taxi calls and sending his fleet to distant parts of the city, Red Hill chaired many meetings in his home about the river with fellow river rats and community leaders. Besides discussing swimming plans, as well as current events like the witch hunt in Europe for Commies and anarchists, talk often got around to the number of bodies that the men had brought ashore from the river. Red had become Niagara's unofficial undertaker, paid five dollars a head from coroner's fees—and sometimes more from relatives of victims—for taking floaters to the funeral home. He figured that, to this point, he'd fished out at least seventy-five corpses. Beatrice tried to keep the stench from Red's clothes out of her kitchen, but she didn't discourage the practice; she told friends, "Will is a good provider. Before we got into the business, often times I'd wonder where our next dollar was coming from, and Will could say, 'Oh, don't worry, something will come up.'" And usually something did, like a body.

Hill was protective of his turf; in 1925, he chastised US authorities for not letting him keep a floater he recovered at the side of the Whirlpool, but which drifted away from him to the American side into the possession of a fisherman, who got paid for it. Nevertheless, the Hills had a little more cash than usual lately, and it came in handy, because the taxi company was not off to a booming start. Red was slipshod in his paperwork and had to be nagged to keep the books straight. Tourism operators suggested he'd get more business if he took the dead sturgeon, silver bass, and salmon out of the trunks of his cabs, to which Mousie, one of his part-time drivers, responded: "Are you kidding? The tourists think it's great. They take pictures of each other and Red holding the coho salmon." Live and dead animals were all over the place in Hill's life; in his cellar and backyard were a variety of fish and fowl, wounded and mending ducks, swans, and geese, which the Hills had rescued from peril. When they got healthy, they were taken back to the wild and released, or shipped to Jack Miner Migratory Bird Sanctuary. Some of the dead fowl were stuffed with arsenic and wood shavings by taxidermists Red and Mousie. Hill also hoped to make money from the US submarine chaser *Sunbeam*, trapped in rocks above Horseshoe Falls, not far from the old scow (which had still not gone over the cataract). In 1923, the $30,000 *Sunbeam* had wandered from its moorings in Chippawa and got stuck at the falls. Unable to salvage the vessel, US authorities sold it to Hill for one dollar, but so far even Hill had not been able to perform a miracle and get it ashore without hiring a giant crane, and he didn't have that kind of dough.

Bea was a good wife; she would lay out quite a spread for dinner for the boys and river rats: thick vegetable soup, deep-dish chili sauce with rye bread, spicy Spanish buns, and ducks soaked in wine. The family was generous. Red took duck dinners to needy homes, and Bea's chocolate and vanilla cakes on the counter were available to anyone who came in the door, albeit she was protective of the birthday cake she prepared for Will Jr.'s twelfth. In 1925, Bea lost another baby, but you would never know it by the way she scrubbed floors, boiled diapers, shopped out of town, and cooked.

***

When reviewing the history of Niagara Falls, the river men figured that everything of importance had been won at least once—the Horseshoe Rapids, the Horseshoe Falls, the Whirlpool Rapids, and the Devil's Hole Rapids—but there were two things that hadn't: the American Falls and swimming across the river below the falls. Riding a barrel over the American Falls would most certainly land a daredevil on a grave of imposing boulders at its base. But swimming the lower river, despite its tricky undercurrents, from the United States to Canada, was a possibility. Several men, including Leach, announced they would do it in the summer of 1925. That, coupled with pledges of Leach and other men to go over the falls in a barrel, motivated Edna Marshall, a reporter for the *Bee* in Danville, Virginia, to write, "A new fever of unrest and searching for adventure has Niagara Falls in its grip." For example, Rene Jacquier, night chef of the Clifton Hotel, was practicing his swimming stroke daily in the river. "I don't know if I'll come out alive when I try the rapids swim," he said. "But I'd like to be the first to do it . . . I have posted a forfeit of $400 pledging that I will—that's a good man's week's salary. I will probably try at night when the police are not so spry—and the new illumination will show me up." After seeing Jacquier's comments in the papers, John White, a budding auto mechanic, challenged him to a race. "I'm out for it, full steam," White said. But on August 30, 1925, Leach beat them to it; wearing a red bathing suit and cocky grin, the old Englishman dove into the water, with Hill rowing along in a rowboat. About one-quarter of the way across, a *Maid of the Mist* boat created a wake and distracted Leach, who had Hill pull him back to shore. On his second attempt, Leach got halfway across, when his false teeth suddenly fell out of his mouth as he was gasping for air. When he struggled to catch them, all he caught was a mouthful of H_2O. The teeth sank, and so did his ambitious stunt. With reporters on hand, Bobby was embarrassed, but promised to make up for it by going over the falls soon.

A week later, on September 26, thirty-seven-year-old Red Hill did what Leach could not—he became the first man to swim across the broad lower river above the old tunnel stream from the New York to the Canadian shore in eleven minutes. Considering the heavy weight and toughness of the water, that was a sparkling time. He used an over-arm style for the first half until encountering a sinister undertow in the middle of the river, at which time he switched to a breaststroke. A crowd of several hundred people was on hand, including his safety man, Mousie Sloggett, friend Norman Beam, and, of course, a reporter. Hill's motivation was to prove something to Leach, who had been making negative comments about Hill in the papers. "Yeah," cracked Leach, "but wait'll ya get false teeth." With his knickers in a twist, Leach planned to go over the falls in October of that year, and one day a fairly large crowd of spectators turned up to watch, but the stunt was postponed, and they went home disappointed when Leach announced he had raised only $119 for the feat, not enough to risk his life.

In the fall of 1926, Hill lost his father, Layfield, at age seventy. Mr. Hill came home from work at the Queen Victoria Park Commission and got the urge to tinker in his backyard garden. With his garden fork in his hand, he collapsed against the front door, blocking the entrance. When his wife, Mary Ann, came home, she could not push herself in, and it was left up to their ten-year-old grandson, Mousie's son, Ken, to scramble through a window to find Layfield dead of a heart attack, still clutching his fork. Good old Lafe. He was a good river man, a good husband and father of five, a military man and veteran of the Fenian Raid. Red had learned so much from his father, from swimming the troubled waters to generosity to treating others and the river with respect. Layfield never attempted a stunt, but he performed many rescues of people and animals. Red cried that night, dreaming of Pa down at the falls in the morning mist with a fishing rod.

The funeral procession started at Layfield's home and proceeded to All Saints Anglican Church for service by the new pastor, Rev. Percival Mayes, then on to burial in the Drummond Hill Cemetery, shoulder to shoulder with War of 1812 heroes. His obituary said that Layfield had been a staunch Conservative and took great interest in politics, but Red had never paid much attention to that. The funeral bill was $226, which included the funeral car, embalming, tie, socks, collar, and sympathy cards. Meanwhile, life and death went on at the river; the body of a one-day-old baby was discovered below the falls, its parents nowhere to be found. Red recovered it.

Until now, Hill had probably been underestimating some of the recoveries, rescues, and daredevil acts he had performed. He had not wanted to give them more than they deserved, yet as his pals pointed out, many local people gave the falls and the Hills less than they deserved. They took the falls for granted and did not appreciate them (tourist traffic and noise did not endear Niagara to the locals, either). Come to think of it, it was rare that the river rats saw any local people down at the river. They didn't seem to care that Sir Adam Beck was the largest hydro generating plant in the world, that the old scow represented a spectacular rescue, and that the city was the number one destination for tourists. They did, however, get turned on by people going over the falls in barrels, and they would soon get more of that.

CHAPTER NINE
THE BOUNCING OF A
BIG RUBBER BALL

The anomalies of life are what make it interesting—the dreams that send youth in search of queer adventures; the successes that sour; the failures that lead to fame; the "mercy murders"; benevolent crimes and stunts on the lunatic fringe . . .

Those millions who wind the clock, put out the cat, eat what their wives cook and pretend to like it, believe in the Ten Commandments and mind your own business still lack a press agent, but they furnish an audience, if nothing else, and what would there be in it for the stunt artist, the stock speculator or the gang leader, if they did not make the wheels go round.

—*An editorial in the Pittsburgh Press on July 6, 1928, two days after Jean Lussier went over Niagara Falls*

He smiled. He was handsome. Charismatic. A rugged New Englander. Cocksure. Thirty-six. A story distributed by the International News Service called him a "gay French Canadian," not as a sexual reference. His life was a dance, a perfect fit for the Roaring Twenties. That's all Red Hill needed in his life, another Bobby Leach (except for the handsome part). In 1928, the new guy in town was Joseph

Albert Jean Lussier of Springfield, Massachusetts, a former carnival stuntman and now a machinist, born in Concord, New Hampshire, and raised in Quebec. He was five-four, one fifty; in fact, Leach and Hill were short, too—a psychologist might say they suffered from the Napoleon complex, small men acting big. Lussier's goals were to become the first American man to perform the Big Splash (Mrs. Taylor had beaten all the blokes, and Leach was English), to buy his parents a small farm, and to "see my picture on the front pages." Lussier was a part-time racer of automobiles and motorcycles, a victor in 1919 of a motorcycle contest from Springfield to Montreal, covering the 302 miles in seven hours and thirty-two minutes.

Thanks partly to knocking heads with Leach at the river and in the papers, Hill was beginning to savor publicity, as well, and he had recently talked about going over the falls in his own contrivance, but he put that dream on the back burner for now; he had six children at home and a wife increasingly irritated with the other woman, Niagara. No one had dared the falls since Stephens's death. Lussier's dream had taken years to hatch, conceived in 1911 when he witnessed Leach's plunge, and from that moment, he was obsessed with beating the famous cataract. A year later, Lussier met Leach and was impressed by how the transplanted Brit was making a fair living on a lecture tour of several countries. For the next sixteen years, Lussier planned his own jaunt over the falls, experimenting and saving dough while performing jobs ranging from salesman to grocery clerk to provide for his wife, Rose, and their two daughters. He considered all manner of vessels and studied diagrams and the shock-absorbing properties of springs, wood, and rubber. "What I wanted to do was go over the falls in something besides a barrel," he said.

> Barrels had been used [three times] before and each time the occupants were badly battered by the fall and contact with rocks below. For years, the idea of a ball has been in my head. I decided at last on a steel frame, with plenty of rubber to break the shock and insure [sic] its keeping afloat.

In early summer of 1928, Hill and his young river-rat sons, fifteen-year-old William and nine-year-old Major, got a preview of Lussier's ball, concealed from police in a barn. These unveilings, these long journeys to the falls, were as much fun as the end result. Meanwhile, William and Major were falling in love with Niagara and trying to outdo one another, especially when the old man was around. Major had just got a part-time kid's job at the Maid of the Mist, painting and clearing debris from the docks, something William had done off and on for years. It was a test for Major's shoulder, which had been injured two years previously when his adopted brother, Harry, accidentally shot him with Grandpa Layfield Hill's old rifle from the Fenian Raid. Harry had been monkeying with the muzzle-loaded rifle, which had been used to turn back the Fenians. Not knowing it was still working and loaded, Harry pulled the trigger, and Major went down with a shoulder wound. It was a minor miracle that their mother, who had been sick from losing a baby at birth, rose from her bed and carried Major to help.

Also in a group this day with William, Major, and another river rat was their twelve-year-old cousin Ken Sloggett. All the boys looked upon Lussier's big rubber ball with astonishment; his expensive invention, started in his garage and completed in Akron, Ohio, by the Akron Rubber Company, was six feet long and nine feet in diameter—one thousand pounds of intricate vessel with nine layers of rubber, inner tubes, and canvas stretched over a steel frame. Actually, it was a ball within a ball; he would be strapped inside the inner ball, and there was a space between the two balls with forty oxygen compartments. Lussier also designed a valve system, allowing him to release air from tanks inside the craft while keeping it watertight, reportedly providing up to forty hours of oxygen. On the bottom were 150 pounds of ballast to keep the craft disciplined in the difficult water. Daredevils and carnies sometimes exaggerated, but it didn't seem far-fetched when he said it cost him seven grand. The only thing Red Hill didn't like about the craft was its color, reddish orange. This was one of the boys' first experiences at a barrel event, and they seemed aware of the perils. Tragedy and danger were tenants in the Niagara River; the week before, a nine-year-old boy from Niagara Falls, New York, had accidentally drowned over the falls, and in nearby Lake Erie, three boats had sunk off Port Colborne. But it was an age of hope and adventure, as well—on June 18, Amelia Earhart had become the first woman to participate in a flight across the Atlantic, from Newfoundland to Wales. Oh, well, at least a man (Charles Lindbergh) had beaten her to that one the previous year. Hill hoped Lussier wouldn't die in his attempt, if only for the sake of his sons being impressionable witnesses.

"Are you going over the falls this year, Pa?" Major said.

Pa quickly changed the subject by telling Major his mouth was open from awe of Mr. Lussier and his ball. "Now, lads," Red said. "You pronounce this gentleman's name Mr. Loose-ee-eh, okay? He's an American, but also French, French Canadian."

"Loose-ee-eh," Major repeated. "American French Canadian."

Lussier announced he was going over the falls on July 4, 1928, which had tourism officials rubbing their hands in glee in anticipation of a lucrative holiday weekend. Another budding daredevil, Miss Bessie Marie Hall of Pittsburgh, a thirty-two-year-old former circus performer, was also planning to go over the falls on Independence Day in her own rubber-lined barrel. According to newspaper reports, she was training through swimming lessons and vaulting in vessels over dams in Pittsburgh. She said she had no fear of the dangerous undertaking and craved the thrill. With flaming red hair and steely blue eyes, Miss Hall said she was born in a circus tent and raised on the death-defying, once riding two horses at the same time. "Her manner is not mannish, but she seems quite sure of herself," said the *Emporia (Kansas) Gazette*. She said the barrel was under construction in New Kensington, Pennsylvania. Hall had asked permission for the stunt from Niagara Falls police, but Superintendent John A. Curry said she would be stopped. Why would she want to do such a thing? "I don't know," she said. "Something just gets into me sometimes and I'd bust if I didn't do something reckless."

One familiar voice was forever silent these days—in 1926, "Perfesser" Bobby Leach, the man whose ego had its own gravitational pull, passed from this cruel world. Accompanied by his wife and daughter, Leach had been on a twenty-nine-week vaudeville tour of Australia, New Zealand, and South Africa, showing motion pictures and telling tall tales of his Niagara Falls glory days, when he slipped on a discarded orange peel while walking down a street in Christchurch, New Zealand. He injured his leg (which had to be amputated), developed gangrene, and died—an ending even the showman himself could not have conjured up. Opined the Ogden (Utah) *Standard-Examiner* in its editorial pages:

> He slipped on an orange peel . . . Death had the last laugh on Bobby Leach. Which is only the tale that insurance companies and their veracious figures tell again and again. Occupations of risk, even plain daredevil stunts, kill so few persons compared with the

can opener, the stair step, the kitchen stepladder and the rusty tack.

The little things again.

Oh, well, Leach's death made all the papers; he would have been pleased. In all, he had gone through the rapids five times and over the falls once, parachuted off bridges and out of airplanes, and performed in Madison Square Garden. He had brought Barnum & Bailey to Niagara, and the tourism operators on tawdry Clifton Hill took notice and started building museums of excess and imagination. Red did not make light of the ironic death of the "Perfesser"; when he had not been going up against the Englishman, he was sort of smitten with him and his verve. He was sorry he never got a chance to tell Bobby a final "you meet the same people on the way up as you do on the way down." Although their relationship had been bitter at times, competition strengthened both of them, and A.L. (after Leach), Red wasn't quite so humble when discussing his successes. Beatrice was sad about Bobby, as well. Living with Red, she got to know all the daredevils and opened her home to them. Poor Bobby. He wouldn't be forgotten anytime soon.

As he had been for Leach and Stephens, Hill became the lead safety hand for Lussier, although he remained leery of Niagara police, who said they would not tolerate such a stunt, calling it suicide and an unnecessary hazardous risk. They wanted to keep civility, especially after Stephens's catastrophe. Hey, Mr. Frenchie, if you want action, why not go down to the Strand Theatre, where *Why Sailors Go Wrong* is playing, starring Sammy Cohen? Indeed, as the big day approached, police searched the countryside for Lussier's oversize playground ball, but it was stored in a barn somewhere at the river's edge. So confident was Lussier that he did not bother to test it in the river. Originally, he had announced he would make his plunge after the ball had been dropped from a plane, but that idea was nixed when airport managers refused to allow a plane to take off towing such a contraption, so he chose to go with the traditional method of having a boat tow him into the channel of the upper river. Although the date of the stunt was well-publicized in the papers, Lussier and his crew kept the time and place for the launch private. And so on July 4, a huge holiday crowd showed up, estimated by the papers at between seventy-five and one hundred thousand, who were glad to be close to the falls, where white spray cooled them from the almost tropical heat.

The journey commenced at small Cayuga Island in Niagara County, New York, several miles above the falls. In the company of a few friends, Lussier donned a blue-and-white bathing suit with "U.S.A." in bold on its tank top, then entered the ball and adjusted the straps for his head, waist, and legs, which would hopefully serve to somewhat break his long fall. The muscular Lussier surrounded himself with cushions, and an aide strapped him with thongs of tarred fabric to the back of the chamber to prevent him from being thrust forward. In his strong hands, he gripped two wooden pegs and sat erect like a Catholic schoolboy in chapel, the interior space just big enough for his body. Also at his disposal was a small cap for loosening the valves in the oxygen compartments to keep him breathing after the ball was sealed. These preparations took longer than expected, and the launch was delayed; finally, with a nonchalant farewell, Lussier told his assistants to seal up the craft, and they towed him out into the river with a boat. Inscribed on the outside of his ball was "Call Me Jean." It was half past two o'clock. At the bottom of the falls, river man Hill waited.

As the ball was surrendered to the current, several small boats that had been following it turned back to the safety of the New York shore. Meanwhile, police didn't see the ball until it was in the middle of the river—too late. Crowds along both banks stopped their sightseeing and focused on the unusual craft, bobbing and weaving in the water. As its seduction always goes, Niagara is careful with you at first, almost lulling you into an afternoon siesta, but then, even before the Point of No Return, it gets irritated; that's what Lussier discovered as the white-water rapids started pitching the ball about, and it lived up to its name by bouncing from rock to rock, wave to wave, reef to reef. Again and again it plunged to the bottom and scraped rocks in the shallow water, and at one point it seemed to strike a glancing blow on the huge steel scow still stranded above the falls, now a tourist attraction. "It looked frail; spectators held their breath, expecting it to be torn to shreds in the terrific current," reported the *Buffalo Evening News*. In reality, it was strong and resilient, but not enough to prevent it from suffering some damage—the heavy ballast at its bottom tore off in the rough water, allowing the ball to turn over and over in the rapids and putting it at serious risk as it approached the falls.

Below the falls, in his bathing suit, Hill waited with anticipation in a small rowboat on the American side. Not knowing if or when the otherworldly ball would appear, he rowed restlessly back and forth, several times moving to avoid the *Maid of the Mist* steamer. He went through several cigarettes, and time seemed to expand as he began to think Lussier had been thwarted by police in the upper river or perhaps stuck on a reef in the unpredictable Horseshoe Rapids. Overhead, *Miss Niagara* of the Sky View Lines and another airplane circled to get a bird's-eye glimpse of the engagement. Then, without warning, an orangey object appeared at the top of the falls, shining in the sun. "There it is!" Hill shouted and threw his arms into the air. Indeed, there it was, an orange ball on the white brink, ready to drop over the middle of the falls. With no ballast remaining to right the ship, it hurled over the brink headfirst. The crowd didn't know whether to cheer or gasp. For the benefit of the doubt, they cheered.

What they didn't see was that in the ball's descent, intense water pressure ripped off an outer cover and water started leaking in. But it escaped the backwash of the falls and soon a current forced the ball out into the plunge pool in the basin of the lower river, and the crowd in the Waiting Room cheered again. If anyone was checking their fob or wristwatches, it was 3:20. Near the falls, Hill adjusted his signature peak cap in the spray and rowed hard toward the peculiar vessel. At first, the ball drifted toward the Ontario Power Company on the Canadian side, then it swung back into the center of the river and downstream toward the dangerous channel that fed the ever-hungry Whirlpool Rapids. With strenuous pulls on the oars, Hill reached *Call Me Jean* before it got into the channel, and looped a rope around one of its wire handles. By this time, the ball was right side up and appeared damaged, as if the rubber had been peeled back and the hatch pummeled by rocks. He wasted no time, worried the ball might be ushered into the rapids' channel, and in its present condition, that could be fatal. "I had to do it fast so he wouldn't suffer exposure at the mercy of the currents," Hill said. He didn't even stop to bang on the ball to get Lussier's attention, if he was still breathing.

Hill later said getting the ball ashore was the toughest thing he had encountered at Niagara, as it weighed more than nine hundred pounds, including the water that had seeped into it. "As the big rubber ball floated past the Maid of the Mist wharf, an outboard motor boat put off from the American side," Hill said.

It had an American policeman on board and he wanted me to pull Lussier into the American side. "Nothing doing," I said. He didn't like that and his propeller started to get tangled up in the rope and made it darned hard for me, so I told him to get the hell out of the way. If he hadn't beat it then I would have slammed him one and then there would have been a real rescue job right from the middle of the river.

With the strong current resisting him, Hill rowed slowly but powerfully toward the Maid landing, but suddenly changed his mind and continued on to Bridge Eddy, near an abutment of the Honeymoon Bridge on the Canadian shore, where a large crowd had gathered. He got the ball to the riverbank, tied it to the steelwork of the bridge, and knocked like a madman on its side. No answer.

"He's dead!" shouted a bystander on shore, closest to the ball, bringing a collective groan from those surrounding the contraption. When Hill knocked a second time, Lussier shouted from inside that he was fine.

"He's all right!" Hill heralded to the crowd, and the groans turned to hurrahs.

Hill tried to talk through the enclosed ball to Lussier, but the latter couldn't make out what he was saying; Lussier could hear the crowd yelling, and he interpreted that as though he were drifting toward the rapids, beyond rescue. The blood left his face. "I thought he had got out to me [in the river] and then missed me and that I had to go on down the rapids and through the whirlpool," Lussier said later. "It seemed a terribly long time until I knew by the ball turning on its side that Red had me all right and that I was on shore . . ." Even then, Lussier feared he would drown not in the river but his own barrel. "The water started coming in and I thought they were never going to get me out. The water was right up to my ears, standing on my head, when [Hill] finally got me in and turned the ball on its side. Everything was jake then." At the riverbank, at least forty men and one woman—Lussier's sister, Madame J. P. Gautiere of Sherbrooke, Quebec—pawed at the huge ball and tried to get inside with penknives, some of them standing knee-deep in water. In the cramped quarters between the river and a stone wall, some pushed others out of the way. As it lay there, bruised and deflated, it looked as though God had taken the air out of the already-strange craft. Several men, including J. Hiscocks, blacksmith at the Ontario Power Company, started hacking at the ball with jackknives to get it open.

Inside the ball, Lussier shouted for his brother, George. When the ball was finally split open, he pushed out through the hatch a cushion he had been sitting on and his black pullover sweater. Hill looked inside to find Lussier sitting, still strapped in, with a blank look on his face and blood oozing out of his temple and cheek, the charisma and handsomeness nowhere to be seen. Then, as light from the hot summer sun poured into the dark, fallen ball, Lussier flashed that fetching smile and was slowly helped out through the hatch, as his chest and arms were not up to their usual strength. But as his body appeared, he thrust his hands up over his head, and the spectators roared and clapped, some of them tossing handkerchiefs and hats into the air. "I was certainly glad to get out and see the world once again," he said. Then Lussier's brother appeared, and the two men heartily shook hands on top of the ball, which sent the audience dizzy with delight. Hill quickly joined them as photographers pleaded with the three men to embrace, which they did, smiling along with the sun, and reporters from all over the world peppered them with questions. Another in the crowd to reach Lussier was his sister, who planted a smacker on the cheek not bleeding and told him how very proud she and his family were. Men sang and children jumped and applause kept breaking out here and there. "I knew I could do it!" Lussier shouted. "I'm tip-top." He then said something in French that hardly anyone could understand, but they cheered anyway.

All of this was being filmed by a four-man camera crew from the National Film Company of Akron, but that didn't stop some mischievous youths and unscrupulous men from hacking chunks of rubber off the ball for keepsakes. Pushing through the crowd, William and Major yelled to their father about the thieves, but he assured them, "Don't worry, I'll get you some souvenirs." They didn't really care; this experience was a shiny souvenir for them. They had seen a craft go over the falls with a man inside, and he was alive, and the boys managed to get in the background of photographs.

Fighting through the well-wishers, Dr. A. B. Whytock reached Lussier, held him by his strong jaw, and examined the injuries—a large gash on his right temple, another on his right cheek, and a third on his left shoulder blade, all suffered, Lussier said, in the terrific bouncing while he passed through the Horseshoe Rapids. He was also quite dazed. "I didn't even think while I was going over—it happened so fast," he said. As the crowd continued to grow and people scrambled down the banks to get close, reporters kept pumping him with questions: What did it feel like to conquer Niagara? Did you pray? Did you think you were going to meet your Maker? Before he answered, the showman talked to his fans and waved to everyone around the big ball and to spectators high up on the cliffs. Then he wouldn't shut up: "When the top was cut off and I breathed fresh air again, believe me it was a welcome feeling. There were several inches of water in the ball already. Ten minutes more and I think it would have been too late." Then he went over his trip from the start: "I tried not to think about anything except getting it over with . . . I went over the falls head first but straps and pillows saved me from serious injury . . . I had really no sensation when I went over the falls [by that point, he *was* praying]. When I landed on the water at the bottom, I got a good jarring up. The ball struck the water and bounced up and down six times, just like a ball being bounced on the sidewalk by a child . . . I really didn't know where I was for a while. I was stunned."

He continued, "Hitting below the falls, the water pressure is so heavy I'm going to the bottom of the river and the first [outer] cover is smashed. Water is rushing in between the two covers and the ball is rolling behind the falls. It circles around maybe five or six seconds and then it's coming out with a strong current. Men are waiting with a boat and no one knows if I'm dead or alive." He said he got cuts and bruises when "the steel framework came in on me sharp. It didn't hurt as much as it might on account of all the cushions I had in there. Everything was fine inside the ball. The oxygen worked perfectly and the two flashlights which I had strapped in kept burning all the time. It wasn't bad."

After the last of the photos and queries, Lussier wrapped himself in a bathrobe and stepped into Hill's boat, along with his brother, George, and reporter Winnifred Stokes of the *Niagara Falls Evening Review*, for a short trip to the Maid of the Mist docks, then they went up an incline to the top of the gorge, almost fighting through happy spectators and several women trying to kiss Lussier (police showed up to make a lane for Lussier's group). Hill then drove the hero par excellence to Hotel Niagara in one of his taxis, where Lussier told reporters in his broken accent about the big picture:

> I suppose the main thing that made me do it was simply the desire to prove to myself it was possible. And then again I was sure that the publicity would gain me contracts of various kinds that would amply repay whatever I spent. I have demonstrated that my theory was correct; Leach went over in a barrel for the trip and the fact I did not get injured as badly as did Leach [in his barrel of steel] is proof that my theory was correct.

He continued, as family, friends, and strangers reached out to touch his sweaty body, asking for autographs: "I have spent more than a year and more than seven thousand dollars on my venture. I have succeeded and I am happy . . . I could do it again, I am sure. But once was plenty for me."

For River Man, it was the third daredevil he had plucked from below the falls, including Leach in 1911 and the arm of Stephens. The next day, the *Evening Review* credited him with saving Lussier's life: "Everything depended on Hill . . . and he met the situation in the same manner in which he has always done when called upon to rescue any person—cool and collected."

Papers across the continent loved the story and the photographs. "To help make a glorious Fourth, Jean Lussier went over Niagara Falls in a big rubber ball and lives to tell the tale," said an editorial writer at the *Joplin (Missouri) Globe*. "It is a small sort of individual who will decry his feat. He risked his life and won. He is entitled to such recompense as the vaudeville houses or the moving picture world will offer him." Gushed the *Standard-Examiner*,

> With the courage of a Lindbergh and with a Lindbergh's luck, with the zeal of a Nobile or a Byrd, with the ancient urge for sudden riches and fame, and with the patience to wait for long years of planning and saving—Jean Lussier was rewarded by realizing his life's dream, to go over Niagara Falls in a rubber ball.

Not long after, a court fined Lussier $113 for stunting, but he did make some money; he was offered several vaudeville contracts and cash to be a spokesman for toothpaste, tobacco, flashlight, soft drink, and bathing suit companies. A local theatre offered him twenty dollars a day to exhibit his ball, but he said he would only do it for five times that amount. Unlike Leach, Lussier apparently didn't let his day in the sun go to his head; his neighbors said he remained a generous and humble man and had time for them when they asked about his amazing trip and career. "He showed me his scrapbooks, two huge volumes filled with newspaper clippings of his daredevil exploits," said neighbor Cecil Burridge. A few days after the plunge, Lussier changed his mind and crowed that he wanted to try the falls again on Labor Day of 1928 with an improved rubber ball. Before that, he said, he would jump off the Woolworth Building in New York while wearing wooden wings on his arms. Shortly after, he adopted Niagara Falls, New York, as his home and set up shop signing autographs and postcards, giving tourists tales about his adventure, and even selling pieces of his rubber ball for twenty-five cents. When he ran out of cuttings from the real stuff, he reportedly went to a gas station, got similar rubber scraps, carved his name into them, and sold them, particularly when a parade was in town. As he went on a lecture tour, theatres and museums proclaimed:

See the Wonder of the World

Jean Lussier

in Person

the Biggest Thrilling Attraction

the Hero of Niagara

One of his prize possessions from the stunt was a souvenir book of the falls, autographed and given to him by Mayor Harry P. Stephens of Niagara Falls, Ontario. When Labor Day came and went with no encore, Lussier said he had postponed his second trip for July 4, 1929, in what he called a smaller parlor ball, which would be six feet in diameter, electrically lighted, and so constructed that the occupant would be able to remain upright during the entire journey. Miss Bessie Hall did not go over the falls in 1928, and neither did anyone else. Privately, Hill told close friends he wished he had done it, although he was concerned about who would provide for his growing family.

Publicity about the affair sparked copycats: James Hardy, an athlete from Toronto, wanted to tightrope across the deep gorge on a rope, if a commercial firm would sponsor him; Molly Semsen of Flint, Michigan, asked for permission to go over the falls, claiming she had already performed dangerous stunts in the mountains of Switzerland; and an unnamed man and wife from Kansas sought to try a Lussier-style rubber ball over the falls, strapped side by side (now that's 'til death doth part). But authorities said they would try to stop any such goings-on. For River Man, it was back to the grind—not long after, he recovered his ninety-fifth body below the falls, sixty-year-old suicide victim Catharine Knapp of Buffalo. She left a note: "Going through the falls. God forgive me. Goodbye, loved ones. Catharine."

CHAPTER TEN
THE GREEK AND HIS TURTLE FIGHT FOR LIFE

Not long after the Lussier wonder, young Major invited a couple of his school chums to the Maid of the Mist, where he was a sometimes child employee, and they fashioned a raft out of debris of boats and trees that had gone over the falls, launching it quietly in one of the few calm spots in the lower river, where there were no channels linked directly to the rapids. There, with pike poles, they pretended to be swashbucklers on their way to the Great Whirlpool, until an adult employee of the docks told them to get ashore pronto or he'd come out and grab them by the ears. Two days later, Major was taken by his father to Morse and Son Funeral Home; there, in a back room, he was told to stand by a heavy table while his father gave him two cork plugs soaked with pungent vapor used to cure people's colds. Skinny Major winced as the corks were pushed up his nose, but he soon forgot that when his father pulled a sheet of rubber off something big on the table. It was a cadaver. He couldn't tell if it was a man or deformed mannequin, so bloated, especially around the stomach and in the testicles, that it didn't seem real. At the Lussier adventure, Major had his mouth open much of the time, but here it was his eyes that were wide. "There," Red said, pulling the corks from his son's nose so that they made a popping sound, "that's what the river does to people." Major took one whiff of the corpse and scooted out of the room. No more rafts for a while.

The following year, 1929, most of the deaths in the river and over the falls were attributed to murder. An investigation by the *Toronto Daily Star* unveiled a disturbing trend: up to twenty men had drowned, probably while rum-running booze from Canada to the United States for as little as twenty-five dollars a load—including nineteen-year-old Hugh Moriarity in a rowboat full of contraband liquor. "All is not harmony along the river front," the *Daily Star* wrote.

> Double crossing and hijacking takes place and there are feuds and gangs . . . the extraordinary thing about the whole sordid business is that nearly everybody around the river front knows what really happened but are afraid to speak. They are in fear of getting bumped off themselves.

An inspector for the US Immigration Patrol said that foul play could not be proven because the rocks and rapids often obscure the cause of death, but he believed they were all members of the "bootlegging fraternity." Red Hill was not one of the dead rumrunners; in fact, he was on the other end, recovering some of the floaters.

The stock market crash also produced a number of suicides, but there weren't any daredevil stunts in 1929, although Mrs. Susan D. Grove, a sixty-nine-year-old gray-haired widow from Hagerstown, Maryland, active in her church and looking for thrills, said she would go over the falls in a rubber ball made in Akron the first week in September. "What's a little danger at my age?" she said. "I have great faith in God and I know He will help me." Her five children helped her more—they wrote to the Niagara Falls Chamber of Commerce to have her stopped. She never made the trip. In 1930, the price of gasoline soared to seventeen cents a gallon, and lines formed for soup and for moving in with the in-laws. If you were making ten bucks a week salary, you counted yourself blessed. There were still dreamers in Niagara Falls, though. There were always dreamers in Niagara Falls—perhaps that's why people always came, year after year, winter and summer, for vacations, honeymoons, day trips, and imagining Oz. Niagara had motels with mirrors on the ceilings, wax museums with Teddy Roosevelt as the doorman, and men and women planning barrel rides over Horseshoe Falls. Even River Man was telling the newspapers he would produce a barrel to become the fifth person to go over with his own rubber ball, and he already had a steel barrel in his yard.

Red Hill Sr. was restless. He was tired of rescuing others, who had the fun. Over the next two years, he made two barrel trips down the rapids into the Whirlpool. On Memorial Day weekend in 1930, he took his barrel into the gorge; six feet long and 620 pounds, including 150 pounds of railroad steel on its bottom to act as a keel. The barrel, which floated on its side, had a manhole entrance fourteen by eighteen inches with a sliding door of steel protected by a rubber gasket. The five-hour ordeal was filmed by the *Toronto Star* Newsreel, starting at the Maid of the Mist docks and spiraling through the swirling rapids, through the Whirlpool and all the way to Queenston, with Hill prone inside on a special hammock, broad straps over his shoulders keeping him in place during the watery rock and roll. The crowd along the banks was in the thousands, and he was elated to be the center of attention again. His wife, Beatrice, who had just given birth to their infant child, Wesley, wasn't so impressed: "The river rats rolled his barrel past my bedroom window. I had to go, so I wrapped my baby in blankets and went down to the Whirlpool. It was cold. I stood there for hours and watched my husband's barrel go round and round in the Whirlpool."

Still, Beatrice, pretty teenaged daughter Edith, and friends kept up appearances—all attired in pretty clothes and cloche hats, worn close to the head, giving them the appearance of aristocracy in the crowd, showing defiance to the Depression. When Hill emerged, wobbly, from his barrel, grinning and wearing a leather football helmet and cardigan sweater dripping with his rescue and military medals, he was mobbed. The scene was too much for Beatrice, who passed out and dropped sleeping little Wesley, wrapped in his bunting bag, who fell into the arms of their doctor, J. H. Davidson, in the crowded gorge.

After the newsreel of his trip was shown at Shea's Hippodrome in Toronto, Hill was inspired for more. Could his barrel beat Horseshoe Falls? It might be small enough to avoid many of the new rocks. As he often said, surviving the plunge wasn't science and sometimes relied more on luck than physics or athleticism, depending largely on what mood or shape Niagara was in. Nowadays, Hill could afford to spend some time on this falls project because he was still able to feed his large family from the proceeds of his taxi company (although 717 wasn't ringing off the hook lately), along with illegal income from bootlegging and rum-running. Whether Hill would launch a barrel over Horseshoe in 1930 or any other year was one for the fortune-telling gypsies on the hotel strip. Whenever somebody challenged him as being all talk, Hill would throw back at them a quote he'd heard somewhere: "Familiarity with danger makes a brave man braver but less daring. He who goes oftenest around Cape Horn goes the most circumspectly." He couldn't pronounce *circumspectly*, but they got the point. Hill wasn't the only one talking about a plunge—the king of the rubber ball, Jean Lussier, was in the papers again for a possible go on July 4, 1930. Two jumps in three years? People were still buzzing about his feat, which had helped eclipse the sad memory of Stephens, and Lussier was hoping for a crowd exceeding the substantial one he had attracted in '28. Rumor had it that he would one day challenge the American Falls with his rubber ball, but that would be absolute disaster, River Man warned, because of its solid floor of boulders reaching to the sky.

Then there was the newest face in town, forty-six-year-old George Stathakis of Buffalo, New York, and it was a bookish, frumpy one, complete with spectacles that likely came with a fake nose, a neatly trimmed mustache, and dark hair combed straight back. People said Stathakis was strange, but strange was usually in at Niagara Falls. Call a guy strange because he said he wants to jump over the falls to find out about the truth in his life? Nevertheless, reporters who interviewed him started referring to Stathakis, a bachelor who had immigrated to the United States from Greece in 1920, as a comical philosopher, a man at a blackboard. Unlike some other daredevils, he was no alpha male and could not hide inside his machismo, and so he didn't try. Stathakis worked as a short-order cook in several restaurants in St. Louis, then for two years at the Manhattan Restaurant in Niagara Falls, New York, while living in a boardinghouse on Delaware Avenue in Buffalo. When he wasn't cooking up bangers and mash, Stathakis was writing books on metaphysics in Greek, including *The Mysterious Veil of Humanity through the Ages*, translated into English. Its narrative had the author talking with long-dead legendary philosophers such as Aristotle, Plato, and Socrates. Stathakis believed in reincarnation and said that in a past life he had been the first man to reach the North Pole, where he proclaimed: "I am king and master of the earth and from this summit I am going to rule and direct it." He believed an expedition over the falls would bring him a financial nest so he could write full-time and expose his ideas to the world. In addition, the emotions and sensations brought on by conquering the falls would offer him a unique mind-set for his writing, he believed.

When he told reporters he was daring Horseshoe, to them it was more proof that he was off his rocker and would never try such a macho stunt. The numbers were with them—probably one in fifty people who talked in the papers about a stunt along the Niagara River actually went through with it. However, Stathakis's plans were well-publicized across the globe by the United Press, well in advance of the event, even though it was supposedly against the law. Stathakis showed street smarts by choosing a busy time for the Big Splash—July 5, 1930. A publicity picture showed him sitting atop his barrel, *Spirit of Niagara*, engulfed by its size and purpose. He planned on making money from the venture through the sale of newsreels, from a Hollywood film of his life, and from writing a book about the stunt, to be titled *From the Bosom of Niagara*. From his hard earnings in steamy kitchens, Stathakis paid $400 to a Buffalo firm, Peter Pfeil Cooperage Works Inc., to construct a colossal one-ton barrel—ten feet long and five feet wide at the middle with a skin of oak three inches thick. (United Press called the vessel a "glorified beer barrel.") Steel hoops encircled wooden staves, a heavy steel casing lined the vessel's interior, and coverings, designed to act as shock absorbers, projected from each end of the barrel and were expected to take the force of the nosedive over the cataract, even if the barrel smashed into rocks. There was cork padding in its walls and a harness to keep the occupant in place, but when Hill inspected the barrel in late June, he warned Stathakis not to dare the falls because it was too large and heavy, offering too much surface area to hit the rocks. But life was a risk, he told Hill, preaching to the choir. Finally, when he realized Stathakis was determined to go over, Hill agreed to be his assistant, and the chef was excited; who wouldn't want Red Hill riding shotgun?

On the big day, Stathakis's barrel was taken from Mang's Boat House at La Salle, New York, and towed by boat to Navy Island in the upper river between the two countries. The barrel was docked briefly on the Canadian side of the island, where Stathakis and his friends prepared a bon voyage. Hill was downstream below the falls, waiting with three of his sons (William, Major, and Harry) to retrieve the barrel. Dressed in a suit and tie (no specs) and fashionable boots, Stathakis appeared on his way to a meeting of accountants, not a date with physical fate. He smiled for the cameras from the *Pittsburgh Post-Gazette*, which was to film every facet of the journey. Stathakis had also made arrangements to go on a post-stunt lecture tour, and he was going to rent or sell his barrel to a museum. Joining George for his journey was his pet turtle, Sonny Boy, reputed to be more than one hundred years old. If he did not survive, the turtle would give a detailed account of the adventure, Stathakis said with a straight face. Also inside the monster barrel were a mattress and a harness to hold him secure and two oxygen tanks with an air supply of three hours. Stathakis was asked if this was enough air to keep him going. "If I don't come up in three hours, there wouldn't be any use in living anyway," he said.

On Navy Island, he was helped into his vessel by friends George Folls and Charles Stathacos, a former employee from the Manhattan Restaurant. Confident, he told Stathacos to prepare a steak dinner for him at five o'clock that night "because this trip is going to make me hungry." Peacefully, he squeezed through the small hole while waving to onlookers and the camera crew. Before the lid was bolted tight, he said he believed the trip would take no more than two hours from the time he was cut loose to the time Hill pulled him from the barrel beneath the falls. As a final gesture, he reached out his left hand through the manhole and gave a good-bye—an effeminate wave, as if to say, *so long, sweetie pie.* The release valve of a tank of air in the barrel was turned and hissed like a snake as the cover was bolted on. In bright sunlight, a boat towed the barrel to a point off Chippawa and cast it adrift at twenty-five minutes past three. At first, the big barrel floated nicely, high in the saddle in the relatively smooth waters of Chippawa, past the eagle's nest high in the last tree on Navy Island. It was sunbaked and hot. It was July Fourth weekend. One could almost hear Hoagy Carmichael crooning his new song, "Up a Lazy River." A large crowd along the banks watched the barrel approach the old scow and the *Sunbeam,* and momentarily they forgot about the troubles of the world while George bobbed and weaved toward his steak dinner. What if *they* were in the barrel? Traffic all along the Niagara Parkway and on the three Niagara Falls bridges was the heaviest on record, although numbers were not revealed; in places along the parkway, it was so congested with automobiles and horse buggies that drivers and passengers had to abandon their vehicles on the road while they went to watch the proceedings. Reporters and police estimated the crowd at twenty thousand.

While on shore, the barrel had looked immense; now it was humbled by the river's building power and became a can of soup in an oversize washing machine. The trip got really serious near the Electrical Development Company, where the barrel disappeared briefly underwater, then headed straight at the *Sunbeam.* "Oh, my God, it's going to crash!" someone shouted from the crowd. To some witnesses, it appeared to strike the old sub chaser; to others, it narrowly missed . . . in any event, it now rode lower after obviously taking on some water. The current carried it back into the midstream, and it heaved and strained, speeding up as it went. At the brink of the precipice, thirty feet from the observation platform on the Canadian side, with a sudden rush, the *Spirit of*

Niagara plummeted down into the roaring chasm. A collective hush came over the thousands of spectators along the railing as it seemed to pause for several seconds at the brink. Then, halfway down, the cask turned a complete wheel and was drawn back behind the torrential wall of water.

"Did you see it? Did anyone see it?" came the cries. Few people took photographs; they wanted to make sure they saw it with the naked eye, a story to hurry home with. Below the falls, a second crowd waited for the barrel to appear, including Hill and his sixteen-year-old son, William Jr., the official rescuers for this afternoon, standing on a rock ledge. All eyes were trained on the misty floor of the river. Meanwhile, nearby at the Maid of the Mist landing were hundreds of spectators, including two doctors and an undertaker ordered by Hill, and two other of Red's sons, Harry, eighteen, and Major, eleven. Along with William, Harry and Major had some trepidation about the mighty falls, but most days they were attracted to their fear as much as they shied away from it. If their pa was here, it was the place to be. Sure enough, heroes of the day were baseball slugger Babe Ruth, jazz singer Louis Armstrong, and aviators Amelia Earhart and Charles Lindbergh. The boys didn't care much for sports, except for some ice hockey, but they admired the aviators, especially Earhart. Their friends at school ridiculed them for having a female as a role model, but they had respect for women daredevils after hearing Pa's tales of the incredible Mrs. Taylor.

When all was said and done, though, their father was their hero number one. He was always risking his life for others. His name was in the papers. He hunted quail and put food on the table. He was a war hero. He'd been assistant to Bobby Leach and Jean Lussier. And Pa had gone down the entire length of the rapids in a barrel and survived! The boys adored their father. According to their mother, they even peed like him. The younger Major was the more impressionable; he absorbed everything his eyes touched, watching like a hawk all of the movements of his father and older brothers. Sometimes he got on their nerves a little by trying to interfere in their efforts, but that's what brothers did; they didn't want to be left out. Fooling around on the docks and waiting for Stathakis's barrel to appear, Major looked like a kid during a mud fight—his soiled shirt was rolled up to the elbows and the collar was wide open down to the breastbone because all its buttons had given up the ghost. He had that mouth-open look of awe again, and his pants were up to the knees, revealing long stockings. He wanted to be more involved with the adults, and yet he didn't want the vapor up his nostrils again. Instead, on this day he spent some of the time goofing off with Harry.

After ten, then fifteen minutes, Stathakis's barrel still had not appeared beneath the falls. Waiting on the ledge, Red started to believe Stathakis was missing for good, trapped in the bosom of the river, or yanked out of his *Spirit of Niagara* by uncaring nature, as Stephens had been ten years earlier. Thank God, Hill thought, he had not taken a chance with his own barrel this day, considering the river's temperament, its "time of the month, like a woman." He put out a small skiff boat and eased as close to the falls as he could get without being drawn under, but he couldn't see the barrel in the heavy mist and curtain of water and came back to shore. "I think the barrel was shattered and is wedged in the rocks at the foot," he told reporters. "Either that or it was holed and sank before it could float from out of the mist. There is not one chance in a thousand of it appearing now." Slowly, the disappointed crowd moseyed back to their automobiles and hotel rooms. Oh, well, they'd seen *something*.

Some of the crowd remained at the Maid of the Mist docks, where one of the spectators was Charles "Sheep" Hill, Red's first cousin, a middle-aged man in a heavy coat in the middle of summer with a nose across his face somebody had used as a punching bag. Sheep was out of *Oliver Twist*, the Hill who never made the papers, a recluse who lived in a cave along the gorge below the falls. Sheep walked up to Harry and Major, and they smiled at him, having seen him several times before, down at the falls. "I heard there wus a man in a barrel," he said to Harry. Sheep's long, placid face and drooping jowls gave him a comical, hound-dog look.

Harry nodded.

"That Greek fella?" Sheep said. "Didn't make it, did he? I told him that barrel was too bulgy."

While they were talking, Red and William Jr. returned from the brink of the falls, and Red came over to say hello to Sheep. He told Harry and Major to either go home for the night or go to Sheep's cave. They went gleefully to the cave. Sheep was born in 1885 to a cemetery caretaker and had little formal education, but after finishing a stint with the local militia, he held jobs as a laborer and helped paint the Honeymoon Bridge. After his father died, he moved out of his parents' tumbledown house and worked winters on a rural pig farm, living most of the year in his cave. When Harry and Major got to the cave after meandering through trees and rocks at the base of the gorge, they found a bachelor pad that had few of the comforts of the city's overnight tourist rooms. Built by nature from huge boulders, its sloping floor offered shelter from the swooping winds of the gorge. Inside, Sheep would snuggle up to a simple campfire with a circle of rocks under a natural chimney hole in the stone roof, and his bed was two old driftwood planks. He never needed a bathtub—his morning wake-up call was windblown spray from the American Falls.

The cave home was actually illegal; trespassing on Niagara Parks Commission property was supposedly against the law, but all the coppers knew Sheep; in fact, they drew on his knowledge of the river's eddies and quirks, as did the daredevils. He hunted mallard ducks with a shotgun, and easier prey included deer and geese that lost their way in the fog and went over the falls; Sheep simply picked the stunned or dead ones from the banks and roasted them over his fire. For veggies, succulent watercress was there for the plucking along the shore. What he didn't eat, Sheep sold at the market; ducks, three bucks a pair. When he needed cash for beer at the Clifton Hotel, he plucked bodies of suicide victims from the river (if he could get to them before his cousin Red) and turned them in at five to ten bucks apiece, depending if the money came from undertakers' fees or relatives of victims. "I'm into beer barrels more than daredevil barrels," he always said, yet over the years he had a front-row seat to the falls stunts. To the Hills, Sheep was a comedy act, but they didn't respect him that much because he never tried to hold a job. But Harry and Major enjoyed their visit and were careful to heed Sheep's warning on the way back to the Maid of the Mist about timber rattlesnakes lurking in the rocks.

When they got back just before nightfall, several hundred people remained beneath the falls, hoping for a resolution for Stathakis—until a rainstorm blasted the area. Harry and Major were sent home by their father, but Red and William remained until the ungodly hour of four in the morning with no sign of the barrel, before finally going home to a quick tea and bed. At six Sunday morning, the sun came up and so did George's barrel. Canadian customs officials at the Honeymoon Bridge spotted it spinning in eddies below the falls; it had been trapped for an incredible fourteen and one-half hours, but received only minimal damage: the steel ends were dented, and some of the hoops were loose. They dialed 717, and Hill came flying. When he got to the scene, he was surprised the barrel had been released by the falls, and said that it happened because the storm had briefly changed the river currents. River Man and William borrowed a rowboat and were able to grapple the barrel in the lower river. As soon as he could, Red reached over and rapped his knuckles on the vessel, but received no answer; and again and again, with nothing in response.

To discourage curiosity seekers, they towed it downriver to a secluded spot, with great difficulty as the cumbersome barrel, loaded with water, kept bumping against rocks. It took ten men, including ex–naval man Walter E. Filer, and a favorable current to pull it ashore north of the bridge on the Canadian side. The manhole was on the submerged end of the barrel, and they needed some time to cut through the scores of bolts that held the lid in place. It wasn't until 11:00 a.m. that they finally pried it off. Inside the custom-made coffin, on a soggy, swollen spring mattress, lay the lifeless body of George Stathakis, still strapped to the mattress, his hair and suit disheveled to the point they would need fixing at the funeral home. The mattress was so swollen, it blocked the entrance and had to be cut and taken out in pieces before the body could be removed. When Stathakis was pulled from the barrel with kid gloves, one of his hands was tightly clutching his nose and mouth. There was hardly a bruise on his body. Nobody said much. There was nothing to say, except from one of the workers of the company that had made the barrel: "We tried to persuade him to have more than two tanks of air, but he said three hours was long enough. There was room for ten tanks in the barrel if he had wanted to take them along."

Meanwhile, Harry and Major were back with their father, and glad to help with minor details, such as pulling away some of the mattress and debris from the barrel. After its terrific soaking, the vessel was shiny and wet, reflecting the sides of the rocky gorge, as well as people's faces, including the boys' expressions of wonder. Harry whispered in Major's ear: "Let's get in it and ride it to the Whirlpool!" But Major snickered. He knew it was a joke because Harry had no interest in attempting daredevil feats. When a newspaper photographer showed up, he stopped snickering and posed with the vessel, which dwarfed him, nearly as tall on its side as he was standing. At one point, Major had his head inside the barrel, left hand insecurely in his shirt pocket, and cursed like one of Stathakis's friends when he smelled the stench. To distract himself, he wondered how big he might build a barrel of his own one day. Meanwhile, William was too close to his father's side to get too much involved with Harry and Major on this day. From the barrel, Red pulled the pet turtle, Sonny Boy, which Stathakis had taken with him. It was alive and apparently none the worse for the trip. "Hey, it's still moving!" William said. Spectators gathering around the scene laughed nervously. The women in the crowd scolded the men for laughing. They said they hoped that poor Mr. Stathakis had been right about there being reincarnation after death. Perhaps he would be more successful in his next life.

Groping inside the water-filled barrel, Red produced a pencil and a pad of paper that author Stathakis had brought with him. It was completely blank. The two oxygen tanks had been opened and Stathakis had drained all the air. At first, the crowd was sad, but chuckles remained for the turtle, which was passed to William for safekeeping. Smiling in the morning light, William was becoming handsome, flirting with ruggedness, with curly red hair, learning to smile differently for the cameras as he held Sonny Boy, and quickly losing his virginity at the river. The crowd at the macabre setting continued to grow, hardly surprising since horror movies had become popular in recent times, such as *The Cabinet of Dr. Caligari* and the vampire flick *Nosferatu*. Many of the onlookers had never seen a dead body. As Hill prepared to tow the barrel away, souvenir hunters, including one with a sledgehammer, tried to break it into pieces, but Red summoned police, and they scurried away. And so, Hill removed the 120th body of his career, towing it to Maid docks before turning it over to coroner Dr. W. W. Thompson. It took several men to carry the body up the banks to the morgue, where Thompson discovered that Stathakis had no water in his lungs, ruling that he had suffocated, not drowned, and estimated he had been dead ten to twelve hours by the time he was taken from the cask.

When it was time for his usual informal press conference, Hill opined to reporters that the barrel had probably received damage in its journey in the upper rapids, perhaps temporarily grounding near the *Sunbeam*, because it was later seen to be lower in the water at the crest of the falls than it had been earlier. And he repeated his theory that the barrel was too heavy, and perhaps its weight kept it behind the falls; it was the only barrel of the five that had gone over the falls that got imprisoned behind the watery curtain. The press conference lasted as long as it took for rumors to circulate that police were considering laying manslaughter charges against those associated with the late Stathakis.

Then, claiming a type of squatter's rights, Hill confiscated the barrel and the turtle and took them to his home on Robinson Street, just one-half mile from the falls. There, for the rest of Sunday, he put them under a tent in his front yard so that spectators paying ten cents apiece could view them, along with his steel rapids barrel. He knew that people would be driven by their curiosity to come, and they were by the thousands. One by one, they filed into the tent to see the aftermath of the daredevil stunt and to pick the brain of the Niagara veteran.

Beatrice placed Sonny Boy in a washtub for viewing, or giving interviews if indeed he would recount the voyage, as his late master had promised. Everybody wanted to hold the turtle or touch the barrel, including Major and William, who were allowed to climb inside it, once they dealt with the claustrophobia.

Hill took the opportunity to entertain tourists and reporters with stories of the venture and of his own life and times, including the true story of another daredevil he knew in his youth, Maud Willard, the first to take a pet with her for a Niagara stunt (in 1901 she had suffocated in her barrel in the Great Whirlpool, but her terrier survived inside the barrel by breathing through a small hole). On Sunday night, Red rocked with Sonny Boy on his veranda, exhausted, too busy counting his dough to worry about fatigue—visitors to the tent had put several hundred dollars into his coffers. For 1930, that was a fat payday at the falls, and it was not lost on the Buffalo cooperage that had made the barrel and was seeking its return from Hill, who they claimed was "reaping a harvest over another man's misfortune." That was one way to look at it—another was that after all those times risking his neck to save men's lives and having little to show for it, Hill was finally getting returns. As he lay in bed that night, Hill thought about Stathakis's unfulfilled plan to write about his experience. That got him to thinking—maybe he should write his own book about his exploits on the river. He could get the wordsmith Mousie Sloggett to help.

As days unfolded and news reports flashed around the continent, the buttoned-down, conservative world did not take well to The George Stathakis Show. "Outraged and humiliated, Canadian and US authorities blamed one another for allowing the tragedy to occur," just ten years after Stephens's debacle. As early as mid-June, Stathakis had publicized his July 5 date with destiny, but since would-be daredevils were constantly announcing their intentions, to police Stathakis probably seemed like just another daydreamer. His death caused shock waves at the Niagara Falls, Ontario, city council, where one alderman suggested stunters be taken to an insane asylum. Other councillors expressed dismay that the Royal Canadian Mounted Police hadn't gone to Navy Island to prevent Stathakis from killing himself. Niagara Falls, Ontario, mayor Charles F. Swayze and city manager H. E. Goddard asked to have authorities place a ban on further daredevil attempts. All of this humbled Red Hill. He wasn't going to be party to daredevil men again; he was tired of being a stand-in for death.

With the steak dinner long cold, Stathakis's body was claimed by his friend Stathacos. His closest relatives, one in New York and the other in Buffalo, were notified by police, and he was buried in a bamboo casket in Riverside Cemetery, Niagara Falls, New York. By July 8, authorities decided to take no action against anyone involved in the stunt, but that didn't stop newspapers around North America from taking shots. Said the San Jose (California) *Evening News*:

> Apparently Niagara, jealous of its power as one of the strongest forces in the world, determined that this little man in his puny contraption of oak and steel should not conquer the falls . . . it was his own life he risked and if he chose to embrace death in so apparently foolhardy a manner it was his business.

The *Evening Review*: "One man pitted his weak strength and puny designs against the might of Niagara on Saturday and today he is lying in a mortuary."

If the caper were one for a Sherlock Holmes novel, it would have been well timed, as the author of the Holmes chronicles, Arthur Conan Doyle, died on July 7. Over the next few weeks, the *Post-Gazette* newsreels of the Stathakis plunge were shown over and over again in theatres, narrated by national broadcasting ace George McNamee with music by the Victor Concert Orchestra, Rosario Bourdon conducting. And so, the Niagara scoreboard now read: three alive, two dead—so far. Hey, maybe there were things that deserved to be in a barrel—pickles, whisky, and oil . . . but a human being? On July 10, while Red was giving a lecture outside his home, some lousy opportunists stole Sonny Boy from George's barrel. Hill jumped into a taxi and chased them to Buffalo, where he lost their trail. From a description of the thieves, Hill suspected they were a couple from Uniontown, Pennsylvania, whom he had recently met. Police in that town arrested the couple and returned the turtle to Red by mail in a wooden box. Sonny survived that one, too.

CHAPTER ELEVEN
ANOTHER RED HILL

Into the next year, Stathakis remained in Red's life. He kept the Greek's jumbo barrel so long in his yard, it warmed his latent desire to finally participate in the fool's game. Another motivator was that people were saying that Niagara had become a death pit, that two of the last three barrelers wound up dead and the only survivor, Lussier, had practically drowned in his own device. River Man revered challenge. He was in his forties now, and his health had never really been restored from Vimy Ridge; if it was to be done, it had to be now. As the bloated oak barrel remained chained to a post in his yard like a pit bull, Hill kept looking at it, examining it, even sleeping inside it on nights he and Beatrice had a tiff about money. The year before, he had gone on record in the newspapers, saying that the barrel was cumbersome, allowing too much surface area to hit the rocks beneath the falls, and his insights had unfortunately proven correct. He'd have to come up with another vessel, perhaps a smaller steel or rubber version, but that could take time and cash. Lussier had spent his life savings on his ball and its lifesaving system of air supply. In the meantime, why let the *Spirit of Niagara* sit in his yard? Red's teenaged sons, William and Major, were pushing him to try a stunt in the river, so why not put the barrel to use in the rapids? He'd had two previous rapids trips, both successes.

On May 30, 1931, the Saturday of Memorial Day weekend, Red was ready to challenge the Whirlpool and Devil's Hole Rapids in what people were calling a haunted barrel; not only had Stathakis met his end in it, so had his beloved pet Sonny Boy, much later. The turtle that Hill had rescued from the barrel had survived the plunge over the falls and been living in it off and on in Hill's yard, while posing for photographs with tourists, until it died of natural causes, with nary a story to tell about its great adventure, as Stathakis had predicted. Hill was not superstitious or religious, apart from occasionally carrying the rabbit's foot his father had bequeathed him; if he had believed in fate or jinxes, he would've driven himself bananas or quit ages before, considering all the crap and horsefeathers he'd been through in his life. Being in hot water had become his natural state of being. But River Man wasn't accepting the Greek's barrel as it stood; he replaced the rusty old bolts and welded two steel strips along the length of the barrel to reinforce the staves. He also installed a special rubber manhole cover for the trapdoor hatch, specifically designed to withstand the pounding he was expecting in the rapids, and at the ready to be quickly opened or closed. You couldn't control Niagara, only your preparation for it. Thanks to the usual hoopla in the papers, a big crowd assembled along the shore of the rapids, estimated anywhere from thirty thousand to seventy-five thousand. With three barrelers over the falls in the past eleven years, and with Red's notoriety as a rescuer, Niagara Falls had been getting considerable ink around the globe, and these things had become like professional sporting events. Today's crowd included newlyweds from Europe, families from New York City staying the long holiday weekend, locals twiddling their thumbs, who got the word when it carried like a flash flood across the twin cities. They lined the steep banks of the gorge all the way from the Maid of the Mist docks, two miles downriver to the Great Whirlpool, and beyond to Queenston on the Canadian side and Lewiston on the Yankee shore near Lake Ontario.

The seven-mile voyage was supposed to start at 1:30 sharp in the afternoon at the American docks below the falls, but there was a slight delay when it was discovered that the motorboat Hill had sequestered under leaves and tarps near the docks overnight to tow him out into the river had been pinched by thieves; instead he had to rent one from the Maid of the Mist. The leader of Red's emergency crew was none other than his seventeen-year-old son, William Jr., undertaking his first official major responsibility on the Niagara, an eager, fresh-faced kid whose lanky frame belied his strength and cunning. First, he helped his father roll the barrel into the water and attach it to the boat. Hearty cheers came from the crowd when a tarpaulin was yanked off the barrel to display its fresh paint—gaily red, white, and blue, drawing attention to itself in the green and sometimes blue water. God bless America and Canada! Midway between two of the three bridges spanning the river, Red left the boat for the barrel. Calmly but with purpose, he strapped himself into a hammock and sat upright with the hatch wide open as the craft started moving down the river. The big lazy barrel was difficult to tow and kept hiccupping onto shore; oh, well, there were no coppers around. These days, the gendarmes were busy closing in on Scarface Al Capone, over in Chicagoland; if they had never arrested Red for his bootlegging and rum-running, which everybody and his brother seemed to know about, surely they wouldn't cuff him for this, with the chamber of commerce backing him up. Despite the negative publicity over the daredevil deaths, barrel jumpers were good for business, and if they went into the river, they knew the risks. Anyway, was there anything such as negative publicity? Although few would openly talk about it, many people came to these things to see a man's life leave his body before their eyes.

When the boat reached the middle of the river, and with his father popping his head out through the still-open hatch, William cut the barrel loose. Cruelly slow was the journey at first, to the applause of the spectators along the bank, as Red put an arm up through the hatch to wave to them. Soon enough, the rapids took possession of the barrel, and it was on its merry way—under the three bridges toward the Whirlpool where, hopefully, it would linger briefly, then with its hefty weight scoot into the Devil's Hole Rapids. Red sealed the hatch tight as the barrel went under the Michigan Central Railway Bridge, where the current Swift Drift got its legs. Downhill the journey continued through fickle, milky water. Strapped inside, Red was a lad again, flying down Murray Hill on a winter's toboggan, as he went through a stretch of high rapids known as the Himalayas.

Look at me! The peaks and valleys took turns violently tossing his craft into the air. At times he was on a bucking bronco in the Old West, and he recalled the adjectives that old Brit Bobby Leach said about his own rapids trip of long ago, God rest his soul. As Leach proved on that fateful New Zealand street in '26, you weren't safe on a sidewalk, so you might as well enjoy life's rapids while you had a chance. Better that than to be one of the millions of left-behinders in the world, who always stayed on the banks. It was good that the rough ride kept your attention away from what was to come—the Whirlpool, where the Niagara River formed its wonderful amphitheater for viewing feats of derring-do, resembling a poor man's Grand Canyon. Encircling the Whirlpool on three sides were the rocky, natural walls of the Niagara Glen—two hundred feet high. Stretching all the way across this gorge on a powerful steel wire was the Spanish Aero Car, a sightseeing ride right out of San Francisco, with patrons shoulder to shoulder, staring straight down into the Whirlpool, awaiting a nutcase and his gaily painted barrel. So many were on board, when the wind blew, the cable car hardly budged. Close to the river's edge in the glen was Red's family—his brother Charlie, sister Myrtle, and wife, Beatrice, and their six other children—teenagers Harry and Edith; Major, twelve; Corky, seven; Helen, eight; and newcomer Wesley, one year and twenty blanket-coddled days. Also on hand were other relatives: Mousie Sloggett and his young son Ken.

On another day, this might have made a fun picnic in the glen, a beautiful rock channel with land and climate unlike any other on earth, filled with peculiar plants and trees as part of the Niagara Falls ecosystem, which was studied in the 1800s by scientists and contributed to Charles Darwin's paper on evolution. Beatrice had just miscarried another child, but she refused to be absent again while Red was risking his wrinkled neck. In recent years, she had tried her darnedest to keep her young ones from the river's grasp, with mixed results. William Jr., Major, and Corky had attended many of their father's recent capers, eager to assist and hungering for their own involvements. Goodness gracious, there were so many sweet girls available—why'd they have to carry a torch for a waterfall? Why couldn't they spend an afternoon at the duck pond? Why did the water always have to be rushing? Anyway, the photograph in the *Niagara Falls Evening Review* of young Major's face at the Lussier plunge of '28 told a thousand words—he never had his mouth open like that when he brought his schoolwork home. Lussier was the big cheese at the falls these days, but Major would see about that when he grew up.

Even Edith got into the act; as a young girl she had stitched pillows on Ma's Singer sewing machine for Stephens's barrel, and as a tomboy who could play ice hockey with the boys at the Victoria Avenue Arena, she jokingly said she might consider her own Niagara stunt one day, over her mother's dead body, of course. When Beatrice found her daughter practicing swim moves in the pool at the Crystal Motel, she grabbed a couple of fags from her husband's Camel pack. Oh, well, maybe Edith's dad would save her again, like he did when her hair was accidentally set on fire as a six-year-old. At river's edge, Edith sensed her mother's concern: "Dad will be all right. Never mind, Ma, a couple of kisses and he'll be better. Everything will be copacetic." Edith was smart—and unique in the fact she was the only Hill born in a hospital; the others were delivered at home, with difficult childbirths. She felt sorry for her mother. "Maybe we should have gone to see that show at the Capitol Theatre instead." Playing at the theatre was *Mothers Cry* with Dorothy Peterson and David Manners. (The marquee: "Why Do Mothers Cry? This Will Help You Understand Their Sacrifice.")

Hundreds, perhaps thousands, in the audience found their way over rocks and through muddy, greasy pathways down the stony amphitheater, even though there were no proper stairs heading toward the Whirlpool. Some stumbled and scraped their shins and elbows. What the hell—who couldn't use some *rock 'em, sock 'em* in this year of Herbert Hoover, this year of the Depression, which was sucking the whole continent down a hole? As with any large throng, they were smoking and gossiping, half of them enthralled by Hill's bravado and the other half wanting to take him down a peg or two, hoping he'd break his lazy ass. Apart from the war and the taxis, had he ever had a real job? "There he is! He's coming!" someone yelled, pointing toward the barrel, in the rapids, on a collision course with the Whirlpool. Beatrice grabbed Helen and toddler Wesley. With cold spray and churning breezes in their faces, the spectators held on to one another, as though the nasty water would reach out and snatch them up, as well. The big barrel, fully intact to the naked eye, ended its voyage through the first set of rapids by bouncing high on the Great Wave.

"Whoa!" the women gasped. "Hurray!" the men crowed. The ovations subsided, however, when the barrel got scooped up and headlocked by the Great Whirlpool while trying to reach the second set of rapids. It was always in the books that this might come to pass. No one said anything, except for a few moans, when the barrel slipped into orbit around the pool's outer edge, accompanied by logs, driftwood, and remnants of a wooden chair, at one time perhaps a child's rocker. Had River Man been knocked into a tizzy? The answer came swiftly as Red pushed two small flags—an American Stars and Stripes and a British Union Jack—through the air holes. "Hurray!" was the response from both men and women. Hill was defiantly and patriotically alive on this hallowed veterans' day, and the soldiers in the crowd started singing off-key versions of old war songs, some so enthusiastic that their poppies with weak pins fell off.

Beatrice and family managed a couple of smiles among them. Their man was a great man. Everybody could see it. "What did you say was for tea tonight?" Edith impulsively said to her mother.

"Spring onions on toast, browned parsnips, Niagara duck." The Hills were not rolling in dough, but they never had to go to one of the Sally Ann soup lines, either, as long as Red's hunting at the falls was regular.

But this wasn't over. The barrel still had to break free of the Whirlpool and scurry around a corner of the glen to continue a lengthy trip down the second set of rapids, the Devil's Hole Rapids, to the twin towns of Queenston and Lewiston. Red didn't leave the flags flying too long; he closed the hatch when it became apparent the Whirlpool was going to have its way and started turning the barrel sideways. Gradually but surely, the barrel got sucked inward, toward the power-packed vortex of the Whirlpool, an imposing vacuum created by hundreds of thousands of gallons of water coiling and pooling—like a huge drain after a plug had been yanked—before it turned out toward the lake. The barrel was seem-ingly shrinking in size compared to the watery monster. Sometimes it stood on its end, sometimes on its back; next time around it was broadside and seconds from sinking. "He might suffocate like that Greek!" cried a woman. And then, oh my God, it did sink, slurped down into the vortex without as much as a trace, to the collective shriek of the crowd. Beatrice squeezed her children and looked away.

"Dessert?" Edith said bravely.

"Neapolitan." From her tone, Bea masked her terror. "And a pot of Salada."

Less than a minute after it disappeared, the barrel thankfully bobbed to the surface, reappearing at another part of the pool. "By golly, he's safe!" Edith shouted. But not completely. The barrel kept messing around in the Whirlpool, to and fro, up and down, in and out, teasing the shore then dallying about the vortex, shrinking at times to the size of a cork. Unbelievably, by Mousie Sloggett's fob watch, it had been held prisoner for the better part of an hour in the tentacles of this giant octopus. Could the same wooden box twice be a coffin? Many began to pray for this daring man, this rescuer of souls. Although each of the family had been christened at birth or as youngsters, the male members of the Hill clan were not religious; but they didn't discourage others from believing or praying, especially when it was offered for their safety. At river's edge, teen-aged William was somewhat worried, but also deep in calculation—when he would get his own vessel for the falls or the rapids, it wouldn't be so damn heavy. Nothing against Dad or Mr. Stathakis, but he'd make his own barrel.

Inside the craft, River Man was hot and tasting his own sweat. It was hard shutting off his mind when the river outside sounded like a thousand violin strings piercing the barrel, bouncing off its walls and his brain. Mortality came at him every few years like an Australian boomerang: those lovers on the ice floe who had not taken his arm across the melting mush; his two baby sisters from black diphtheria; his buddies gored right beside him in the war; and his wife's four miscarriages. Did they all make it to Bea's heaven? And how many times had the Reaper been at his door, on the Ice Bridge, straddling a rope to get to the old scow, and lying with the wounded and gassed in No Man's Land with Jerry sniper fire over his head at a mucky hill? Not many things gave Red Hill the heebie-jeebies, apart from the dentist, daddy longlegs spiders, and getting water up the nose, into his sinuses, bringing that sharp, burning sensation. When these things happened, he was usually sitting around. Red Hill did not sit well, and neither did his sons; that was one reason they were lousy in church and school. All the while, in the lame-duck barrel, Red talked to himself: *Keep your wits about you. When the barrel tips head down and the ballast and the rabbit's foot don't do their work, stay low and keep your eye on the hatch, ready to seal it. Breathe, breathe, breathe! Don't kill yourself with panic. First you overcome yourself, then the river.* With a small flashlight, Red could see the barrel was taking on water, apparently from an imperfect hatch cover or an unlucky rapids ride.

Why didn't he catch this during the preparation? He'd felt helpless before in his life, and he hated it. He was starting to feel like an old man. Fitting a war vet should die on Memorial Day, poppies on the ground. Was it possible he knew how to be savior but not saved? The violins were now intensely playing Mozart's requiem for death. There was, of course, another problem—the most qualified guy to save him was trapped in the barrel. William Red Hill, 1888–1931, RIP. He recalled the official tribute the Twin Cities had bestowed upon him less than three weeks earlier. "Red Hill will long live in the memory of the residents of Niagara on both sides of the border," wrote William Laughlin, mayor of Niagara Falls, New York, in an official statement, cosigned by H. P. Stephens, former mayor of Niagara Falls, Ontario. "A man of seeming iron nerve, of wonderful daring, and always ready to help those in danger."

Red thought of his family on shore. They were still young; why had he put himself in this position? Who would take care of them? Who would Bea remarry—maybe that Robby fella at the bakery? Wonder how much wonderful daring he ever did? The barrel was a steam bath, and only water squirting into his face from leaks helped cool him. Anger was one fuel that kept him going, as well. Good God, he hoped that motion picture guy from Buffalo had finally shown up; he hadn't seen him when the rowboat had towed him into the rapids. Jesus. Would the major publicity be left up to his autobiography, which was being bound and released this very day (the last chapter of which was presently being lived)? He tried to roll with the punches: *Keep your wits, man! Dance with the river and don't fight it—it's a passionate partner. Think of Bea and the little ones. It's nature's way of survival, remember—life flashbacks are not an old wives' tale; you've got to get home to them. Remember Robby. See in your mind how the rescue will come about and how you will swim to safety. You can be the new Houdini.*

At shore's edge, newspapermen were furiously scribbling play-by-play accounts of the ominous events, but by midafternoon, the *Evening Review* had to go to press with the outcome hanging in the balance:

RED HILL IN WHIRLPOOL, BARREL IS LEAKING

RESCUERS ON WAY WITH ROPES

Newspaper boys with shrill voices distributed copies of the still-inky first edition among the crowd, for ten cents more than usual. "Come and get it! Read all about it!" Voices rose, and fathers told their sons to put the papers under their arms as souvenirs. Then, without warning, the barrel was kicked away from the vortex to the friendlier edge of the Whirlpool. The crowd sighed, and Beatrice and her children laughed giddily and started talking about dinner again as it righted itself. Quite unexpectedly, the hatch opened up and, lo and behold, there was River Man's thinning hair, sticking up, and then he started peeping around like a gopher awaking in a fox's den. "Get me a boat and get me out of here!" he shouted, his voice cracking. "Hurry, I'm drowning!" Water started pouring into the hatch, so he quickly shut it. Some people screamed, others offered suggestions:

"An airplane—we need an airplane to get him out!"

"For the Good Lord's sake, somebody toss him a rope!"

"Where is the fire department?"

"What about lowering somebody from the Aero Car?"

According to the paper, firemen were en route, but two other more realistic options were Hill's sons William Jr. and his older brother Harry, both exceptional swimmers. Already, as leader of his father's emergency crew, William was standing on the edge of shore with one end of a thick rope, of 250 feet in length, around his waist. He was sporting new trunks and a tank top, which Beatrice suspected he'd purchased for ninety-eight cents in the spring sale at Rosberg's downtown. The Roaring Twenties had become the Thrifty Thirties. "That barrel is jinxed," William shouted. "I'm not just going to hang around and watch Dad die." But he would be toast, as well, if he swam into the vortex. In and out of the colossal drain, his father was trapped like that nitwit Mr. Stathakis had been behind the falls. The river kills fools, but it should not treat his father with such blatant disrespect, such happenstance. Near William, Beatrice shuddered and had run out of things to say years ago. She knew something like this might happen in the morning, when she'd noticed the tank top under his shirt. Adjusting the rope around his waist and encouraging two sturdy men to hold the other end of it, William secretly wondered if this was a little arrogance on his part—was he really up to saving Red Hill? What had he accomplished so far in his life? Drive a little taxi for his Pa's company? Watch Dad at the scow as a youngster? Swim a little, argue with his brothers, flunk school?

But no one else was about to leap into the maelstrom; even Red's brother-in-law, Mousie, and friend Roy "Skike" Healey were hesitant in these uncharted waters—everybody talked a good game down here, but few knew what in the hell to do. Sure, William was scared stiff, but he'd go anyway; wasn't that the definition of courage? He'd seen what was left of bodies out of the Whirlpool, their lifeblood gone somewhere else. In 1883, Captain Matthew Webb, formerly of the British Navy, who had successfully swum the English Channel, drowned like a rat in there. But Captain Webb wasn't a Hill, so William kept his cool. Keep your emotions for your energy, your focus, the task. Keep your wits, your courage. It takes more than a power stroke to rescue. Pa was always harping on those things.

This partly cloudy afternoon in May could have been the time to shine for an unheralded member of the Hill family—Red's adopted son, Harry. Everything was set up for him to succeed and gain the recognition he had sought from his adoptive father, his family, and the thousands of fans of Niagara daredevils. From the huge crowd, Harry may have been most qualified to get Red out of this pickle. Not long before, Harry had helped Red recover a suicide body near the Whirlpool. He was a little wild and a little unpredictable, but he could swim like a sonofabitch. Having just moved out of the Hill homestead, Harry was now living with his adoptive grandmother, Mary Ann, where he could focus a little more to get his head straight after accidentally shooting Major in the shoulder with the old rifle, having trouble at school, and getting into more than one accident while driving Red's taxicabs. Even though he was the first son of Red, Harry had discovered through government papers that he was not a Hill after all, but a Boltz.

After a frustrated Beatrice miscarried in 1912, she believed she could not have children, and they adopted Harry as a child, two years before she discovered she had been mistaken and gave birth to William Jr. Harry had been born in Waterloo, Ontario, the son of a factory worker and reportedly the grandson of a Prussian general. His father died in an accident when Harry was a child. Sibling rivalry or not, Edith and Helen said that Harry was sometimes mean with frogs and that he was a crazy stuntman at the wheel of the taxicabs. The real Hills were daredevils, and Harry didn't feel so much a Hill when the others were around; oh, well, as the oldest, at least he didn't get hand-me-down trousers from his brothers—they got his. He did feel more of a Hill when he was alone at the falls with Red, when there were no crowds, no hoots and hollers, no barrels being spit out of the falls or the rapids, just him and his dad. It didn't matter what the birth certificate said; he was Dad.

To impress and share with his father, Harry had been training in the past year to become a champion swimmer—three or four hours a day he would practice his strokes in calm waterways near the falls; at Dufferin Islands near the wreck of the old scow, and in Chippawa Creek, hoping to qualify for a swimming competition at the Canadian National Exhibition in Toronto. He had even beaten William in a marathon race around the small islands, and the latter was still red-faced about that. Harry was Rudolph Valentino handsome, and his black hair was always combed over his forehead, helping to hide his dour expression; he was forever wiping the bangs away when he swam. On this day, Harry was potentially ready to help his struggling father out of the Great Whirlpool, but for some reason, he gave way to William. Part of the reason was that Beatrice was encouraging William, not Harry, to get out there in the water in the new trunks he had bought on sale.

As the barrel inched closer to shore and the great drain was turning its attention to other wayward artifacts, William announced he was ready to swim out and retrieve the barrel. With the rope held on shore by, of all people, the Hills' family doctor, Dr. J. H. Davidson, and others, William dove out as far as he could and went into a pattern of long, powerful strokes with the end of the rope in his gritted teeth. Flat feet didn't seem to bother William while getting up and down the rocks in the gorge and certainly not while swimming. Although he had not been able to defeat his father's record of swimming across the lower river below the falls, this was a race with more on the line. "Legs, legs, legs!" he told himself. His legs were strong from ice hockey and scaling the cliffs. When he was five, his father had tossed him into the river, just as his father had done before him. *Do it yourself. Focus on what must be done, not who is in the barrel.* On shore, the crowd egged him on, pleading for divine intervention.

Not in the annals of the river's history had anyone swum this far into the Whirlpool and returned to be quoted on it. Beatrice and her other children were holding hands, praying silently. On his first attempt, William got to within fifteen feet of the barrel, but briefly burned out and was knocked off course. The second time, it was to within ten feet, and soon it became three strokes forward and two back as the heavy currents restricted his movements in the water; it became like fighting an alligator on its turf. To the old-timers in the crowd, the scene was reminiscent of how Red had slowly reached the men trapped in the scow above the falls in 1918 while snotty-nosed William had watched. Finally, after what seemed an eternity—more than twenty minutes—William, cold from the river's pounding and exhausted, got close enough to the barrel to reach his right arm out and grab one of the steel rings on its side. After nearly losing grip, he clamped on, took the rope out of his teeth, and tied it around the ring. Surprisingly, his father's hand reached through the partially open hatch and clasped his son's hand like he had never done. Junior scrambled, lanky as ever, and finally got aboard the big barrel to help his father out of the trapdoor. Red was able to clamber out, and they both slumped on top of it on the edge of the Whirlpool. "Go!" William shouted to the men on shore. The burly brutes had gathered behind the rope, tug-of-war style, and they pulled it home, laboring, as it was incredibly heavy and three-quarters full of Niagara's best stuff.

Oh, the reaction on land. To the *hip, hip, hurrah*s of the men and squeals of the ladies and girls, the two Hills were able to raise their spent arms in victory. For a good thirty seconds, the clamor of the crowd all around the glen humbled the roar of the Whirlpool. Slapped with exposure and soaked to the skin, when they reached shore, Red had problems with his equilibrium, but the showmanship still had legs as he got the newspapermen to write down his every word. "I'll never pull another stunt where my life is in danger, so help me," he said, between blowing long breaths. Mousie and Skike Healey put their shoulders under him to keep him up. The first portion of the rapids had been thrilling, and his stomach felt a little queer, he said, and at times the barrel was stifling hot and other times, with water splashing inside, frigid cold. In the Whirlpool, he said, he had become worried when it took on water each time it went down and thought, "Well, this is good-bye for Red." In the end, water had been up to his shoulders in the barrel. Thirty more minutes of that, and he would have been toast. More than anything, Red wanted the reporters and everyone else to know that it was his son who had saved his butt: "I'm damned glad to be out of here. He's shown that he's game. He has more courage than I have." Then he put his arm around William and repeated, "You have more pluck than I have." William would have been embarrassed, if he'd had any energy left. Red encouraged photographers to take their picture together. "He even looks like me, see?" He moved his face back and forth so everyone could see their profiles, revealing a red welt like somebody had whacked him in the kisser. William would be the next river man, Red said. "Look at what he's done here today. He's done it before, you just haven't noticed until now." They'd done it together, and how.

"How gladly Hill held on to his son and hugged him," said bystander Cecil Burridge. The usually deadpan Sr. was aglow.

William laughed, cool and nonchalant, until he couldn't control his shivering, then the words came out fractured: "There was n- n-nothing to it. Now, do I get all your medals?" He had never really told his father he loved him. Now he didn't have to.

"Gimme a smoke," Red said to Mousie while Dr. Davidson took his pulse. Away from cameras, father and son had a puff together, blowing exaggerated rings toward the defeated Whirlpool, even though William didn't smoke regularly, like some of his river-rat buddies. "That smoking could kill you," the doctor laughed. Red suddenly remembered something and pulled his old rabbit's foot out of his pocket and gave it to William. His son shrugged his shoulders and at first didn't want to take it, but he did after Red kissed it for luck.

As this was going on, an out-of-towner in a three-piece suit pushed his way close to the Hills on the crowded shore. "*He's* Red Hill?" the man said, obviously expecting a giant. "Him?" If you didn't know any better, the man who had clambered out of the barrel, wiping his nose and receiving thunderous pats to his back, was fatigued and worn from coming out of the local wire-weaving plant, a left-behinder. Sometimes when you looked at Red's expression, there was nobody home. But nothing could take the joy away from this day. Locals told the naysayer to scram and gave him the bum's rush, although they were careful not to harm the woman on his arm; she had some chassis on her.

A teary-eyed Beatrice tiptoed through the rocks and draped her husband with dry beach towels. If photographers were waiting for a hug and a kiss of sweethearts, they'd have to wait until nightfall. She almost had to force it out of herself that she was proud. But, you know, William and his father were always doing nice things for people. Beatrice didn't know this, but when she would get home that night, the local wireless (radio) station would be playing her favorite, "Rhapsody in Blue," a request from her husband. Not wanting this day to end, people continued to cheer long and hard, and their voices echoed throughout the gorge and down the rapids. Major, Harry, and the other kids cheered, as well, but at times it was uncomfortable in front of all those other people. Couldn't they just congratulate Pa in their backyard? Major didn't feel that way, though—with mouth agape, he gathered up any artifacts he could find from the scene and made sure his younger brother, Corky, didn't get them. His father was a happy man until he realized that the motion picture chaps from Buffalo had not shown up and there would be no newsreels for next Saturday's theatres. And there were scant few donations collected from the Depression crowd. "There's no money in stunting. I'm through," Red sighed, mopping his face with a towel. Little Major looked disappointed, yet he didn't believe it. Red might not have, either, because he stayed around for another hour, beating his gums.

With halfhearted bravado, William was going to get into the barrel and finish the planned trip to Queenston/Lewiston, which would be his first official daredevil stunt, but he let his father talk him out of it (good thing—his half-price swim trunks were falling apart). After she'd had enough, Beatrice hustled the children home, and Harry went to drive the cab and answer queries about today with the fares. The next day, the *Toronto Daily Star* proclaimed: "Saturday's spectacle introduced a new Niagara hero in the person of William Hill Jr." He was tomorrow's man.

It didn't take long for a cigarette company to seize the moment for newspaper advertising:

FIVE HOURS AT THE MERCY OF NIAGARA . . . THEN
A BUCKINGHAM

It quoted Red: "After being lashed and buffeted about for five hours in the rapids of Niagara, my first thought on coming out of my barrel was for a Buckingham. They're a splendid cigarette for steadying the nerves."

BUCKINGHAM, TWENTY FOR TWENTY-FIVE CENTS, NO COUPONS, ALL QUALITY

Harry continued to help his father at the river. A few weeks after Memorial Day, the memorable day, he and Red recovered the body of an unidentified man from below the falls. The man, who wore a black belt and a bloodstone ring on his finger, was believed to be the victim of a bootleggers' feud. They took the remains to Morse and Son Funeral Home. A short time after that, Harry and Major got to go with their father to scout Horseshoe Falls for a potential plunge in a rubber ball. Some woman was planning on stealing Hill's thunder and walking across the falls on a wire like the old French tightrope artist Blondin, but Red Sr. would show them. William was supposed to go check out the falls with his father, but he had the flu. Actually, that was a cover story—the real reason was that he got hog-tied with the rope he had saved his father with, by Harry and two bully buddies, and was left to struggle in the cellar of an abandoned garage for the afternoon. William was too humiliated to report it. Major also had something to report right after William got into all the papers for rescuing their father—he rescued a swan from the gorge, or so he said. Later that summer, William continued to take on more responsibility, recovering below the falls the head and trunk of a suicide victim, then, while vacationing in Ontario's Muskoka region, he pulled a drowning woman from a lake. That was the final straw—he was William Red Hill Jr. The family was tickled pink, except for Major. For a while after that, he was calling himself Major Hill Jr. That bothered his father, so William settled for Bill for now.

CHAPTER TWELVE

FRANNY

"My mom's going to kill me," Franny Bowen said.

Bill couldn't hear his girlfriend's words, drowned out by the roar of Horseshoe Falls looming directly above them, almost devouring them.

She tried again. *"My mom's going to kill me!"*

The young lovers were sitting on a wet rock, holding hands in the presence of a world wonder. In this lazy summer afternoon of 1933, thunder and misty rainbows took turns seducing them, then threatening them.

Bill smiled and moved his lips to form "I hear you."

Franny kissed him, but not too hard. Over their shoulder was his sister and Franny's best friend, Edith Hill. She was two years younger than Bill, but quite a capable chaperone. Franny giggled at Edith, then put her lips to his ear and pretended to whisper: "First of all, I shouldn't be down here. And secondly, we're from different churches . . . and, by the way, your father's going to kill you if you keep talking about going over the falls!"

Bill wiped mist off her cheek and talked into her ear. "I can't worry about that. You'll have to worry for both of us, honey."

"But remember that man a few years ago—that cook!" Bill and his father had recovered the Stathakis barrel and his body a hundred yards from where they were sitting. When Bill pointed out to Franny that three others had survived in barrels since 1901, she countered that the world's foremost expert on the falls, his father, Red Hill Sr., said even he would never attempt the stunt. Edith, along with his four brothers, had mixed feelings on that. Half of them were jumping into the river, and the other half were trying to pull them out.

By age nineteen, Bill's other passion was women. Every time he went to table 10 at the Falls View Observation Tower Restaurant in '33, he ordered bacon, lettuce, and tomato sandwiches (no mayo) from waitress Frances Bowen, even though the young outdoorsman was used to shotgunning ducks and roasting his lunch on an open fire in the windswept haunts of the gorge (outdoorsmen had an advantage in poor financial times). Franny was yummier than practically anything on the menu—a tall, slim drink-of-water brunette, who emerged from the steamy kitchen as a debutante à la Bette Davis or Claudette Colbert. Several times a week, he would saunter in and chat with Franny while his BLT attracted flies, and the best part was, he did not have to discuss the issues of the falls with her, even though one of his dad's daredevil barrels was on full display directly across the street, its cherry redness reflecting the sun. They could talk about her potential future, or just giggle. Red wasn't the only customer interested in Bowen. One of these holiday weekends, a Hollywood director was going to stroll in and, while completely ignoring the popular observation deck, discover her waltzing across the floor with a plate of bangers and mash.

In those days, women liked to be swept off their feet. Red didn't mind about that—he was competitive in ice hockey, dating, and of course, beating other daredevils to the punch at the river. At home, he had a big drawing card—big shots like escape artist/moviemaker Harry Houdini would come to kiss Red Hill Sr.'s ring and discuss the mighty Niagara. Bill seemed to have a need to impress women; it gave him more courage to slay the dragon at the falls. And he was willing to take chances in courting; apparently, one night he took Franny to a speakeasy in the Prohibition days of "dry" Niagara Falls, New York, and, after it was busted by the cops, they spent an hour in the back of a paddy wagon (yes, her mother would have indeed killed her if she'd found out).

Although he was a name in the local newspapers, young Bill was not a catch for every woman in town. Yes, in many ways he was traditional, a polite young gentleman who lived with, and got along with, his parents, and he often wore a suit and tie, but, alas, inside the buttoned-up exterior was another bloke. While he was easy to talk with, there was an inner purpose, an inner rapids, as the shrinks might say, and a need to prove something. As a hockey player, he was on championship junior teams, and two of his buddies, Max Kaminsky and Gus Mancuso, went on to play in the National Hockey League. Bill had professional hockey dreams, too, and he loathed it when anybody called him an average player. He loathed being called average in anything. When he met Frances Bowen, Hill had to swallow his pride as a tourist guide making peanuts. These were grind-it-out days of the Depression, but individual heroes were flourishing, like hockey player Howie Morenz, US president Franklin Delano Roosevelt, Babe Ruth with his $80,000 baseball salary, and Tarzan the Ape Man, who could lead the masses out of the jungle of mediocrity. Even on a local level, Bill was joining his pa in his growing hero status; after the Whirlpool rescue, he received a postcard from an unknown female admirer with a bold, handwritten note: "JESUS SAVES BUT THE HILLS SAVE AT NIAGARA." He kept it under clothes in a bottom drawer at home.

After a few weeks of brunches and delicious necking in the kitchen pantry, Bill and Franny started quietly dating, and they would often go to hear the new record-playing machine—a jukebox—in the lobby of the Capitol Theatre. Bill began referring to Franny as his BLT Gal: Bacon, Lettuce, and Terrific.

If everything sounded hunky-dory, it was not. There was a big problem with the relationship, which kept them from announcing their love to the world. The Bowens were devout Roman Catholic and attended St. Patrick's Church. A Catholic needed special written permission to marry an outsider, and the non-Catholic partner needed to agree in writing to the education of his or her children to the Catholic faith. This was out of the question, since the Hills were dyed-in-orange Anglican and attended All Saints Church. While Bill was not overly religious, his grandparents, Mary Ann and the late Layfield Hill, were charter members of the local Orange Lodge, and England-born Mary Ann sometimes antagonized Catholics by parading with a chest full of medals in front of St. Pat's Church, mimicking an Irish accent. Boy, oh, boy, would that ever go over like gangbusters with Franny's kin. "Like the priest keeps his back to us during mass," Franny once said to him, "we must keep our backs to one another in public."

According to family members, Bill took Franny on a second illegal "booze" date—a rum-running excursion from Niagara Falls, Ontario, across the river in a speedboat to the United States, with liquor on board for Prohibition sale. His father had for many years run an illegal bootlegging operation in his home. William Sr. had also been a rumrunner, sometimes escorted by Bill and his brother Harry, delivering booze across the river above the falls—in the most dangerous of daredevil acts—to avoid authorities. U.S. federal officers would pursue them to the Point of No Return, but no farther unless they were willing to risk life and limb for the sake of one more arrest. Many of the boats of other rumrunners were drawn into the Whirlpool Rapids and over the falls, killing their occupants. Sometimes Detroit hijackers were to blame, attacking the rumrunners, stealing their load of booze, and setting the men adrift over the cataract. Most of the deaths in the river and over the falls in that era were attributed to murder. Bill and his father got fifteen dollars a corpse, and sometimes more, from various sources for bringing the floaters out of the gorge to funeral homes. Bill felt he had to contribute to the family coffers and occasionally drove a cab for his father's taxi company. But his dream was to gain sponsors and publicity for a barrel plunge over the falls.

Mostly, Bill and Franny went for clandestine dates off the beaten path along the river. He introduced her to nature's beauties and secrets, such as Bridal Veil Falls, the smallest of the three falls, tucked between the American Falls and Luna Island on the United States side. There, on a warm autumn evening, they rocked quietly in a rowboat beneath the crashing water, and were blessed with a rarity—a lunar rainbow; a smiling full moon bounced its rays off water droplets in the air, turning the mist into a colored rainbow. Bill explained moonbows had been a regular occurrence before 1925, when the Niagara Parks Commission began illuminating the falls at night (to this day, they can be seen on occasion.)

Franny was not Bill's first gal, but she was the first he took Down There, which the family sometimes referred to as the gorge, to try to catch the moonbows. The first time she peered into the gorge, her perky Cossack hat falling off, Franny gasped, and touched her rosary beads. "Who would venture Down There? Mary, Holy Mother of Grace . . ." Nevertheless, she felt safe with Bill, so once every week she followed him Down There. While other young couples would rather see Clark Gable and Jean Harlow in *China Seas* over at the Capitol Theatre, Bill saved his cash for the 1927 Chevy one-ton truck being offered for 145 bucks at Wells Garage. The gorge was a strange, and some might say a creepy spot, thick with trees and foliage, nearly one thousand different types of species, and in spring it was showered with peach blossoms. During their walks, they learned much about one another. He discovered that Frances Dorothea Bowen was born in Toronto before coming to Niagara Falls when she was eleven. Her father died when she was young, and she lived with her mother, Hilda, a cook, and her two aunts, spinster Veronica Gardiner and Phyllis W. Gray, a widow and bookkeeper, in the redbrick Jubilee Apartments downtown, where middle-class people kept a stiff upper lip in the economic storm. The upbringings of the two lovers were opposed in ways other than religion; Frances was an only child, while Bill was from a big, gregarious family. The Hill lifestyle wasn't as rigid as many in town, and people were in and out of the homestead every night; neighborhood kids would even be allowed to transform the sofa in the front parlor into a circus trampoline. Other things turned some traditional people away from the Hills, who were ale drinkers, keeping half the patrons at gorge-side taverns fascinated with tall tales, and the other half turned off by a family they felt were bums without regular working hours.

Franny didn't know about all this, or didn't want to. Away from the security and confidence that the tower restaurant provided, she was not quite as certain what she wanted, or needed. She looked to the sky to see images in clouds that inspired her. Fresh out of high school, she wasn't sure if she wanted to continue living with her mother, or to apply for the temporary assistant bookkeeper's position in the *Evening Review* for six bucks a week, which asked for "preferably a student of unquestionable character and references." Franny was a nurturer—in her senior year of high school, she jeopardized her mathematics mark by staying home for two days to hold a cold cloth to her mother's migraine, and in that she reminded Bill of his mother. Most likely, Franny would eventually seek a husband; after all, the unemployment rate was more than 20 percent. As well, women were submissive and, by 1933, had had the vote for only thirteen years. She wasn't sure if she wanted to meet a doctor or solicitor, as her aunts encouraged, which seemed a natural progression: from waitress to nurse to solicitor's wife. Sure, you had to change your name, but it would appear on a shingle over a pine door. One thing she knew for certain was that if she really wanted William Red Hill Jr., she would eventually have to follow him down into the gorge, even though her aunts had warned her about "young men these days . . . the young bucks." And so, she did, taking his left hand for the descent once a week.

His sister Edith recalled being a sort-of chaperone on several of their dates in 1933 and 1934. Bill was close to his sister, who was a tomboy, a strong swimmer who loved going to the river and picking her brother's brains about the moods of Niagara. The three got along just grand. As the angular Frances walked down crooked steps into the gorge, fingers intertwined with her man's, she looked pretty in her checkered spring suit, a black skirt with inverted white checks—although the casual shoes with laces didn't quite match. Over her shoulder, she carried a plain cloth bag with picnic ingredients, including Eccles cakes and cheese sandwiches made at the bakery from pure milk bread. Bill loved that. Yes, at first he had been attracted to Franny as someone who might push him to greater heights, but now he loved the way she helped him to relax, to snuggle. She called him Buster. Here we go again with the names. To his family, he was Bill. To outsiders, tourists, and newspapermen, he was Red Hill Jr.—ever since he rescued his father from that sinking barrel in the Whirlpool in 1931. To Franny, he was Buster when they snuggled on a picnic blanket.

The rocks and crevices along the bank were tricky, and even while stationed on flat land, Franny was self-conscious about her tallness. The winding journey required some input, picking your landing spots and keeping your ankles in their sockets. At times, she pinched the skin on Buster's elbow, and yet she could turn on an athletic side when it was called for. She could dance and roller-skate and play softball with Edith and the gals; just weeks before, and with considerable glee, Franny had won the ball-throwing and young ladies' race at the picnic of the Blue Bell Rebekah Lodge in Queen Victoria Park. The yellow ribbon did not go with anything she wore, but fashion was not always everything.

They walked near the Whirlpool, where Bill noted that four stuntmen and -women died while daring to swim or barrel the rapids.

"There," Bill pointed out to the women in a monotone voice. "Peter Nissen of Chicago, a bookkeeper, powered the world's smallest steamship, *The Fool Killer*, successfully and bumpily through the lower rapids. He died a few years later in a hot-air balloon over Lake Michigan."

"Bill's a tour guide," Edith chuckled.

He continued, "Carlisle Graham, a cooper from Philadelphia, was the first to navigate the lower rapids . . ."

"Don't tell us," Franny laughed. "They did it for women!"

Bill looked a little annoyed, but Edith picked up the pace, noting that women held their place in daredevil lore—Martha Wagenfurher had beaten these rapids in a barrel, and the first person to survive a plunge over Horseshoe Falls, of course, was Annie Taylor.

From his emotion, Franny could tell Bill Jr. wasn't far off from attempting his own first stunt, perhaps, God forbid, the Big Splash. She didn't like it. Franny loved being one with the outdoors when it concerned making a tomato garden or meditating in a pine forest, but not to challenge Big Nature. It was hard becoming one with Big Nature, and a lot of daredevils were finding that out to their chagrin.

The three young people walked a little farther down the gorge, beyond the crooked danger signs, until civilization vanished, until explorers had the right of way again, along with the water moccasins, the salmon, and thirty-pound sturgeons. In a grassy area, Bill wanted Franny to take her shoes off so they could feel closer to the earth and have a picnic, but the most she would allow was to remove the delicate wristwatch he had given her for her birthday from his cash share of carrying a suicide victim out of the gorge. "We mustn't cross the river on stones, must we?" she said. Franny didn't like the same water as Bill; her idea was to be in cottage country, sitting in shorts on the dock of a serene lake, letting her thoughts be the only things bubbling on the surface. However, she was sometimes fond of rushing water from a distance; for instance, she loved to hear the sound of Niagara Falls from the Jubilee Apartments, when it came through open windows like a faint melody. On the previous night, she had propped her bedroom window open with Aunt Phyllis's painted ceramic frog and fallen asleep to the lullaby of Niagara. But that was troubling her now in the gorge because she suddenly realized she had left the window open, and there was rain in the forecast that would likely spoil the frog or dampen her mattress. Aunt Phyllis would find out, and that would make it even more difficult to live in the apartments. Already, it was stifling and smug in there, especially if you were in Unit 4 at the same time as your mother and two aunts, with all the physical closeness and the opinions and the old ideas and clichés (rather than actual conversations) and the radio constantly barking about the horrid economy and the whiff of yet another vanilla pound cake on the stove.

Down in the gorge, the air was purer, even considering the aroma of seaweed, and you could let your ideas blossom. Bill talked to Franny more down here—although their words were often hard to comprehend over the breezy trees and roar of the cataract—and he laughed more, too, even loudly. He was different here, more cocky. He knew everything backward and forward; once he spent every evening for a week studying an eel returning to the same spot to feed on sand flies while standing on its end. "Oh, Red, why do boys exaggerate?" Franny asked, smiling. And whenever a new piece of hydroelectric construction popped up, he discovered how the water's course was affected.

"Welcome to my world, my job," he said proudly. "Don't laugh—you see that wristwatch I bought for your birthday?"

"I know! I know the story, William!"

"Well, there *is* money to be made down here, buckets of it. Just last week, a guy swam through the Whirlpool and now he has agents and publicity men from New York after him!" William Kondrat, a teenager from Chatham, New Jersey, had become the first person to swim through the mighty Whirlpool and survive. Franny stopped short of laughing at Bill because he had bought that wristwatch and because on some days, he went to the river in a white shirt and tie, which she, and quite a few others, considered peculiar.

On this afternoon, however, Red took a break from work. He told Franny and Edith to hang on a minute while he ducked back into the woods off the dirt trail, fraught with brambles and devil's paintbrush, and soon returned coyly with two purple trilliums. He handed the first to his sister and the second to his woman. Both of them blushed. After picnicking for a half hour, they finally reached the foot of Horseshoe Falls, where everything was soggy and slippery. Standing on a small ledge, they gawked up into the face of the falls towering above them—but only in stages, because it was overwhelming with its controlled wildness, its water roaring over the cliff like some royal mane.

Edith managed a full breath, then smelled her flower. "Tell Fran about the real Maid of the Mist."

Bill smiled and pointed slowly to the base of the falls. "It's told that Lelawala was a princess in the Ongiara tribe of the Iroquois nation. Some believe she was sacrificed to the gods over the falls in a birch-bark canoe. And now she lives behind the falls as a friendly spirit . . . the original Maid of the Mist."

"Lelawala!" Edith said. "I'm not sure if I believe this in one gulp, but people say she has been seen at times from the *Maid of the Mist* boat, when the mist is blowing a certain way in the gorge."

Bill was smiling a lot today. "The Rhine in Germany has its Lorelei; we have Lelawala. I know one thing—Niagara got its name from the Ongiara tribe. Early in the evening, especially in summer, they say she has been spotted by honeymooners, and brings great luck to them."

Suddenly, Franny didn't look nervous anymore but excited. "Really?"

"You two could use some luck," Edith said.

Franny nodded. "Pretty please, with sugar on top. To tell you the truth, I thought I saw something behind the falls one day . . . a misty figure, or something."

They looked intensely at the base of the falls, but it was difficult to see through its thick and intricate veil of rushing water.

Bill tossed a stick into the river to see how it reacted. "Around these parts, you see something new every day—new currents, new minks, water rats and wildlife, new sightings. Niagara surprises me every day."

"It's our town, our society, which needs something new," Edith sighed. "We need a new way of thinking about religion, and how we treat one another. In this crazy world, you could use a spirit to protect you two."

Franny touched Edith's hand and squeezed it while they watched Bill look at the falls. His body half encased in silver mist, he moved a little closer to the cataract, where he braced himself on a boulder, in awe and yet trying to feel in sync. He stood strong and didn't let its power stare him down. For five minutes, he couldn't take his eyes off its breadth and width, its serpentine brink winding wonderfully twenty-two hundred feet from America to Canada, then he lay down on a rock, closed his eyes, and just listened to its glorious thunder and the wind singing soprano through the glen. Franny didn't look at the falls anymore, but rather at the look on her man's face. She turned to Edith and said, almost sadly, "I don't know if I can compete with that."

This day ended with a big bang. As they prepared to go home up the gorge, Bill had them stop halfway for a breather. While they were leaning against a tree, he respectfully reached inside Frances's blouse to gently touch the chain she always wore around her neck, which seemed to be revealing something.

Edith scolded him in a playful way: "Watch it, mister! Buster!" The necklace had been in Franny's family for several generations, reminding her of Thanksgiving dinners and a carriage ride on another birthday. Besides touching the chain under her blouse, Bill kissed Franny's smooth, olive-colored cheek. She excited him, in some ways similar to the manner in which the river excited him, but mostly, throughout the course of a day together, she calmed him. Suddenly, when he brought his fingers out of her bosom, something fell softly to the ground. Edith's eyes popped open. Good God, it was a gold ring. A wedding ring had fallen off the chain, and Bill wasn't fast enough to retrieve it without detection. Edith's expression said everything. "Yes," Bill sighed, putting a hand on his sister's shoulder. "We've up and married!"

Red Hill Jr. had given Franny a gold ring and his family's revered name in a marriage ceremony before a justice of the peace and strangers who became witnesses. Like the river, there was a side of him that was impulsive, fast flowing, and unpredictable. It reminded Edith of the story of her parents' impulsive wedding—by a JP in Lockport, New York, on Valentine's Day 1911. After shedding a tear, Edith changed her expression to happy and hugged both of them. "Lelawala be with you!" she chuckled gleefully. Bill was the first of the children to get hitched.

CHAPTER THIRTEEN
TURBULENCE

For Franny, the marriage without consent was a daredevil move, attempted only after months of prayer. Of course, by this time she had it drummed into her by her man that the greatest risk of all was being yourself in a world of scrutiny. Hydro men in fedoras and three-piece suits were changing the river, he said, but should they be allowed the power to change you? Accustomed to the Hills' every move ending up in print, Bill kept his frustrations to himself. People from across the world poured into Niagara Falls to showcase their love for one another; with embroidered silk hearts attached to their vehicles, they took hundreds of photographs for unborn grandchildren and embraced one another before thousands of people in the hotels on Clifton Hill—and here he was, sneaking kisses in the gorge and making love in the back of a sedan behind the Nabisco factory. Niagara Falls was the last place on earth for a secret love.

It was such a pity, because the feminine Frances would've looked fabulous in a white gown. But it was what it was. The bottom line—Bill wanted to be the first to give his father a grandchild. Another generation of Hills! For their honeymoon, he took his bride back to the gorge and carved her name into the side of one of the Maid of the Mist boats. He called her Mrs. Hill only when no one was around. Edith hugged them both at every opportunity. "Well, you didn't make Mrs. Solicitor," mused Edith, "but you could become Miss Niagara Rapids!" The newlyweds told no one else about their marriage and continued to live apart for a year, meeting privately on weekends. It sometimes made Franny question her faith. Didn't God want them to be open and happy? At times, Franny felt like Baltimore divorcée Wallis Simpson, who was dating Edward VIII of England, who threatened to renounce his throne if the world did not accept their love. When she told Bill about that, he promised to go over Horseshoe Falls in a barrel, with her name printed on its side. That honored her, but she asked him to please do something different—perhaps build her a garden of roses (his grandfather Layfield had been chief gardener in Queen Victoria Park). It was obvious to him by now that Franny was more interested in working with nature than poking it.

But the planning for his stunt was well under way. In research, he closely studied the contraptions of the five people who had gone over Horseshoe between 1901 and 1930. He discounted the barrels of Annie Taylor (wooden bongo drum of sorts) and Bobby Leach (eleven-foot, steel cylindrical cask), even though they had some benefits and had protected them from the Grim Reaper. Stephens's steel and wooden death barrel had been crushed by the might of the Falls. Stathakis's one-ton monster had survived the Falls and later the Whirlpool with his father, but young Bill most admired the huge rubber ball of Jean Lussier, which had been recommended by Red Sr. because it had the best opportunity to bounce off the rocks beneath Horseshoe. Not wishing to spook Franny, Bill didn't go into the details of these barrels with her. Instead, he told her he was indeed planning on making a rose garden for her.

However, Bill's ambitious barrel plans were abruptly derailed. In summer of 1935, Franny went shopping in Buffalo with friends and ate a tuna-fish sandwich at a restaurant. On the train ride home, she developed stomach cramps, and when it got worse she was taken to the Niagara Falls (Ontario) General Hospital. At first, no one was certain what the matter was; she was admitted to a ward, and Bill stayed at her side with a single rose in his hand. He was worried, but despite the tubes and the ointment and the smells, the hospital could not sap Franny's beauty, and her shapely figure stood out under the white sheets. No one could take that away from him.

One of the hospital receptionists, Alice Sills, was so touched by Bill's caring and tenderness, she wrote a poem for the couple:

> We feel sad, and yet touched, by the caring,
> Of the nice man who comes once, twice, three times a day,
> To kiss his love and thank the nurses . . .

Although friends donated blood for her transfusions, Franny's condition deteriorated. Her mother placed a Bible by her bedside and kept vigil, along with Bill, Edith, and their mother, Beatrice. A sheet-white Bill felt helpless. He had rescued countless animals and people from life-threatening situations, and yet for the one he loved most, he could do precious little. Bill and Franny were confused and scared—were they being punished for their unblessed relationship? Was it time for confession? Like most of the men in his family, Red was not religious, but some things were worth praying to Jesus about.

On Thursday evening, August 29, 1935, just before sunset, Niagara Falls fell into brief darkness from a power failure after twenty-one-year-old John Peters climbed up a hydro pole and was electrocuted and killed. Also on that day, Queen Astrid of Belgium was killed in an automobile crash. On the following day, the BLT Gal, Frances Bowen Hill, died of a ruptured appendix in the hospital. She was twenty-one. Bill told Edith that she was two months pregnant. It would have been the first grandson for Pa. Franny was gone before she could announce her marriage to her Buster, plan birthday parties for all the Hill kids in a Norman Rockwell painting—and gone before she could trade sarcastic barbs with her famous father-in-law.

Funeral services were held at the Jubilee Apartments, where her bedroom window was left ajar with a ceramic frog in order to let the lullaby of the falls inside, followed by mass at St. Patrick's Church, where students from St. Patrick's School sang a hymn in Latin. Many floral tributes and mass cards poured in, and Father F. R. Paulding officiated. In a sea of gray faces, the pallbearers were Bill's adopted brother, Harry (Boltz) Hill, and five family friends. People told one another what a nice girl Franny was, and yet some were uncomfortable about her life, as well as her death. One of her aunts, Miss Veronica Gardiner, refused to believe that Franny and Bill had entered into matrimony. "They never lived together," she snapped at a journalist. And yet, when Franny was lowered into an unmarked Catholic grave at the Fairview Cemetery (R Lot 185), official records listed her as a housewife. Hail Frances, full of grace.

Over the next few days, life went on at Niagara Falls, where big crowds turned out for Labor Day, the last big tourism weekend of the year, and there was the usual stuff, such as "Dancing until Dawn" with Jack Crawford and His Band at nearby Lakeside Park in Port Dalhousie, where the sweet melody of "Stormy Weather" drifted out onto Lake Ontario. Bill took his wife's death hard. He trudged into the gorge alone to sit, legs wide, on a big rock out in the water, staring at Bridal Veil Falls, without a lunar rainbow, playing with Franny's wedding ring. For once, he looked right through the falls without seeing them. The Horseshoe Falls was no more of a help—Lelawala was nowhere to be seen. Franny's mother, Hilda, took it even worse. She left town, fell into ill health, and was eventually admitted to a sanitarium. Some people say Hilda had a nervous breakdown.

But life indeed did go on. Summer passed almost directly into winter that year, and on December 15, 1935, the seventh offspring of Bill's parents, Red Sr. and Beatrice, was born. While Beatrice was in the hospital, having health issues with her baby girl, Red Sr. got a local radio station to play for her "I Love You Truly." Beatrice sent Bill to the registry office to officially name his baby sister Margaret Rose. But he did not. He registered her as Frances Margaret. It would not be the only lingering memory of Franny for the rest of his life. He still wanted to go over the falls for her.

Meanwhile, Bill's spirit was sometimes distracted from its grief by the advances of Alice, the nice receptionist from the hospital, and the failing health of his father. Into his fifties, Red Sr. was having health problems and wondering if his rescue and daredevil days down at the river were numbered. He was coughing with lung problems, wearing rubber dentures, and developing ulcers from keeping things inside, and his face was hard and dry as a desert. And yet, a child's gleam remained in his eyes. When he felt up to it, Red spent more time with Bea and the kids. He still had enough strength and style for dancing, sometimes with one of the most stinking rich men in North America, Harry Oakes, and his wife, Eunice. What a strange relationship that was. In the early to mid-1930s, Hill briefly relinquished his title as the most telephoned, if not the most talked about, man in town to Oakes, a Yankee from Maine, who had come to Canada as a prospector and mining engineer and struck gold.

Oakes so admired Hill for his daring, high profile in the community, and ability to work with his hands, he hired him as his gardener. Oakes's mansion was a thirty-seven-room Tudor dream with beautiful lawns, a golf course, and from atop its roof, the highest view of the falls. Red Hill, gardener? Hill was a man of many odd jobs and the owner of a fourteen-car taxi service. His green thumb came from his father, Layfield, who died with a gardening implement in his hand. After work, the Hills and Oakes would sometimes go dancing together, which was shocking to some locals because, despite his millions, Oakes had few friends. By this time, the Hills (like Annie Taylor in her day) were dance instructors, and they showed the Oakes a step or two. On some summer evenings, the foursome went dancing at the Erie Beach Casino in Fort Erie in Hill's big Buick McLaughlin, the flagship for his taxi fleet. As he often did when in company, Red would wear a sharp navy-blue blazer with an embroidered crest of the Royal Canadian Legion, Branch 51, a waistcoat, tiepin, and shiny shoes. For a night dancing to the Tommy Dorsey Band, Beatrice would dress simply, yet compellingly, with a white Gibson Girl top and an artificial rose attached to her necklace. There would be little makeup, but occasionally she would let her brown hair down. They looked like anything but Mr. and Mrs. River Rat. Red told his wife that one day he would ask Mr. Oakes to fund a plunge over the falls.

In 1935, Red Sr. had enough energy to open a souvenir store near the river, housing several of his daredevil barrels. The store had two big windows facing the street and a bold sign right across the top of the windows and the door:

SEE THE BARRELS THAT WENT OVER THE FALLS

MEET RED HILL IN PERSON

LIFESAVER—NAVIGATOR

ADMISSION FREE

Nearby was a refreshment stand: ginger ale five cents, hot dogs and hamburgers ten cents. People who might not dare to go into the water could touch the barrels and imagine. The whole family was motivated, even the women—in a way the shop validated their lives. There was a real building for river rats, after all! The prize piece of the museum was Red himself. In the *Who's Who* book, he was listed as a lifeguard, with his name next to politicians, ambassadors, and chief ecclesiastics of religious denominations, men with long titles behind their names. With that book not far out of reach, he would sit out front on the sidewalk in a rocking chair like an old eagle, looking to his old hunting grounds, dressed on a sunny day in a white shirt, chatting and waving with honeymooners and locals, waiting for the river to come to him. Even Beatrice sometimes sat, legs closed, on the sidewalk in a polka-dot dress while little daughter Frances Margaret played with a red wagon. In a back room were hidden cigarettes and a cot Red used whenever he and Bea quarreled. They split up a couple of times, usually when he was drinking too much, and once Red rented an apartment next to the souvenir shop at the Royal Hotel. During domestic squabbles was the only time Bill saw him cry. On the whole, though, their long marriage remained stable, and an inspiration to Bill and his siblings.

Following Franny's death, Bill never gave up his plans for going over the falls, but his father urged him to ease into it with a warm-up—a trip down the rapids into the Whirlpool. Apart from the deadly cat-and-mouse game of smugglers versus authorities in the upper river, stunts were few and far between in the 1930s. However, in the summer of '33, William Kondrat, an eighteen-year-old from Chatham, New Jersey, became the first person to swim through the mighty Whirlpool and survive, where others, including the fabled Matthew Webb, had succumbed. Kondrat, a big, husky blond, had hitchhiked from New York City to Niagara Falls with friend Arthur Hecht. The two young men went for a swim in the river on the US side just below the falls, unaware of the rapids downstream, because they had never been in Canada. "When I nearly reached the Canadian shore, I discovered that I was in a swift current and decided to turn back," Kondrat later said. But he was caught by the heavy current and carried all the way through the rapids and through the edge, then into the eye of the Whirlpool, where he was sucked underwater by the vortex, several witnesses said. "Somewhere I'd read to escape an undertow was to swim with it. I tried that and suddenly was tossed thirty feet into the air," he said. Eventually, he made it to shore. "My arms were virtually useless, my lungs filled with water . . . my brain was in a fog, and I fell over. The strange part was . . . I wanted a drink of water."

By the time the river was finished with him, Kondrat was stripped naked; in fact, he hid behind bushes on the banks and called to an employee of the Spanish Aero Car to get him overalls. Back upstream, his friend Hecht was able to swim ashore before he reached the rapids. The whole thing happened too fast for the Hills—or anybody else—to be summoned for rescue, but Kondrat was picked up by authorities and put in jail overnight on charges of vagrancy and unlawfully swimming in the river. However, a judge released him, saying he was too courageous a man to be treated as a tramp. When interviewed, Kondrat explained, "I needed a bath and wanted a swim and got both." With this, he was briefly hired to tell his story at the Lafayette Theatre in Buffalo with the nickname Tarzan of the Waters.

Meanwhile, Niagara tourism was getting more popular, partly due to radio broadcasts that featured the roar of the falls and tales of heroism by the Hill family. Scheduled stunts, however, remained scarce, although in a nutty scheme in 1936, a Chicago man talked about riding a horse over the falls, but it never came about, and two years later, a Kentucky woman wrote to the mayor's office in Hamilton, Ontario, near Niagara Falls, for permission to go over the falls in a rubber ball. She didn't want her name publicized. In 1937, Jean Lussier announced plans to make his second trip over the falls in nine years, but authorities responded negatively to all requests. That year, Police Superintendent John A. Curry of Niagara Falls came up with the idea of answering mail from the daredevils with a sudden-death pamphlet, featuring pictures of the headstones of those who had died going over the falls or in the rapids, hoping it would deter risk takers. One of the biggest media events of the time occurred in the winter of '38, when one of the world's premier steel arch bridges, the Falls View (or Honeymoon) Bridge—connecting Canada and the United States at Niagara Falls—collapsed because unprecedented ice jams crushed its abutments. About one hundred journalists and two thousand spectators waited for the groaning bridge to collapse into the gorge, along with Red Hill Sr., who predicted the bridge would collapse several days before it did. It was rebuilt as the Rainbow Bridge.

Around that time, Bill helped his pa develop an intricate trolling device, the Red Hill Grappling Rope, a series of grappling hooks, sinkers, and bobbers for recovering bodies from river or lake beds and sold to fire departments and lifesaving associations for $150. With his father, Junior also maintained a lifesaving boat, with trailer and equipment, for use in the river.

In the late 1930s, when his grief for Franny became at least manageable, Bill began dating Alice Jean Sills, the receptionist and switchboard operator at the hospital who had written poems for him and his dying wife. Alice was three years younger than he. While Franny had been ill, Junior hadn't paid attention to Alice's figure, lovely brunette hair, and snappy dresses, but now she seemed a divine gal, five foot two, eyes of blue. In an immaculate white dress, she looked like someone from a far-off city who would visit Niagara Falls in a pristine hotel. Her brain was just as impressive, making her a smart miss who had always been near the top of her class, and by 1936, she was assistant secretary-treasurer of General Hospital, as well as a doctor's secretary. She had a good mind for figures; everything had to be worked out. In their courtship, Alice and Bill enjoyed outdoor excursions—picnicking at Watkins Glen, New York, tobogganing the hills of Pelham, Ontario, and swimming at Waverly Beach in Fort Erie, where Alice was mistaken for a model in her swimsuit. At times, though, her personality had a hard exterior, and she didn't seem sentimental, according to the Hill family. She was so closemouthed, you could tell her secrets about the river, and she wouldn't spill the beans. In 1940, Bill and Alice got married, but, true to form, they didn't tell anybody about it at first, until (if this sounds familiar) a gold ring appeared on her finger at the dinner table and gave away his second hushed marriage in succession. "We were shocked and looked at one another around the table," said his sister Edith. Religion was not a factor, as both families were Protestant.

Alice wasn't sold on the river and her groom's obsession with it; almost right away, they moved to a modest bungalow in Fort Erie, nearly twenty miles away, where children could swim in the cerebral part of the Niagara River. There he got a job at the Fleet Aircraft plant, making parts for Allied air forces in the Second World War. Unbelievably, a Hill had left Niagara Falls. Alice took a leave of absence as secretary for Dr. J. H. Davidson and became a housewife. Another reason Bill went to Fort Erie was to play on the hockey team sponsored by Fleet. He was a good teammate and enjoyed being with people. His younger brother Corky got a job as a stock chaser at Fleet and became the team's stick boy. Major and Wesley weren't into hockey. Harry played some hockey, but not at Fleet.

Actually, Niagara Falls was not the place to be during the war; tourism was down with no daredevils on the river. Maybe it was a good time for the Hills to take a breather, but Bill's river-rat chums worried he'd catch a hefty dose of domesticity and never be back. Alice became pregnant, and Bill was thrilled that he would be giving his parents their first grandchild, but there was stress during the pregnancy as Alice's mother died in January 1941. On February 26 of that year, Sally Hill was born at Douglas Memorial Hospital in Fort Erie. Junior hid his disappointment that it wasn't a boy, but she had his wide forehead and big bright blue eyes—and, of course, there were such things as river women (companies were still bugging Edith to get into a barrel). "Spitting image of you," Edith said to him. By two years old, Sally was a pretty little girl, resembling actress Shirley Temple with a bow in her hair.

However, not long into their marriage, it became clear there were compatibility problems. For one thing, Alice didn't like Bill driving to the falls on his off day. "They were definitely opposites—Mom very driven and ambitious and Bill very laid back and relaxed about life . . . a dreamer who loved the Niagara River," Sally would later write in a self-published book, *Niagara's Daughter: Memories of a Girl Named Sally.* "Finances continued to be tight, but they were very happy and in love and they both loved me. My father dreamed of being famous one day, and his dreams consisted of being able to conquer the falls in a barrel."

"They had nothing in common," said Alice's twin sister, Agnes.

"Alice was a nice girl, but she didn't approve of the publicity the Hills got," his adoptive brother Harry said. Neither did Harry, who went to Ohio to marry a woman he had met there while visiting his biological brother Walter.

***

The Niagara River in Fort Erie was quiet and calm, and you could float only so long on your back until you had to drive to Buffalo and drink. At one point, Alice moved back to Niagara Falls with their daughter to live with her mother-in-law, Mary Ann "Granny" Hill. "Eventually, finances caused the breakdown of our little family," Sally wrote. Still, Bill put on a good face. Although he had an amiable nature and was easy to get along with, sometimes he kept worries inside, and by the early forties he'd developed ulcers and was taking lots of Pepto-Bismol.

For a while, Major moved in with Bill in Fort Erie. As they grew into young men, Red Jr. and Major developed a rivalry, not only for their father's attention but also for space in the newspapers. Being six years older, Junior had a head start on everything, but Major scored points, especially when he became the youngest sergeant in the Canadian militia, at thirteen, in the mid-1930s. Military hero Red Sr. was proud, and so was Ma, as long as Major stayed away from the river, which, of course, he did not; his close-up experiences at the Lussier and Stathakis barrel jumps left an imprint on the lad, and he vowed to try his own stunt one day soon. At home, Beatrice spent more time parenting than did her husband, unless they were at the river. She hoped the boys' rivalry would continue in school, but neither Major nor Junior got a high school diploma; instead, they learned street smarts and river smarts and talked their way into part-time money by convincing companies like RCA Victor to send their wooden cabinets over the falls to test their strength (some survived being waterlogged, others were turned into toothpicks). The brothers remained close, though, especially while living together in Fort Erie.

In 1942, Bill and Alice got back together, with Bill coming home to Horseshoe and moving to the falls to live with her, Sally, his mother and father, his grandmother, Mary Ann, and their cat, Mickey, in a big old two-story home on Stanley Avenue.

CHAPTER FOURTEEN
PASSING THE TORCH

In the early 1940s, Red Hill Sr. wasn't doing so well. Just after turning fifty, he developed heart problems to go along with his ulcers and the lung issues he'd had since the gassing in the first war. Friends and family knew it was serious when he stopped going down to the Maid of the Mist to poke around for duck decoys and floaters. The last time his son Wesley remembered Red going into the gorge, he killed a pheasant for supper with a chunk of ice. Following that, he was home a lot, sick in bed. He wondered if he'd made the right choices in life, got his sons to follow the right path. Then he heard the falls through an open window. "I guess I'm all washed up as far as fighting the river is concerned, but I still feel the same about it," he said. Lying in bed day after day in the new family home on Victoria Avenue, and in and out of the hospital, the fabled river man had a lot on his mind besides his own mortality—Major had gone off with the Canadian Army to fight the Second World War in Europe, Harry was embracing another family in Ohio, everybody seemed to be out of money or work, and Bill and his wife were resuming their marital troubles in Niagara Falls. "Eventually, the stress took its toll and Mom and Dad separated bitterly," daughter Sally later recalled of her parents' separation. "Mom and I moved in with her two [m]aiden aunts in a large Victorian home."

On May 14, 1942, Red's brother Charlie received a Western Union telegram from Beatrice: *To Charles Hill, 242 Lemon St., Buffalo, N.Y.: "Brother Red Died*

Seven Thirty This morning—Mother. William Red Hill had gone with his boots off. After suffering a heart attack at home, he'd been rushed to the hospital, where he died two days later. Although most everybody could see it coming for some time, they couldn't believe that River Man's life had ended in the hospital with other sick mortals. Even the fierce river he challenged and tempted and the sniper's bullets in the war had not stifled him. His two quiet sons, Wesley and Corky, were still living at home at the time. May 14 was Wesley's twelfth birthday; he went to Kitchener Street School that day and during a morning class, his teacher, Mrs. Gladys Thompson, pulled him aside. "Wesley, your mother telephoned. She wants you to come home."

"They told me he died—they were supposed to let him out of hospital that day," Wesley recalled. He had already been helping his father and brothers fish bodies out of the river for a few years and was hoping to learn more. On the inside, Beatrice was devastated; on the outside, she maintained some stoicism: "William Hill was a tough man, a real tough man. After he was wounded so many times in Europe, and then got those terrified men off the scow, we had five more children. They say he died of his war wounds, but it was the river that finally finished him off. Being sick didn't stop him. He was always going Down There on some rescue when they needed him." His daughter Edith said the night before Red died, she saw it in a dream. "I dream in Technicolor," she said. "I saw Dad in a red barrel with his eyes closed. It was vivid; a Hawaiian wreath was around his neck . . . in the morning, my brother Bill came to the door and told me Dad had died." Junior also told her he'd made a promise to his sickly father that he would one day go over Horseshoe Falls in a barrel. His father had tried to dissuade him, but said that if he was going to go through with it, he should choose a light barrel, perhaps of rubber. He got condolences from Alice, whose own father had died at fifty-two when she was just fourteen. Newspapers and wire services across the world carried the story of the man synonymous with Niagara Falls. Who could ever replace him? His funeral was probably the largest ever held in Niagara Falls, Ontario, attended by hundreds from both sides of the border, including river and war veterans, who came to praise him and consider their own mortality with a backdrop of enough flowers for a greenhouse in Queen Victoria Park. Even wayward Harry came from Toledo for the funeral. The bugler R. Haise played "Last Post" and "Reveille," and piper D. Forrester played the lament on the bagpipes. "Niagara has lost her best son and his name will remain eternally in history," said falls survivor Jean Lussier, who had developed a strong kinship with Hill. Even Maxim T. Gray, general manager of the Niagara Parks Commission, which sought to end all daredevil stunts, later gushed that there were not enough words to describe Hill's meaning to the community and that "one might almost say that the recent history of the Niagara River is bound up, quite intimately, with the life of this man."

"My inspiration all through life has been my father," Red Jr. would later write. "He taught me how to face dangerous situations and the meaning of courage. Everything I know about the Niagara River, he showed me . . . he was fearless, yet gentle, kind and unselfish and helped many a needy person, or wildlife." Beatrice was heartened by all the tributes, including a letter sent to her all the way from Kingston, Jamaica, containing a newspaper article that had been printed in 1939 in the Kingston *Daily Gleaner*, which said,

> [Red Hill] is one of the most gallant and daring men that has ever lived in our day . . . he has given the best years of his life in supplying daredevil thrills and hair-breadth rescues to many. He has no regrets for he is blessed with two sons [Red Jr. and Major] who are determined to carry on the work once started by their illustrious father.

The only thing missing from Red's résumé was a trip over the falls, and that was a topic of conversation at his wake; he'd talked in the papers of doing it, but loved the river too much or hadn't found the correct barrel or didn't want to end up like barber Charles Stephens, who left a widow and eleven children. But in the end, there was no money in the river. Old Red left a life insurance policy of just $420, and his family couldn't provide a proper gravestone for him. The good news was that Beatrice could burn his IOUs.

Local poet F. A. Hardwicke chimed in:

> O, life-long Hero! Silver bright
> Be those long rivers of delight
> That bear thee to the mystic sea
> Of all-enfolding Deity

When Red was unbelievably gone, not only Junior but Major and Corky, as well, sought to take the guardianship of Niagara from fallen hands, or at least a share of it. Certainly, Major carried on the work of his father in the military. While Junior was in Fort Erie, putting the family's legacy on hold, Major enlisted in the Canadian Army. Junior didn't go to war, for reasons not clear; some said it was because he had a leg injury from work on the river; others said he just wasn't interested in the military, although for a time he was a local air raid warden, waiting for invaders who never came. Next to the river, the army was Major's great passion. He learned to fight early as the young pip-squeak with older brothers Bill and Harry, albeit he sometimes got hurt when he couldn't keep up with them in sports or at the river. Eventually, Major followed his father and grandfather as a member of the Lincoln and Welland Regiment, the local arm of the Canadian Army. He made sergeant as a teenager and by 1938 was guarding ships along the Welland Canal. In 1939, Major married a young woman he met at the regiment, Margaret (Peggy) Hanna, a nice girl, plain by most accounts but fun-loving and personable. They had one child, Margaret (Molly), born in 1941. Peggy fancied Major partly because he was a nice guy and a gentleman, who would carve dollhouses for children up the street. Their letter writing sustained him through the war in Europe.

Actually, a series of calamities could not stop Major from entering the European Theatre. The army questioned his health, particularly the shoulder injury from Harry's wayward Fenian rifle, which required several operations to fix, and then there was the foot problem incurred at nineteen; while trying to whittle an ingrown toenail with a knife, he developed blood poisoning in a big toe, and doctors had to surgically remove it at the joint. Then, in 1937, Major suffered a machine gun bullet wound at a rifle range, and in 1940, while wearing army boots in training, he reinjured his foot, dropping a case of ammunition on it, and spent five weeks in the hospital. "If I had my druthers, I would have rather have been gassed like Dad," he said. But Major worked hard and convinced the army he was ready for combat; he certainly looked the part in his beret and khaki battle dress. Being a marksman didn't hurt; on the range, Major was usually five out of five bull's-eyes from fifty yards with a .303 Lee-Enfield service rifle and was also efficient with an automatic Bren Gun. By 1941, Private No. B-88308 was shipped overseas with the Lorne Scots Regiment. He fought in major skirmishes in Dieppe in France and Casablanca in North Africa in 1942, Italy in 1943–44, and Corsica in France in 1944. He was wounded several times, once by a hand grenade, which he lobbed over a fence to save himself and several comrades. In a postcard to his mother from England at Christmas 1943, Major wrote: "Please don't worry. Received the pepperoni, powdered eggs and dried bananas. I'm tickled pink. As Always, Your Son. Cheerio!" By '44, Major had made many missions behind enemy lines with parachute jumps; he had always been fascinated by free falling, and that became one of his allures at the falls. "Only parachutists know why the birds sing," he would say. In a letter to wife Peggy from Italy that year, Major wrote:

> I've seen plenty of action lately and have a damned healthy respect for Jerry [Germans] . . . I'm roughly fed up with Italy and this Wop lingo . . . I'm waiting for a glass of Labatt's at Legion 51 [in Niagara Falls] to shoot the well-known B-S!

Major scaled a mountain in Italy and saw some of his friends killed beside him, but he had courage and was just as afraid of daddy longlegs spiders as he was of the Germans; one night he struck a match in an old Italian castle and found them crawling around him before blowing them away with a flame-thrower. However, on one occasion, Major got drunk with a buddy and went AWOL, visiting his cousin Ken Sloggett, an army sergeant, stationed in England. Major came home to Niagara in 1944 with several injuries, including shrapnel in his leg, and he could not get steady work or proper housing. Bored stiff with no outlet for his nervous energy, Major told a reporter, "Excitement, that's all there is in life." Apparently, the excitement was too much for Margaret, and at one point she briefly left with their daughter. Sad but determined, he got involved with the falls and the river again; eager to follow his father, he started planning his first stunt—a trip down the rapids and, perhaps later, a plunge over the falls, but he had a hard time adjusting to civilian life and couldn't get going. Friends and relatives noticed he'd changed, or had been adversely affected by the war. At times, he was nervous, even shell-shocked. While Major wanted to beat his brother Bill to the punch with the first daredevil stunt of their generation, he couldn't focus properly or put a rescue crew together.

***

Junior's focus was suffering, too, and he was depressed about a bunch of things. In 1943, his work in Fort Erie blew up. He was charged with stealing high-speed drills from his employer, Fleet Aircraft. The publicity was a blow to the family, but he was acquitted in court, albeit discharged from his job. That was a turning point for him. He had to go back to the falls. While he was packing up, he came across a postcard from an anonymous female admirer: "JESUS SAVES BUT THE HILLS SAVE AT NIAGARA." Ah, yes, that had been sent a few days after he'd rescued Pa from the Whirlpool in '31. It revived his spirits, and over the next few weeks, Junior changed his mind about life. He was not a full-time domestic or factory worker; he was a river guy, an outdoorsman, Red Hill Jr.

As his father was falling into illness and despair, Bill had promised he would take up the engagement on the river. There had been no daredevil stunts at Niagara for more than a decade for a number of reasons. For Junior, life had undergone many bumpy transitions: the Depression, Franny's death, his father's death, constantly trying to console his mother, Alice leaving him with their daughter, and the specter and effects of World War II. But the war was winding down—time for action. Without question, he was going over the falls, but first he planned shooting the rapids in one of his father's old barrels, which did not sit well with his on-again, off-again spouse, who wanted no part of the river and the meager finances it brought her husband. Alice bought a house for herself and their daughter in downtown Niagara Falls for $3,000, away from him. Junior was upset, but, like Major, turned his energies to the river. While earning some money as a tour guide, game warden, and manager of the family souvenir store, he put together a crew and decided to dedicate his first daredevil act in 1945 to his father, hoping to use money collected from spectators for a memorial to him. "Knowing his great admiration for his father and his longing to emulate the Old Man's feats, I quickly swung behind this great adventure," said one of Hill's team, Skike Healey, a friend of the family, owner of one leg and a sense of humor about it. "I promised him my full support." This was no small matter for any daredevil's rescue team, who could be charged with manslaughter if their man died in the river.

Major swallowed his jealousy and joined the crew, along with Corky and Wesley, for their brother's first barrel ride down both the Whirlpool Rapids above the Whirlpool and Devil's Hole Rapids beyond it. The twenty-one-year-old Corky had not yet dared a stunt. He was about the same age as Junior when the latter had rescued their father. A calm fifteen-year-old, Wesley didn't seem enamored by his family's fame or stunts; as a tot in 1930, he had fallen from his mother's arms on the banks of the Whirlpool while his father was trapped in a barrel. Apparently, though, he had inherited his father's rescue genes and training; in fact, he was named for Wesley Morse, proprietor of the funeral home where the Hills took floaters. Wesley described how he recovered his first body: "Dad got the call there was a body in the Whirlpool. I stood on the bank with Bill and Dad said to me, 'Take a rope, swim out, and snag the body with hooks.' I said I wasn't going to do it. I was scared. But he wouldn't take no for an answer, so I swam out maybe seventy-five yards into the Whirlpool. I got near the body and threw a rope over it. The hooks caught, then Dad and Bill pulled the body in."

The vessel Junior chose was his father's steel barrel from the 1930 trip through the rapids, six feet long, three feet in diameter, and 620 pounds, with six-inch bulkheads at either end and 150 pounds of railroad iron ballast at its bottom. Stenciled on the sides of the steel barrel were some of his father's achievements:

- Girl Saved from Burning Building, 1896
- Bobby Leach Saved from the Whirlpool, 1910
- Ignatius Roth in 1912 Saved from Ice Bridge, and Several Others
- Sniper Red Hill, Seventy-Fifth Battalion, Gassed and Wounded in World War I, 1914–1918
- Only Man to Navigate the Upper and Lower Whirlpool Rapids in a Steel Barrel and Live to Tell the Story, 1910 and 1930
- Rescued Lofberg and Harris, 1918, from Upper Rapids
- Swims Niagara from the US Falls to Canadian Side in Eleven Minutes, 1925
- Jean Lussier Saved from Drowning after Going over Falls, 1928
- 117 Bodies Taken from Niagara River
- The Only Man in Canada or the US Who Can Wear Three Life-saving Medals

No pressure riding in that vehicle! By 1945, Junior had left his innocent looks and was somewhat ruddy-faced, with a muscular yet average build of 150 pounds on five feet eight inches. In a three-piece suit and tie, he could have been an insurance salesman; however, no insurance company would touch his lifestyle; in fact, they rarely touched river men at all. For this project, Junior got lots of play in local papers. Authorities weren't impressed—Chairman Gray of the Niagara Parks Commission, in charge of the Canadian side of the river, said the stunt would be against the law and every effort would be made to stop him.

Indeed, on July 8, 1945, police stopped Junior in a car on the Niagara Parkway, but the barrel was nowhere in sight. Instead, his crew chief, Mike Marrazzo, and his teenaged son, Charlie, and others had sneaked the red barrel out of the souvenir shop at three in the morning, lowered it 250 feet down the Niagara Gorge, and tied it to a tree.

It wasn't police, but local youths who interfered; they discovered the barrel after daylight and cut the rope, allowing it to roll partway down the gorge. In early afternoon, Hill, along with several friends and journalists, found the barrel had dropped over a fifteen-foot cliff and suffered a large dent, partly to the man-hole cover. When they got the barrel to the water's edge, Hill could hear people coming through the thick brush at him. "The law's coming and I'm going!" he told his crew, jumping through the small hatch, putting on his father's football helmet, and strapping himself into a tight harness as he lay on a hammock to close the world out. The steel barrel was small, claustrophobic. The helmet had a bar in front to protect his mouth (he still had his own teeth, even though he played hockey). Moments later, he was pushed off by one of the reporters. It was time for initiation. He just wished his dad had been here to see it. The last time anyone dared the rapids, Junior had saved Senior from the Whirlpool in '31. On that day, his father gave him his lucky rabbit's foot. It was in his pocket for this trip, and he kept touching it to make sure it was there. Beneath the old fur, it was bony, but to him, its pungent smell was another part of Dad. Junior would later describe his stunt in his published pamphlet, *True Facts of the Death Defying Barrel Trips*:

> Half an hour before I was cut loose just above the first set of rapids, I knew that I was taking an awful gamble . . . it was like going to almost certain doom—because I discovered just before the trip that the rubber manhole cover protecting the opening had been sprung badly! . . . I knew that it would be almost suicide to go on with the trip with the barrel in that condition . . . but all those people were on hand to see it. I couldn't disappoint them. And I couldn't have anyone say that Red Hill was a coward.

Indeed, a tremendous crowd showed up—estimates were between two hundred and three hundred thousand, lining up all the way from the Maid of the Mist landing, atop bridges across the gorge, through the rapids, and beyond the

Whirlpool—not to see his father or Bobby Leach, but him. "Luckily, the end of the war in Germany allowed everyone to relax a bit and look for escape from the intense strain of the war years," Healey later wrote. For the first few seconds, the barrel rode as smooth as silk—thanks partly to steel plate weighting down the bottom and adding stability. But soon the rapids plucked the barrel from the water and promptly tossed it twenty-five feet into the air. Already, the damaged vessel started taking on water, some of it through two air holes that had been plugged with corks, which popped off with the noise of a .45-caliber revolver being shot. Stinging water shot up Junior's nose, like the nails of a creature from the depths, trying to poke its way into his brain.

> I thought of my wife, my child, my brothers and my mother . . . then I thought of my dad, and all my worries seemed to disappear . . . suddenly, the barrel shot high into the air as it hit the first wave—and came spinning down. A few drops at first, and then a steady shower of water hit my face, soaking my clothes and body. The barrel rolled, pitched and tossed like a cork. One minute I was right-side up and the next I was hurled upside down . . . I gasped for breath as the water struck my nose and mouth . . . For what seemed like ages, I was subjected to the worst pounding I had ever had in my life. The barrel crashed sharply against rocks . . . my elbow, knees and shoulders were battered and bruised as they struck against the steel insides of the barrel. I was sure I was doomed! Then came smooth water—I was through the first set of rapids.

Junior was in the Whirlpool, and his fans and crew worried, remembering how Senior had been trapped there in 1931. Waiting at the finish line, six miles downriver near Queenston, Healey got the word. "The Whirlpool! I couldn't get beyond that point," Healey said. "Knowing the river as I do, I could visualize so much better than all the hordes of spectators the possible failure of the mission. Was he even now whirling, whirling, whirling . . ."

At one point in the Whirlpool, while his barrel was the right way up, Hill was able to open the hatch and look out. "It was a great sight," he later said. "The current had taken the barrel to the edge of the pool and coming toward me were my two brothers, Major and Norman, in a rowboat. They caught hold of the barrel before the suction of the pool swept me to the center." With a strong rope, the brothers towed it to the far side of the pool to discover five inches of water in the barrel, and it still faced a trip all the way down through the second set of Devil's Hole Rapids. "It looked like sheer suicide to go on, but in spite of protests of my brothers and friends, I decided to complete the full trip as my dad had done," Junior said. As he got out and stretched his legs, the crew bailed out as much water as they could, and the barrel was pushed offshore once more and into the Devil's Hole Rapids.

> As I closed the manhole cover, I could see the strained looks on the faces of those on shore . . . the current caught the barrel and it shot downstream. Then the barrel was whipped around suddenly—going forward, then twisting back and slamming hard against a partly-submerged rock ledge. I knew this dangerous place and I dreaded it. No one could help me. I would have to take a pummeling until the current worked the barrel away . . . My neck cracked every time the barrel smashed against that rocky ledge . . . That seemed to continue for an hour, then the barrel shot away and down the river.

Through the Niagara Glen in the next portion of the trip, the barrel drifted into stiller water. Hill cautiously pulled out one of the air plugs and could hear the crowd on the banks: "He's coming in! He's coming in!"

> I eased back the cover and I could see the tops of the trees. I lifted myself up and waved my hand to them. Just as I was going to stand up, the current caught the barrel and I dropped back and slammed the cover tight. The barrel sped toward the rapids . . . catpulted [sic] right up into the air, as if shot by a giant cannon . . . water gushed in through the leaky manhole cover . . . . a dozen times the barrel leaped high out of the water and dropped back with a thunderous crash . . . every bone in my body seemed to ache and I was completely drenched with water all around me inside the barrel.

The barrel remained in rough waters for another fifteen minutes before it made it to the finish line in the steady waters of Queenston, a stone's skipping from Lake Ontario. A big roar went up from the thousands along the banks.

"Suddenly, to the acclaim of thousands, I saw a red gleam around the bend," Healey said.

> No one will ever know the thrill I felt as I reached up to slide back that manhole cover for the last time. I breathed a silent prayer to my dad, whom I felt had been with me, and had brought me through safely.

A motorboat came out to greet the barrel, and Hill's crew grabbed his arms and hugged him. "Exulting, I started toward the barrel, proudly helping Red onto our boat while the news cameras recorded this for posterity," Healey said. "We had won, our plan had succeeded." On shore, Junior, suffering only bumps, bruises, and an upset stomach, was greeted by his mother, who had tried to talk Bill out of the stunt, but not so much that she would leave her men alone with it. She had attended all three of her late husband's rapids trips, and now she had to be both mother and father to Bill. His on-again, off-again wife, Alice, was not here—she had more disdain for the river than Beatrice.

Before the stunt, Alice had been quoted as saying she "didn't feel very good about it." However, prior to the trip, their four-year-old daughter, Sally, had said she wouldn't be afraid to accompany her father in the barrel. Meanwhile, adrenaline flowed in the Hill crew—until collections from the huge crowd were brought in. It totaled just $300. At first, Junior couldn't believe it, then his handlers told him why—all along, police had been dispersing the crowd and the collectors. Perhaps they were embarrassed that he had publicized his stunt and yet they had still been unable to stop him. Hill had wanted to collect enough money for two memorials for his father—a piece of lifesaving equipment for public use and a monument.

> I never have been able to understand why this municipality and district have not erected a memorial to my dad, who rendered such great public service to this area . . . The Niagara River is one of the most dangerous and treacherous pieces of water in the world and a great many accidents and fatalities occur each year along this river. There is a need for mobile lifesaving equipment located at a central point. This could be rushed behind a car or truck to the scene of a river accident, and many lives might be saved.

That night, while his first stunt was happily making the rounds in his head, Junior and Beatrice went to Red Senior's grave to lay a wreath. The day's emotions were obviously too much for his mother, who suffered a mild heart attack.

CHAPTER FIFTEEN
ROLL OUT THE BARREL BROTHERS

A third daredevil emerged in the Hill family. On July 20, 1945, Corky conducted his first stunt, taking his place in the family's laurels. Rugged, with a husky build and strong jaw, Corky loved the outdoors, especially swimming, fishing, and hunting rabbits and pheasants. He had the perfect seasonal job for a budding river rescuer and would-be daredevil, as a handyman at the Maid of the Mist, painting boats and keeping the area around the docks clear of debris, at fifty cents an hour. Already the garage at the Hill residence was a clearinghouse for lures and duck decoys that washed up on the docks. Corky risked his life for animals as well as people; once, he suffered severe rope burns when he was lowered on a rope by Junior and Skike 125 feet down the slippery Niagara Gorge to save a cocker spaniel that had fallen into the gorge. Whenever he was at the river, Corky had a look of resolve, if not quite the look of destiny that Major sometimes posed. In a suit and tie, he could have been an apprentice banker. He was courageous away from the river, as well. Classmate Nancy Reynolds remembered Corky as a boy in school: "He was my first champion. He beat up a kid who was picking on me." And now as a young man, he was playing the fast and rough game of hockey on roller skates, where you had to be careful of the pole in the middle of the local arena (Wesley wasn't and broke his beak). Like most of the males in his family, Corky was mild mannered, talking with his deeds. With his handsome face and wavy reddish-blond hair, he was attractive to the ladies.

They also liked the fact that, like his parents, he was a good dancer, especially in the waltz. However, Corky was already planning on marrying his girlfriend, Joyce Kerridge, a slightly plump, pretty brunette, a little loud at times but caring.

In 1945, Corky had the distinction of swimming across the lower Niagara River, midway between the American Falls and the Rainbow Bridge. All the Hill boys were indoctrinated swimmers after having been offered to the river not long after discovering their legs. Wearing swim trunks, he rowed from the Canadian side to a spot near the American power canal, then jumped into the devious currents. At first, he received the benefit of the current coming out of the canal, then went into long, resolute strokes, hand over arm, with a rope in his teeth to pull the rowboat behind him. He had to be careful he wasn't sucked underwater, because near the American Falls, a mini plunge pool could eliminate your visibility and lead to disorientation. As he swam, a crowd of several hundred gathered to watch. Confident and focused, he forged to the Maid docks, where he disappointingly discovered he had not broken his father's record of eleven minutes. It was, however, still a daring feat for a young man who had been known for recovering floaters and rescuing deer from the turbulent waters. And he had achieved something neither Major nor Junior had tried. "I knew that I could do it. So I decided that I'd do it without telling anybody." There had been no prepublicity for the swim, but tourists at the docks gave a round of applause. One would think Corky had a bright future as a daredevil, if he were to choose that path. Major was glad for his brother, but annoyed that he had now been beaten to the punch by both his brothers and did not yet have a stunt to stencil on a barrel.

Not long after, somebody came up with the nutty idea of Junior and Major having a barrel race over the falls. "Roll out the Barrel Brothers" was potentially gangbusters, a sure way to rustle up a big crowd, media attention, and some cash, which thus far had eluded the Hills. However, sibling spats started up immediately. Where would they start from? How might a winner be determined, assuming they survived: over the falls first, to the Whirlpool first, then Queenston, with points for each? Two of their father's barrels were still around—the steel version, which Senior had used in 1930 and Junior in 1945, and the wooden barrel that became Stathakis's coffin in 1930 and Senior's victorious ride and rescue the following year. Eventually, each man talked of putting together brand new barrels for the Big Splash. When Lussier caught wind of this, he wanted a piece of the action, although his plan was broader; now a machinist in his late fifties in Dunkirk, New York, he announced he would sail his big rubber ball over the falls, out through Lake Ontario, and along the St. Lawrence River to New York, where he would attach himself to an ocean liner and cross the Atlantic. Lussier was grandiose enough to try to do it the legal way—by getting permission from the Niagara Parks Commission. Well, good luck with that one, *"mon ami,"* the brothers told Mr. Lussier. Tightrope walkers were also talking about a comeback; in 1946, Arthur Trosi, aka the Great Arturo, of Miami, announced he would cross the gorge on a wire, but left without getting consent. A year later, the great-great-granddaughter of fabled tightrope walker Blondin was turned down for a similar performance. Most of the time, Major and William didn't bother asking permission for barrel stunts along the river; better to ask forgiveness later. Alas, by 1948, the brothers Hill still had not put barrels or rescue teams together. Lussier was no closer, either, having been denied permission in 1947 and 1948, then in 1949 he was turned down for his request to go over the American Falls, a stunt that surely would have been suicide.

Instead, "Roll out the Barrel Brothers" manifested itself in other ways. During a bout with depression, a destitute Major spent ten months in a reformatory in 1947–48 for stealing several mechanics' coats from the back of a truck, then trying to sell them in a bar in Niagara Falls, New York. "I am not a habitual criminal," he wrote to the parole board. "I have learned my lesson and I realize I have disgraced my family's name, which is known all over the world for rescue work." He penned a poem:

> If Old Red, my Dad
> Could see . . .
> Just how his life's
> Affected me . . .

Still, Major made the most of his time in prison, making dollhouses for children at Christmas. Not to be outdone by his younger brother, Junior went to the slammer, too—he got sixty days in 1948, relating to a stint as a deputy game warden for the province of Ontario. He was convicted of theft by conversion of $3,753 in government funds for the sale of fishing and hunting licenses. Junior told the court he overdrew the account, believing he would make up the money from stunting. "Bad bookkeeping and carelessness are to some extent responsible for the fix you're in," Judge H. F. Fuller told him. Certainly, they liked him in the Welland Jail, where he cooked delicious wild ducks for the inmates, and they didn't want to see him get released, according to his sister Margaret (Major reminded everybody that he, too, was an excellent cook). Nevertheless, friends and family were surprised; nobody else had a criminal record. It was a real come-down for Junior, who had recently been awarded a citation for lifesaving and a certificate of merit from the Canadian Society for the Prevention of Cruelty to Animals for his saving many deer in the river. When he got home from jail, his clothes were waiting for him on his front doorstep—the marriage was off again. Alice had had enough of borrowing money from her brother-in-law, the promises of a big payday at the falls, and scrambling day to day to make ends meet. Junior was allowed to see his daughter on occasion, and he would take Sally on excursions into the lower Niagara River to fish in a rowboat with their spaniel, Pal—"much to Mom's disgust. Pal loved the water and would spend the time jumping in and out of the boat," Sally would later recall. "Life vests were not mandated then and Mom would have a fit every time my Dad mentioned going fishing, fearing that Pal was going to cause us to capsize." But father and daughter loved sharing time together. Family was integral to the Hills.

Then there was another setback—the family lost their sacred souvenir store and all their memorabilia in a public auction. Hundreds of people and tourism operators crowded into the shop to pick over artifacts of the Hill legend. Three barrels belonging to Junior and his father were auctioned for $2,900 to the operator of a souvenir store in Hotel General Brock, along with hundreds of clippings, pictures, and souvenirs. The money went to several of the Hills' creditors. As their legacy was being taken from them, Junior and Major remained in the Niagara game, although Junior started drinking fairly heavily. Thankfully, Horseshoe Falls was still there, like a guardian angel. If everything was right with promoters, film companies, and book publishers, they could be set for life financially. If only the falls smiled on them. On Labor Day weekend of 1948, Junior beat the rapids for a second time in his father's fixed-up 1930 barrel before a crowd of what some newspapers estimated at one hundred thousand. Police didn't intervene, but he had to be rescued from the Whirlpool again by Major, Corky, and Wesley. Junior took a pounding in the barrel, which was tossed forty feet into the air by a wave, but he wasn't seriously hurt. When naysayers criticized him for taking more chances, he pointed to the fact that, just two weeks earlier, a five-year-old boy had died after his dog's leash jerked him forward on the sidewalk and he cracked his head. Hey, it could happen anytime (remember

Leach?). That was no consolation to Beatrice; she was suffering from fainting spells and made a resolution to avoid daredevil stunts. The stunt didn't help Corky, either; he missed work and was fired from his job at the Maid of the Mist.

By 1949, "Roll out the Barrel Brothers" remained on hold, but both Major and Junior were planning individual trips over Horseshoe. The way Major talked, he had no choice but to get into a barrel, burdened not only with the pressure of becoming the next Red Hill, but to distance himself from the reputation he was getting locally of being a drunk. He was no sissy, according to Ken Sloggett, himself a war veteran, but had the shakes from the war. "They call Major names, and sometimes he can be full of baloney and hatch up a few tales here and there, but he has more nerve than anyone around here," Sloggett said. "He'll try things no one else will dare, not even the other Hills." And there was a third pressure—to reestablish the Hill family's good name in the community.

***

For a number of reasons, it wasn't until 1949, when he was thirty, that Major made his barrel debut. First of all, it seemed a generational thing—Junior was thirty-two for his initial splash in 1945, and their father was in his forties when he made his first planned rapids excursions (his first in 1910 had been impulsive, in Bobby Leach's barrel). Of course, if one went strictly by falls jumpers, none of them had exactly been young: Annie Taylor was sixty-three, Leach fifty-three, Stephens fifty-eight, Stathakis forty-six, and Lussier the youngster at thirty-six; strange, since daredevils in other events tended to be much younger, usually young bucks full of testosterone with something to prove in swimming, racing, or skydiving. Another reason for Major's neglect of a stunt was the terrible speed bump of the war against Hitler, when he'd been ducking bullets and giving as much back, and then getting his family onto some sort of even keel when he returned to Niagara. He had to scramble to make dough, he'd spent time in the slammer, and his wounds and shell shock from the war slowed his motivation and momentum.

On July 31, 1949, Major slipped into a steel barrel for a trip down the two sets of rapids, Whirlpool Rapids and Devil's Hole beyond the Whirlpool, with the goal of beating Junior's time of five hours. Major said he had the vessel to pull it off—a cylindrical device people were referring to as the *Torpedo*, a sleek ten feet six inches long and three wide, weighing a relatively light 620 pounds, only three-quarters of the weight of the steel barrel used by Junior and their father. And *Torpedo* carried very little ballast. What Major was counting on was the unique barrel's steel fins on either side, connected to levers inside that Hill would control, giving the craft supposedly good maneuverability in the rough water. That was expected to come into play to avoid the strong vortex of the Whirlpool. With Major helping in the design, *Torpedo* was constructed by Myer Delduca, proprietor of Niagara Sheet Metal and Welding Works in Niagara Falls, Ontario. Inside, it had an oxygen tank and cork plugs in the sides so he could peer out. Painted red, white, and blue, *Torpedo* was fragile enough for it to be a challenge—its steel walls were exceptionally thin at just one-eighth of an inch.

Major and his team, which included Sloggett, Wesley, Corky, and, yes, rival Junior, secluded the barrel in the gorge on the night of July 30 to 31. The skinny Major was dressed in blue swim trunks, a white T-shirt, a padded life jacket, and a soft leather crash helmet. In the barrel, he reclined on a padded mattress and held the rabbit's foot that his father had given to Junior, who lent it to him for this trip. It was mangy but was still comforting. As he touched it in his pocket, he showed confidence, claiming that after the rapids and the Whirlpool were navigated, he would "lean back and relax" for the rest of the journey downstream to Queenston. "It was a confidence so secure, that unlike his father and brother, he left no orders for a rowboat to wait near the Whirlpool in case of emergency," according to the Dunkirk, New York, *Evening Observer*. However, privately Major had doubts. As a youngster, he had seen Lussier nearly drown and Stathakis suffocate at the falls; even the best-laid plans of mice and men could collapse in the hands of Niagara, he told friends. Too often, something you might not account for could leap up and bite.

Major's journey began from a concealed point below the Rainbow Bridge; the *Torpedo* moved slowly under the Whirlpool Rapids Bridge and took on the first set of white, foamy rapids. He thought of his wife and daughter, waiting downstream, then focused on rolling with the punches the rapids started throwing at him. The Great Wave tossed the light vessel high into the air, which gave the *Torpedo* enough momentum to fly through the side of the Whirlpool; the fins on its sides also helped Hill guide it away from the vortex. After a short time, it circled within twenty yards of the shore, where Junior and Wesley were waiting to reroute the barrel for the second leg of its journey. Recalling the problems his father had with the Whirlpool in 1931 and his own problems with it in 1945, Junior felt he had to act quickly, and he jumped into the water, swimming out to the barrel. With the help of Wesley and Sloggett, he pulled the barrel ashore to an area under the Spanish Aero Car (the tourist cable car across the gorge) known as Thompson's Point. They found Major all twisted in the barrel, sweating and semiconscious. The mattress he had been sitting on had broken from its moorings, and Major was sliding around on it. As they refastened the mattress, Major was adamant he wanted to continue the trip, so they pushed the barrel back into the water, away from the Whirlpool. He was an army vet, a tough guy.

Then the Hill team encountered something they hadn't expected—a swirling eddy between them and the Whirlpool. It grabbed *Torpedo* and held it fast for thirty minutes, then an hour, but they let it founder because they expected it to eventually kick out toward Queenston. Two hours later, it still hadn't happened; finally, when the barrel circled close to shore, Junior swam out once again and brought it back to Thompson's Point. Major prepared to get out, and a decision was made to pull it farther away from the eddy, then put it back in the water, but as Major got ready to step out of the hatch, currents caught the barrel and slammed his left leg against a big rock, and he shouted in pain. They carried Major to shore, laid him down, and attended to him as he lay battered and bleeding. With his leather helmet, he looked like a football player who had been ambushed at the goal line.

A large crowd was beginning to form along the bottom, as well as the top, of the Niagara Glen. Soon Acting Fire Chief William Wade and several firemen came down the banks with a rescue basket and a five-hundred-foot rope. The Aero Car was closed to tourists and set up as an unlikely rescue center—265 feet above where the injured Hill lay prone. What came next was one of the most spectacular rescues in Niagara history. Two other ropes were tied to the long one to form a lifeline from the Aero Car all the way down to the shore. A rescue basket was tied to its end and lowered from the Aero Car down to the victim. Gingerly, Major was placed into the basket and, painfully slow, brought up to the Aero Car, sometimes twirling as it climbed. Finally, Hill was brought to the top of the banks; what a story for sightseers to take home to Albany or Albuquerque. Up top, Hill was rushed to the Niagara Falls General Hospital, suffering from suspected internal injuries and a fractured leg. Rumors spread around the gorge, and then the city, that Major was on his deathbed. However, it was established his injuries were not life threatening—abrasions, bruises, and aggravation of an old war wound to his leg—but he was shaken and decided not to finish the second leg of his trip anytime soon. "I'm sorry I disappointed so many people," he said. "I promise I'll make the complete trip the next time I try—probably Labor Day."

Hill stayed overnight in the hospital, but another ugly rumor started making the rounds—that Junior was ready to finish Major's ride through the Devil's Hole Rapids for him, just as their father had done, without thanks, for Bobby Leach. Brother, did that ever bring Major to life; next morning, he marched out of the hospital without notifying the nurses. When a doctor heard of this, he said Hill was too weak to finish the trip in the rapids. At first, Major went straight by taxi to Junior's home. There, according to Major, the conversation went something like this:

Major: "What do you think you're doing?"

Junior: "I thought you were unable to finish the trip. Remember, we hauled you out of the gorge like you were dead."

Major: "Leave my barrel alone!"

By telephone, Major rounded up his team, including Sloggett, and returned to the Whirlpool. Limping, with his left knee in a bandage, he got back into his barrel and was pushed off, five hundred yards below the Whirlpool, to avoid the uncooperative eddies of two days previous, and toward the Devil's Hole Rapids. Almost right away, these rapids pulled him and slammed him through a series of water-covered rocks. His father always said the Devil's Hole Rapids were more fearsome than the Whirlpool Rapids (a statement challenged by other daredevils). It was often a wild ride, particularly near the Queenston Power Plant, where currents kept it for about an hour, but the confident Major opened the hatch and waved to spectators. After two motorboats brought the barrel to shore to end the trip, his wife, Peggy, and daughter, Molly, embraced him, and he was led away, his weary arms slumped over people's shoulders.

"How much was collected [in passing the hat]?" he asked.

"Two dollars and fifty cents," Sloggett said. As they often did, police had discouraged the collection, but Hill remained upbeat: "This was my first stunt and I learned a lot." Next for Major was the falls, but the only thing that happened in the remainder of 1949 was that his marriage of eight years to Peggy started to break up. He wanted to beat Junior to get on board for the start of the television era; September 12, 1948, had marked the first international TV broadcast ever made in the Americas, when WBEN-TV Buffalo broadcast from the falls.

CHAPTER SIXTEEN
JIGGS' JINX

The year 1950 kicked off on a Sunday. Fitting—time for a breather, starting on a Sabbath, for a new decade without world war or Depression. As in any new decade, of course, tensions were part of life. President Harry S. Truman ordered the development of the hydrogen bomb in response to the detonation of the Soviet Union's first atomic bomb the previous year. The Cold War was under way, and Major Lloyd Hill didn't know how to fight it; his life was action. He had returned to Niagara with a limited pension, an injured body, and psychological and emotional scars people didn't seek help for or openly talk about, except to make fun of.

Although he was a returning hero of sorts, Major found it hard to get a job, even as a tour guide around Niagara Falls. Frustrated, he started drinking draft beer and Captain Morgan rum, and his marriage to Peggy remained on the rocks. Destitute, he sold his rapids barrels, with the undertaker's coffin straps, for $650 to pay debts. The one thing Major could trust was the falls. It hadn't changed through the war; it was always the same—beautiful, powerful, independent, arrogantly provoking people to beat it. For some time, Major had been talking in the newspapers about becoming the first Canadian to defeat the falls. No one had dared the Big Splash for two decades, since Stathakis ran out of air, bringing outcry from politicians. By 1950, bookmakers were taking odds for someone tackling the falls within a year. Major was the most likely to try it at odds of five to one, followed by Junior at six to one, Lussier at seven to one, and Major's tomboy sister, Edith, at twelve to one. (Major was tired of hearing Lussier's yapping in the papers about a proposed second trip. "Crap or get off the pot," he would say about Lussier.)

Annie Taylor would roll over in her pauper's grave at Edith's odds; no woman had attempted a stunt in the river since she had in 1901, although several others had crowed about it to the press. Men were always fighting for the spotlight, but Edith, who had been getting encouragement from an enterprising American company, just might try the falls. Her relationship with Major had been spotty ever since they were kids and she'd saved up all those Smiles 'n Chuckles candy wrappers to get a fountain pen, only to have Major go and break it. But Major and Junior were the legitimate contenders. "They were fighting and hard-headed about almost everything . . . even who was a better shot with a rifle," said their twenty-year-old brother Wesley, who wouldn't get involved because he loved life too much. For now, their own brother Corky was sticking with breaststrokes in the river.

Major and Junior each wrote pamphlets about Niagara, but neither pamphlet was as good as their father's. And, of course, they sometimes rivaled over suicide bodies, waiting in rain macs under the Rainbow Bridge to see who would pull out a floater and get fifteen bucks for bringing it in. Their tallies of victims plucked from the river, dead or alive, depended on who you heard it from, but Junior likely had a slight edge. If it was possible for family scrapbooks to battle, it happened. In their constant telephone calls to Winnifred Stokes at the *Evening Review*, Junior managed to garner headlines by running for city alderman (he lost), and Major got his share, thanks to his war record. Junior didn't have any war medals, but he had more local lifesaving certificates. In the game of love, they were both good-looking, but not necessarily husband material. When he controlled his frown, Major could be more handsome than Junior, who was not aging particularly well, like his father at the same age. In his legion blazer with its embroidered crest and war medals, Major was debonair, but the brothers' record with women was checkered—both were having marriage problems. Horseshoe Falls remained the most coveted flame. "They wanted to show who the better man was—and in the end that was always measured by who would go over the falls first," Wesley said. "I told them it would be fatal. What was there left to prove?" Edith chuckled when she heard that. "I suppose Wesley doesn't have anything to prove to his brothers, or himself? Brothers are always fighting."

Like others before him, Major chose a summer weekend for his trip over the falls—Sunday, July 16, 1950. On his team were three men respected in metal works in the city—Anthony "Jiggs" Rufrano and Norm Cummings, co-owners of Cataract Metal Works, and Vince Kerrio, proprietor of Kerrio Metal Works, who would go on to become a notable politician. With designs from Hill, the men produced a custom-made cylinder barrel from stainless steel, similar to *Torpedo*. *Jiggs' Jinx* was bullet shaped, twelve feet long, and weighed 728 pounds, with red stripes and a red nose like a small spacecraft. It had a double hull and oxygen in case he got caught under the falls like Stathakis, and the *Evening Review* called it the best barrel to date for going over the brink. The vessel was somewhat similar to that of Bobby Leach, who had survived his 1911 plunge but had been injured and shaken emotionally for weeks afterward. Wood was not the way to go, Major decided, after seeing Stephens and Stathakis perish beneath the falls as a lad. Rubber was an option once considered by his father, but more expensive, and he didn't have the dough. In preparation, Major and his assistants and potential promoters held cloak-and-dagger meetings in hotels, keeping their plans from the police. Junior didn't attend the meetings; after their argument at Major's first stunt the year before, he wasn't asked to be on the crew. Anyway, Junior had his own idea for a falls barrel—a rubber ball with a thick outer cork coating.

As a boy hungry for action, Major had attended and even assisted in plunges, and he was constantly studying the river, especially quirky currents that were always coming up as hydro companies assumed more of the water. Recently, the Hills believed they had found a black hole underwater near the mouth of Lake Ontario, perhaps the original site of Niagara Falls before erosion took it backward, and they warned skin divers to be wary. Despite popular belief, Major insisted there were no rocks at Horseshoe's base, except close to the Canadian shore. "And the water at that point is about forty per cent air which will cushion my drop so much I don't even think I'll feel any impact," he said. "The knowledge that my dad, brother and I have gained on our previous trips on the Niagara River have helped us in saving forty persons from death," he said. "I intend to prove or disprove all my theories as to the currents and formations of the falls by going over it. All other persons who have gone over the falls did so strictly in do-or-die situations. I have theories to vindicate."

As a bonus, Major had army training in parachuting, skiing, mountain warfare, amphibious landings, demolition, and weapons. He knew what it was like to plummet great distances. For luck, Major had a set of cocked dice and the number thirteen painted inside the barrel. "He doesn't need good-luck charms," said Al Salci, owner of the Erie Hotel and one of Hill's managers. "He's got the river all figured out." Bookies in Niagara Falls, New York, disagreed, posting odds of six to one that he wouldn't make it. "I'll be around to laugh at those fellows Sunday night," Major said. An unidentified hotel owner was on his side, telling local papers he was offering to bet twenty-five grand on Major.

During all the publicity, Major had a reconciliation with his estranged wife, Peggy. The night before the stunt, they met in a local hotel room, and a photo of them sitting together on the corner of a bed was published by the *Welland Tribune*. "Women," Major always said. "They bring out the worst in a man—his conscience." Indeed, it was key for Major to have his family with him on his big day. "A lot of people are hanging crepe for me, but my wife and daughter aren't among them. In fact, I know my daughter would get into the barrel with me if I asked her." He was pretty sure that Corky, Wesley, and even Junior would be there for him, but they weren't on his rescue crew; there had been some tension among the brothers lately about who would be first to go over the falls. Their cousin Ken Sloggett was becoming the most reliable river man for Major and would do almost anything for him. Major was not in top shape for a plunge. Usually with 150 pounds on his six-foot frame, he was dangerously down to 130—he was still hurting somewhat from the 1949 trip through the rapids. As well, shrapnel that remained in his leg from the war got aggravated from time to time, as did his childhood shoulder injury from Harry's wayward shot.

From early morning, the crowd started to build around the falls. Everybody wanted to see Major and his new barrel and the first attempt at the falls by the ballyhooed Red Hill family. An estimated fifty journalists were on hand, and those who could locate Major hounded him all morning as he tried to hide his barrel in the weeds off Chippawa Creek, a mile above the falls. Some reporters caught up to him as he got into a truck in downtown Niagara Falls, Ontario, but Hill raced away and lost them in traffic, worried they would attract the cops. By noon, crowds were up to an incredible twenty deep at the riverside; some people had been sleeping in the park and others in cars overnight to establish a good vantage point.

Hotels and bed-and-breakfasts were overbooked, bridges hopelessly jammed. One of the largest crowds ever, estimated by several papers at two hundred thousand, had the day's largest pre-stunt picnic in the northeast. "They came from everywhere," wrote Tom Williams of the *Toronto Telegram*. "They shoved and pushed and fainted and fell. And they screamed blue murder when they couldn't see what they wanted to see." Police were on duty, but more to correct the crowd than to stop a daredevil. "To onlookers," mused Williams, "it appeared that the Parks Commission knew a good tourist attraction when it saw one, and wasn't trying too hard to prevent Hill taking the big drop. Thousands and thousands of dollars crossed counters and you couldn't get a pair of binoculars in town."

At the Waiting Room, as the Hills often described the Maid of the Mist landing, Peggy was with their daughter, Molly; the Sloggetts; and some of Major's other buddies. Peggy's presence was as important to Major as her letters to him while he was fighting overseas. She showed no signs of apprehension. "If anyone can do it, he can," she said. "He lives in these waters. Anyone will tell you he was born in the big Whirlpool here. Oh, yes, Major can do it." Their daughter, Molly, agreed and smiled: "I know Daddy will be all right." A few minutes later, Peggy told another reporter, "It's a stunt. If he comes out alive, he comes out alive. If his time has come, his time has come."

If you were a fan of Niagara daredevils, you got to know the docks at the Maid of the Mist. You got used to pacing below the falls and passing time by watching gulls and fish wounded from the plunge. Drama crackled in the air. Promoters smacked their lips about a potential movie based on this event, in which Hill made up with his wife, defeated Niagara Falls before a screaming crowd, and rode off into the sunset. When told the background music could be "Ave Maria," Major chuckled, "Now, don't that beat all." There were two sets of promoters fighting for the right to sell the Hill story—one local group run by his friend Salci and the other from Toronto. Hill favored the Salci group, but the aggressive Toronto group was trying to negotiate with newspapers and magazines for exclusive rights to photographs and the inside story of "the man who beat all odds and was finally the first Hill to go over the Falls."

The Hills' adoptive brother, Harry, was not here, but driving a bus in Toledo (clear the streets of Toledo!). Initially, Major announced in the papers that his barrel would be lowered into the river just two hundred yards from the falls, but, fearing the coppers would set up a trap there, he decided to launch at Hogg Island off Chippawa Creek—the closest launch to date, except for Leach, who also set sail from the island. The creek was being scouted lately by a movie company for a Technicolor film starring Marilyn Monroe in which a woman would ride an out-of-control boat in the upper Niagara, headed for the falls, but somehow she would be rescued. The Chippawa was a slow, lazy waterway where Major and his brothers had played and swam as kids. It felt comforting to him, even though critics suggested launching at that point could create problems, causing the barrel to ground from currents along the Niagara shore before it got to the falls.

In early afternoon in the weeds and shallows of the creek, Major climbed into his steel barrel, giving thumbs-up to a small crowd around him, including two members of his team, Frank Morosco, a Dominion Foundries and Steel Company worker in Hamilton, Ontario, who had never met Hill until the day before the stunt, but was a friend of one of Hill's aides. Knowing Morosco was a sharp swimmer, they recruited him to take the barrel out into the river, along with Jerry McAndrew of Niagara Falls, Ontario. With two men in the water, it would be easier to push it out of the weeds, into the Niagara River. Major wore a softly padded football helmet and a scowl, like those times he waited to parachute from a plane over enemy lines. There was no going back. He was ready. A gathering of perhaps twenty people discovered the secret location and crowded near the barrel. Also at the launch site were more than a dozen picnickers and spectators, who jumped out of cars when they saw the activity. Suddenly, there was noise and confusion. "Don't get so excited," Hill said, speaking into a microphone held by a cameraman. That sounded funny, since Major liked excitement, but he knew it was time to close the hatch on all of his distractions. "For something this deadly, you gotta get everything else out of your mind," he always said. "You gotta forget your wife, your kids, your job, and your fear . . . most of all your fear. The distractions can kill you."

One of his aides, Lou Pellet, helped secure Major into the barrel. "How do you like the chesterfield we fixed for you?" Pellet said of a hammock he lay on.

"Fine, everything's fine," Hill said. "Dad's out there . . . I can feel him. I'll see you at the bottom of the falls." Major reached into his pocket and realized he didn't have the rabbit's foot, which Junior had loaned him for his rapids trip the previous year and taken back after they'd had a spat. Oh, yeah, and Junior didn't like the fact Major had tried to color it red with cheap dye and it turned out purple.

From the inside, Major helped the men put the cover on the hatch to seal him up. One of them tightened it with a pipe wrench, then the men smacked the side of the barrel to notify Hill that he was ready to go, and he slapped back from the inside to acknowledge.

188

"Let's go, gang," one of the men yelled.

In nothing but their swim trunks, Morosco and McAndrew jumped into the creek and pushed the barrel toward the Niagara River. It was ten past one o'clock in the afternoon. They were accompanied in a safety motorboat by Hector Cote, a Niagara Falls garage operator. First trouble—just after leaving Chippawa Creek, the two swimmers remained with the barrel for too long, and the swift current picked them up and carried them toward Horseshoe Falls and away from the barrel. No problem—Cote would simply bring them aboard the boat, and they would watch Major's barrel carry on toward destiny. But as much as he tried, Cote couldn't get a good grip on the two men in the water, and they needed both their arms to keep control in the troublesome current, which was faster and more difficult than they had expected. Cote decided to motor back to shore to get another man to help him. Meanwhile, the barrel with Hill inside drifted down the river alongside the two men. Onshore, Salci shouted at the top of his lungs for Cote to turn the boat around and make another attempt at saving Morosco and McAndrew before they beat the barrel over the falls with no protection. "Use a rope!" Salci shouted. "Get those men out of there before they go over!" Spectators on the bank screamed above the seagulls.

"I've got miles of rope!" Cote barked, piloting the boat back to shore. "What I need is another man to help me." Cote looked toward a dozen bystanders, but some said they couldn't swim and others turned their backs and walked away to the road. The frustrated Cote turned the boat back toward the men, but his motor failed; it had overheated after the propeller had been tied up with weeds near the shore. Sheepishly, he looked out into the river as the men were being swept away. They were on their own. At first, they swam bravely and strongly, but the current was stronger and carried them toward deadly rocks in the rapids, ready to tear them apart. Finally, less than half a mile from destruction, currents seemed to shift, and the tiring Morosco and McAndrew somehow made it to the Canadian shore through sheer willpower. They collapsed on the rocky banks and were picked up by more of Hill's men and taken away in a car. "I'm glad I didn't eat much before we went in," Morosco said, throwing up a little. "For a while, I thought the three of us [including Cote] were goners."

Spectators gasped, but then cheered as they saw Hill's barrel coming down the river, close to shore. Less than a mile separated Major from his dream, or nightmare. The huge crowd moved as one, some along the river and others down into the gorge. "Children were sent flying, aged men and women were pushed and bustled by the wildly-excited throng which lined the banks of the Niagara for miles," Tom Williams wrote. "Many collapsed in the heat and at one time, the ranks were pressing so hard that it was feared they were going to drive people on the edge of the railing into the thunderous rapid waters below." In the distance beyond the falls, Professor Robert B. Kleinschmidt at the keyboard of the Carillon Tower played "Cruising Down the River," as he was oft to do at big events. It was difficult for any one person to get a clear view of the barrel's adventure, from its start in the Niagara River all the way to the edge of the falls; the river was winding, with lots of hats and pushy arms in the way, but from the launch point, you could see as far as the old scow, still lodged in the river twenty-five hundred feet above the falls, a monument to the rescue by Major's father. God, he was tired of seeing that old scow; why didn't it just uproot and go over, once and for all? As it passed, the barrel got roughed up near the scow, tossed around by the accelerating speed of the white water.

Way down below the falls, Peggy, Molly, and thousands of others were informed by portable radio that the barrel was in the water. They waited, hearts pounding, cameras ready. And waited. Five minutes slowly became ten, time passing in milliseconds, but still no Major Lloyd Hill. Peggy squeezed her daughter's hand almost too tight. Below the falls, Junior, Corky, and Wesley stayed close to a small boat, even though they were not official members of the crew. Sunday was getting really sweaty.

"Where is he?" Corky said.

"He didn't go through with it," a cynic said.

Junior gave him a dirty look as Wesley kept scanning the river below the falls with binoculars.

Amateur eyewitnesses kept seeing false alarms—logs, geese, light refracting the wrong way. Suddenly, Peggy heard a jumbled telephone or radio message from the docks: "He's been caught . . ."

"Oh!" she exclaimed.

Up top in the great mist-making machine, Major was still in the barrel, but it had been snagged in a cross current and flung toward the shore, less than five hundred yards from the brink, where it got caught by an eddy in a hydro forebay, a small reservoir capturing some of the river's water. It was a bay of stone walls, with a small waterfall coming out of a power plant, offering good viewing for the crowd rushing to the railing. Again and again, the barrel was bumped and bounced against the stone wall. Men in white shirts and short hair and women in colorful frocks leaned over the railing, some taking chances for a better view. Some shouted: "Major—keep going! You're almost there!"

Close by, the rumble of the falls beckoned. It appeared the barrel had been damaged. If it went over the cataract now, would the chance of Hill perishing be increased? Some of his aides arrived and were puzzled about what to do. "The bullet-shaped barrel gleamed in the hot sunlight as it whirled around and around," Williams wrote. "Every once in a while it was forced under the falls but always shot to the surface amid heavy spray. Finally, it rolled almost to the side of the power station wall." Was Major to die—or worse be embarrassed—in a fake waterfall? The barrel was trapped for the longest time, giving opportunity for more of Hill's crew to come up from the Maid of the Mist to check on him. This type of calamity had never happened before at the falls.

"Get it out!" someone yelled, sparking hydro workers to go after the barrel with pike poles. They and some of Hill's crew helped pull *Jiggs' Jinx* ashore, but it took time to hook the barrel, which kept slipping away and threatening to go back under the small waterfall, or continue down the river to the mother of all falls. Finally, several brawny workers pinned it down and hauled it ashore. In all, it had been in the forebay for a whole hour.

Next came a war of words between Hill's friends and assistants and the hydro crew. "He'll be killed for sure," a bearded hydro man said.

"No, it's still in the plan to go over," Salci said. "Major wants nothing to stop the trip."

A Niagara Parks Police officer cornered Salci. "If he goes over the falls and gets killed, you're responsible. He's staying here. Get him out!" Another cop said the last man to cut the rope at the Chippawa Creek might also be held responsible. As workers tried to hold the barrel beside a wooden weir, McAndrew had recovered from his near-death experience of an hour earlier. This time, he tied a rope around his waist, leaned out into the water, and tried to grab the barrel before it slipped back out over to the small waterfall, but he missed and nearly fell into the drink again. The barrel danced madly in the swirling eddy, resisting rescuers' attempts to fasten it to the weir, and it kept banging violently against the wall. Until now, there had been many ways the falls could kill you—suffocation, drowning, heart attack, ripping off your limbs. But death by ramming a stone wall?

"Let the fool get himself killed!" an onlooker yelled.

Suddenly, Junior and Corky showed up from the lower river. "Let me through, I'm his brother," Junior said. Elbowing his way through the crowd, he jumped over a steel picket fence around the forebay and promptly cut open his hand and started to bleed.

By this time, McAndrew had managed to get atop the barrel and was tugging at its steel lid. He put his mouth beside the air hole. "Major, Major, are you all right?"

There was a muffled reply.

"He's alive!" McAndrew shouted. About five hundred people roared.

Suddenly, Junior stepped back. "Aren't you going to help?" someone asked.

"Nope—there's too many bosses."

McAndrew was handed a heavy monkey wrench and began twisting the bolts that separated Hill from life or possible death, but too many people got into the mix, and it became a slow, confused operation. Some police officers tried to help, while others were pushing the excited crowd back for fear they might fall into the river. Rescuers finally got the barrel to stop rocking by pulling it through a hole in the wall to calmer waters. It was another twenty minutes until the barrel could be opened. Finally, a thin, trembling hand poked out of the hatch. Major's pale face and sinewy neck showed through a small hole. He blinked wildly as the sun hit his green eyes in the dark barrel. Rescuers reached for his scrawny arms. There was nothing to him, and the crowd looked in amazement. Had he lost weight during the ordeal? And he had been soaked through two air holes, which had previously been plugged.

"Put me back in the barrel, you fucker!" Major screamed at Corky. Arms grabbed him, pinned him, and Major struggled furiously while cursing a blue streak, but he was helpless against so many, and they plopped him onto the grass in a small park bordering the river. "If you'd left me in the barrel, the eddy would have eventually thrown me clear." There was some evidence that Major believed his words; he had not turned on the oxygen tank inside the barrel, saving it for the falls. But he looked as old and beaten as his kapok-lined jacket. His fingers were shaking noticeably.

"He looks twenty years old than I thought," a man said to Sloggett, who had arrived from below the falls.

"Fuck you," Major said to the man. "This is all bull."

Hill still had to be hauled over the safety wall. A rope three inches thick was looped through his armpits, despite his moans and groans to be left alone, and several men hauled him up and over the safety fence to a catwalk above the falls, but not before he cut his hand on the back of the barrel. Before somebody could get to him with a first aid kit, Major's friends and family hustled him away to a nearby panel truck. By this time, a massive crowd had converged on the small park, and it was hard getting Hill into the truck. Suddenly, Peggy and Molly were there. Peggy kissed her husband hard, and Molly hugged him, although "Ave Maria" was nowhere to be heard. "The crowd went mad," Williams wrote. "Children fell and were trampled. Even hearty men couldn't stand against the hooting mass of humanity that was swarming all over the little park."

They finally got Hill into the truck, which slowly worked its way through the crowd and then bumper-to-bumper traffic on the Niagara Parkway. Back at the weir, Hill's rescue team screwed the lid back onto the barrel and pushed it back out of the forebay and through the rapids toward the falls. It was the only safe way they could retrieve the barrel from the river, down at the Maid docks. After less than a minute, *Jiggs' Jinx* sailed in a wide arc over the brink of Horseshoe Falls, about thirty yards from shore, and crashed into the steamy, roaring maelstrom. Professor K, still thinking Hill was in the barrel, played "Nearer My God to Thee." When the barrel popped up in the plunge pool, many of the thousands along the banks gasped and cheered, believing Hill was still inside. No sooner had it taken the long dip than it was tossed up against boulders at the base of the falls. Rescuers got the damaged barrel open, and of course, Hill was nowhere to be seen. Some thought he'd been tossed out, or escaped. Others, believing they had been tricked, became angry, and cries of "phony" and "yellow coward" filled the air.

Back at the Hill camp, Major was equally furious. His friends told him they'd had his best interests in mind in pulling him out when they did; they were afraid the oxygen tanks had been damaged by the small waterfall and that Horseshoe would have killed him. "I told you I was going over," he said sternly. "I could feel [the barrel] spin like a top through the upper rapids and I knew when she keeled over and I was on my head. I knew my position by peeking out the air vents when she was upright . . . you should have let me." The pummeled barrel was taken to Cataract Metal Works, where about one hundred people came to see it. From looking at its dents, they wondered if Major would have survived the big plunge. Still, his barrel might find a second life; although there was a considerable dent along its length and other dents had all but caved in the air chambers at each end, it had not sprung a leak. "We could fix it for another run," Rufrano said. "But to pound out the dents, we'll have to take down the steel plates and send them back to the factory to be rolled again." As emotions dissipated, Hill's crew went to the Erie Hotel on Bridge Street, headquarters for the event, and Salci ordered drafts on the house. They had been hoping to host a celebratory press conference, but instead it ended up a bit of a drunk fest. Junior said the barrel had not been placed in the river at the right spot. Major argued that he expected to get caught in the eddy by the forebay but anticipated his men would push him back out without interference from authorities. Offered Kerrio: "We learned a lot by putting the empty barrel over the falls and think we can use our knowledge to advantage."

Two days later, Major announced he would try the falls again, likely on Labor Day. Hill made no money on the quest, but he was later fined thirty-six dollars and costs in a magistrate's court for careless driving and operating a truck without a license in connection with the incident on the morning of the stunt. Hill told the court that he was simply trying to escape from reporters.

On August 7, Major successfully rode *Jiggs' Jinx* through the Whirlpool Rapids, but it received more damage, and he retired the barrel. At the Canadian National Exhibition that summer, he was paid a handsome $3,000 to display it and tell people of his exploits. Eventually, Major could envision his barrel, dents and all, in a new Hill souvenir shop or museum. Creditors had confiscated the Hills' other barrels, but he could start anew; the second half of the century could be his. Meanwhile, a local anonymous businessman thought a falls plunge could be made safer—he went to the *Evening Review* and suggested that someone could make a big rubber ball, perhaps twenty feet in diameter, for a different daredevil to ride over the falls each Monday, adding dollars to tourism coffers on a day when visitors usually left town. That idea never took legs, but over the rest of the summer, Major planned his next falls trip. He had to hurry, though; Number One Son was planning a stunt in a rubber ball. And then there was New York interior designer Leslie Sander, who put in an order for a barrel with the metal works that had manufactured Hill's barrel. Sander was known for gluing together 167,000 toothpicks to make a sixteen-foot replica of the Eiffel Tower. Such men came to Niagara Falls.

CHAPTER SEVENTEEN
THE THING

And now, apparently, it all comes down to this day, August 5, 1951. As he pauses under Ussher's Creek Bridge, a mile upriver from Chippawa, for his crack at Niagara Falls, suddenly Red Hill Jr. is older than thirty-seven; his sandy red hair is receding, like fire is slowly engulfing him, and lines gain hold on his face. Yet, as he waits his chance to become the first Hill and first Canadian-born to go over the falls, he remains, at least on the outside, carefree, with a charming smile for well-wishers and those on his rescue team, including his uncle Mousie Sloggett and his son Ken, Norm Chandler, and friend Al Sedore, a truck driver who will pilot the boat to get him into the river. If you know Bill, though, and are paying attention, you'll notice a slight pinkish discoloration on the corner of his mouth, possibly Pepto-Bismol, and a few cigarette butts in the grass. Since Alice left him, he has been drinking and smoking. As daredevil and river rescuer, though, he is of broad shoulders and tight vision, a man with his eye so locked onto something, he is willing to dismiss most else, including the catcalls of local doubters. Early this afternoon, as the sun searches its beam under the stone bridge where Hill and his team are hiding from police, it is hard to tell what is going through his mind, but those who know him know: *avoid the cops, stay in control, but make your excitement work for you, and, by all means, if you are thrown out of the barrel, get clear of the plunge pool as soon as humanly possible.* To the derision of many, including some of his own family, Junior has chosen for this perilous trip a vessel unlike any other before it at Niagara—thirteen inner tubes bound by cotton webbing and wrapped in an old fishnet, with a fourteenth for the hatch, which he will pull in when the edge of the falls gets too close. Draped over the barrel is a canvas sign: *The Thing*.

Some people around the bridge look at the barrel as though it's from a cheesy museum on Clifton Hill. Last night at the Rapids Tavern, in a final strategy session over Carling drafts, some guys tried to talk Junior out of it, and even some of his handlers were worried about the fragility of *The Thing*, but he wouldn't back down: "It's gotta be light and buoyant, so it won't be dragged underwater and hammered down. It's the tons of water pounding you down that does the damage. I've got it all figured. The tubes will act as a cushion when I hit. The long and wide tubes will be like shock absorbers. I won't go deep, and that way I'll miss the rocks Down There that are the real danger." He claimed the barrel would be the safest thing ever to travel over the falls and bristled at the observation of Jean Lussier, who said he "wouldn't go down the Chippawa Creek in that thing." Bill had tried to keep last night's conversation light: "Why, I've never even received a scratch from the Niagara . . . the only chance I ever took in my life was the day I got married. Going over the falls is far easier than going to the altar." Bookies chortled, but don't buy it; they're offering odds of seven to two against him, that he will die with water in his lungs from a river he knows better than anything he ever learned at Buchanan Street School. They emphasize that two of the last three daredevils with barrels sturdier than his didn't live to tell reporters about it, and that nobody has even attempted this in two decades. Although he's never said it in so many words, Bill seems to believe that when the moment of judgment arrives, Niagara will wash over him like a protective veil, perhaps as his sister Edith says, to be caught in the arms of the spirit Lelawala. Before Red left the tavern last night, workers dolled up its main dining room with red, white, and blue streamers; white T-shirts with images of the falls; and gladiolas in vases on the speakers' table for the postplunge party to be held later today, when *The Thing* will be on a stage for people to touch and admire.

Suddenly, back at Ussher's Creek, Norm Chandler, a balding, middle-aged tinsmith who helped Hill design *The Thing*, and others in the team start barking instructions to one another. "How ya feelin'?" Chandler says. Normie had been talking up a storm this morning, but has said precious little since. The dark look on his jowl speaks for him.

"Swell, like a million bucks—ready to go, Normie."

"Focus." Yes, focus, Bill. Remember the recent experiments you performed with branches near the old scow, the notes you made of the New Niagara, about the tiny changes that have occurred in the currents since the latest hydroelectric construction (for example, just two months ago, the US Army Corps of Engineers was planning on curbing erosion of the falls by better water distribution). One can never forget that to find the right current is tricky, dead-or-alive stuff, which will keep *The Thing* from entering the falls directly above the hidden boulders that have turned other barrels into tombs. You don't go up against the falls with only a barrel, but with experience and a game plan. Nowhere in sight, however, is a simple life jacket, despite the pleas of his mother Beatrice last night. "That would take the kick out of the show," he said. Some time ago, he stopped listening to the women—Ma and his three sisters, who are waiting for him now below the falls after kneeling earlier at All Saints and offering the hymn "Whispering Hope." Beatrice forgave Junior's recklessness years ago, just as she had grudgingly forgiven her husband before he died, because "it is something that gets in their blood and you can't stop them. All I say to them is that they are in God's hands and once they are on the river they are on their own." While he doesn't do what they say anymore, it has taken years for Bill's guilt about the women to subside, especially over Ma, who sometimes passes out cold at these spectacles, but he loves them dearly for caring and keeping him topped up with hot towels and hockey toques sewed on the rickety Singer in the parlor. This very morning, his sister Margaret fixed him his all-time preferred breakfast—pork chops and fried potatoes—but he flatly turned down his family's final plea to quit the project, telling them, "If I survive, I'll be famous. Maybe I'll get on that TV show [in June, the first color broadcast was transmitted from CBS in New York, featuring Ed Sullivan]. It will make all the papers in Europe and I'll be famous in the States. Maybe they'll put me in the wax museum on Clifton Hill. If I don't make it, I won't know, anyway."

Years ago, Bea had stopped saying, "If you loved your family, you wouldn't do this." How could she blame them—it was obvious even God didn't listen to her anymore. Now, in the soft afternoon, she waits downriver on the edge of a dock, on pins and needles, in the Waiting Room, along with her sons Major, Corky, and Wesley. For this stunt, they are not officially in his team, but they are his family. Not everyone is on Bill's side; many of the local yokels at the tavern are always giving him the gears for his lifestyle and dreaming. Oh, it's perfectly all right, and even interesting, for an American daredevil to charge into the tavern, like that brave Taylor widow, or a Brit like Bobby Leach, or a transplanted American Greek such as Stathakis, but for a guy who lives in an upper apartment on Peer Street? All that these critics remember is what happened twenty years ago, when they popped you one in the school yard and made you bleed. Hell, they *knew* Red Hill Jr.; how could he be *somebody*?

"You try the falls and you're gonna fucking die," one of the locals slurred last night. Junior looked at the guy, who happened to be a lifer at the local paint factory, like he was already in a wooden box. "I'd rather get hell for something I did than something I didn't do," Bill said, but not in a condescending tone. In a cooler moment, he added, "I'm through waiting. This shooting the rapids has been practice stuff. I'm going over the falls. I've given it a lot of study and I'm going over. I'm as good a man as my father was. Now it's time to prove I'm a better one." He did not say it with a huge ego.

Everybody has a different theory why Junior is getting ready to stretch prone in a rubber cocoon and cast off. And he is constantly giving them clues; just five hours ago, among his last words to Margaret were "Life as it stands now is not worth living without Alice." In the past six months, as much as he has tried to let the roar of the river occupy him, Bill cannot shake the image of Alice the first time he had seen her at the hospital with that twinkle in her eye, attending to his dying Franny, or the way she had touched the back of his hand the second time he saw her, or the day she gave birth to Sally. For a moment, watching him there on the bank of Ussher's Creek, as his jaw slips temporarily, one suspects he is going to drown in sentiment. However, he tells Chandler that if this doesn't work out, he has had a good life. He had the best father in the world, who taught him the basics of life and the outdoors; he has had wonderful, if somewhat competitive brothers and sisters; hundreds of friends; the beautiful Franny; a wonderful daughter; and a scrapbook of deeds—swimming the lower river twice, rescuing his father and Major from the Whirlpool, and twice beating the rapids. He's led a life of being alive. If he is to go out on this day, he wants to go out alive. Could his life be better? Sure, and it will be, but he has to remind himself he has already lived other people's dreams, and today they have turned out in the tens of thousands just to watch him live them out, and others have come to visit the dark part of their soul that wants to see a man snap his spine.

Right now, he has a crowd many times the population of Niagara Falls waiting for him—estimates by police and media range from two hundred to three hundred thousand, lining up along the banks, in the windows of the Foxhead

Inn, on the Rainbow Bridge, in the Carillon Tower, and in the middle of the road on this muggy afternoon, all along the riverbank—Yankees, Canucks, tourists from Berlin and Bombay, people with all colors of skin, with Ohio and Quebec on their license plates, and a man in a military uniform running with long legs, his medals flapping—all waiting for a double rainbow, or a miracle, or *something*. Business is booming—taxicabs squeezing between double-parked automobiles, hawkers selling red rock candy, and young women on wooden carts, peddling everything from vinegar 'n' fries to Lucky Strikes. The brides and grooms are temporarily distracted from their shiny rings, and they are not gazing at tiny Bridal Veil Falls or the chunky *Maid of the Mist* steamboat down in the lower river, safely under the rainbow. For once, they have not come to pay homage to the great Niagara; they are looking for a little barrel in the river. No wonder the cops don't seem to be making much of an effort to stop the illegal stunt. Surely, with all the commotion in the media the past couple of weeks, they must know that he, his barrel, and his growing team are under Ussher's Creek Bridge. Twice already a police car has passed over the bridge, taking its sweet time rumbling over until Bill could hear every tread.

Suddenly, and out of character for him, Hill gets excited. Somebody has let his spaniel Pal out of a parked car. "Who let the dog out?" he says, almost shouting. "Get her back in the car, she may get hurt." As they put the dog back, Junior suddenly thinks about the photograph in his wallet of Sally posing with him on his father's old rapids barrel; she is four or five, sitting in her blond Shirley Temple locks on the front of the barrel in relaxed waters as Red holds her with one hand and points to something in the distance with the other. It's his favorite, and he asks Chandler if someone is protecting his wallet with the photograph in it, and Chandler confirms. Bill has kept with him the rabbit's foot his father had given him in the fantastic rapids trip of 1931. He looks at it; why did that damn Major try to color it with cheap dye?

As they report back from the brink, no one in Hill's team has seen Leslie Sander, the New York designer who said he will also plunge over the falls in a barrel on this day. And no one has seen Sally in the crowd. Children are allowed to watch all of this unfold, of course, but they are not to take part, as Bill and Major had done as kids. In fact, kids are all over the place, dressed like their parents and acting like their parents, and yet they would never be permitted to mimic what Mr. Hill is about to do. Really, they should all be farther up the parkway with their cousins and nephews, rolling in picnic blankets or throwing a baseball around and taking color snapshots with the sun overhead, but that wouldn't get their central nervous systems thumping. You have to feel for people who allow their hearts to beat fast only while standing behind a protective railing, watching someone else, Bill has said. No, he isn't Bill right now. He is Red Hill.

Time for a final barrel check. The tubes seem okay, tight but not bloated. Inside are straps to hold him in place, donated by the Morse and Son Funeral Home, leftovers from coffins. The barrel is painted silver with the large sign *The Thing* draped over it. It still smells like Chandler's garage, where it has been hidden overnight, but there is enough room inside to breathe. When his father was in the hospital for the final time in 1942, he told Junior that, if he was going stubbornly through with it, he should make a falls barrel as airy as possible. Amazed tourists stand back to give Hill and his team room to put the barrel into the water. He drinks a half beer someone hands him. "Thanks, my mouth was dry," he says. A dainty monarch butterfly floats just over his head, and Hill tries to get it to land on his arm, but it refuses. He shrugs, then gets his finger wet in the creek and runs it across his barrel, causing a squeaking noise. The air smells fresh, and he takes a deep breath. But, as he senses many in his team are nervous, Junior forces a beer fart and everybody laughs. "You stink," his cousin and aide Ken Sloggett says, giving him a thumbs-up.

"Smoke?" Chandler says, offering a cigarette.

"Trying to quit," Hill chuckles. "Isn't that the old joke about the guy before they hang him?" If he's scared, Junior isn't giving it away; as he tends to the barrel in shallow water, no sweat is visible on his wide forehead. His countenance is flat, with his hair nicely combed and controlled, and he wears a used pair of trousers and a tan sport shirt, like a bloke ready for a day of bass fishing with soft-shelled crabs. Junior never does things with a lot of noise; they make noise after he does them. What he is doing is trusting himself. As he vividly imagines a positive outcome, he knows it all comes down to trusting yourself, your thirty-plus years on the river, living with the mallards, all the research you've gathered with soiled hands, your knowledge of the ebbs and flows, and the day you plucked that starving mutt from the Whirlpool under the Spanish Aero Car and grinned as he licked your ear.

He's ready, so he and Chandler tie the barrel to the back of Sedore's motorboat. The launch site is near Major's of last year, but they won't repeat some of his brother's goof-ups. His barrel is lighter and should keep romping right over the falls, rather than drifting to the hydro pool, and he won't let any of his men swim the barrel out into the Niagara River. With newsreel cameras rolling, Sedore tows the barrel out where the water is deep and green, where ducks sleep on automatic pilot, and teenagers often dangle toes from air mattresses. There, Hill gets out of the boat, climbs into the barrel, and takes off his shoes. Calmly, he lies on an air mattress in *The Thing* and adjusts a leather football helmet fitted with two metal rods to guard his face, making him look like Red Grange, the old football player. Brilliant sunshine illuminates everything—the homemade barrel, the sparkling green Ussher's Creek, and then the Niagara River—and especially the funny look on Sloggett's lips. You can't ignore that—it is a look of uncertainty. But Hill still smiles as he holds the hatch open. The only frown comes when he hears Pal barking from the car.

***

Red Hill Jr. is finally on his way, as soon as he had lost the reporters, the helpers, the hangers-on, the naysayers, and that waitress at the Foxhead Inn, who promised him a date when he was finished. He is tucked inside his barrel, alone with the Niagara River. Finally, there is no one to answer to, except something he had been worshipping for all of his life. In many ways, he has been alone on this project all along; not even his father wanted in. After he waves farewell through the open hatch, cameras whirr, and he is in the Niagara current—with ten minutes and a mile or so to go. What awaits? That is only one of the imperative questions of the day, and another is "Why would a man get inside a contraption to go over Niagara Falls in the first place?" Everybody has an answer.

His mother:

> William, my son . . . I tried to talk him out of it, but he wouldn't listen. His Pa and Major never listened, either. That stupid river called to them and it got in their blood so they couldn't think straight anymore. I pleaded with Bill right until the end. He just kept walking out of the house and toward that river like it was pulling him on a string. A big car scooped him up and I said a prayer. You know, I always used to worry my children would grow up too quick. Maybe they never grew up.

If, indeed, this is where Bill wants to be, he is getting a once-in-a-lifetime view, because he's keeping the hatch open for as long as he can. According to his plan, just before reaching the crest of the falls, he will close the hatch from inside; right now, he is simply drifting and lollygagging in the upper river's friendly neighborhood, across from the eagle's nest at the end of Navy Island, where he had watched a mother proudly hatch her eggs five years before, where he had saved a deer from getting snared by the current. The barrel is slowly turning, rolling, almost pleasantly so. Why, Bill?

Friend Bud Sinclair:

> I guess he had to do it. He couldn't stop himself. He was driven by an urge bigger than himself, bigger than Niagara. I told him he was crazy. I told him if his father was alive, he'd disown him as a fool, but he said his father would have gone over with him. You can't fall one hundred and seventy feet without being seriously injured or killed. I told him to give up this suicide and grow old and fat drinking ale.

Hill can now probably see to his left the tidy middle-class bungalows of Chippawa, and he will know he is coming close to the Point of No Return, where only Superman can reach him. In the big picture today, if one takes the vulnerable barrel and the incredible danger out of the equation, the scene is quite lovely in the six hundred yards spanning the river above the falls, Canada to America, a sparkling stage of rippling water and sunlight. And yet all around the barrel currents swirl up and down, in and out, although in the end it is always a steady race downhill toward the big ending. Once he starts spinning, he will know he has given up control, and yet he probably loves all of it and always has. He can't always say the same for many things that have transpired in his life on shore.

Ken Sloggett:

> He was at his wit's end. His wife had left him, the family souvenir store was out of business, there was the scandal of going to jail, he had no money and Major's try at the falls had been a laughing stock

to many people. In his mind, going over in a barrel was the only thing he had left. I told him he was in the hands of the Good Lord.

And now Bill passes small islands in the fast stream, overpopulated with gulls and other fowl, who, until *The Thing* came by, thought they'd seen everything in the river. As the silver vessel spins around, he must be catching a glimpse of power plants on the American side, run by those institutionalized, civilized people—the status quo. And yet, for all of their independence and quirky habits, even the Hills have some good old-fashioned reputation in the community.

Major:

> My brother had to stand up for our name, and all the things we'd done. He didn't want people to think he was a coward, a quitter, and so he didn't wait as long as he should have to get the money for the metal lining in the barrel. I think a dead hero is better than a dead coward every day of the week.

As word of the oncoming barrel spreads, crowds circling Horseshoe Falls have become larger than they were last year for Major; in the areas not sprinkled with mist by angels, Bill can likely see people sitting precariously over the safety railing at the brink on the Canadian side—people who will snap fuzzy, long-distance photographs and take them home for a piece of plastic in their album. There will be incredible coverage in the papers and on the radio stations and the new television stations. One day, somebody will do a book or movie about him, and then he will never die.

Sloggett:

> He did it because he knew all the spectators would be there and all the papers and the news reels would be there, and he thought he would become famous. He said if he survived, he would be rich and famous and the family souvenir store would open again.

Indeed, journalists have been parked in the premier vantage points for several hours, waiting, anticipating, writing prose, hoping to become Hemingways.

Niagara Falls *Evening Review* reporter Clive Jacklin calls it "one of the zaniest daredevil exploits ever attempted," and yet he brags he has been given preferential viewing areas by the Hill team.

The Toronto Globe and Mail:

> Whatever might be said of the individual who risks his life, for the crowds of thoughtless people who come from far and near to gape at the spectacle, there can be nothing but contempt. It is a sad commentary on Twentieth Century civilization that one hundred thousand people could have found nothing better to do on a pleasant afternoon.

(And yet, the *Globe and Mail* published a money-making story about the stunt the previous day on its front page.)

Probably the last thing Red Hill Jr. sees before he closes the hatch is the huge crowd from all over the world rimming the falls. Some spectators will later say they saw the barrel starting to break up as it bounced up and down in the Horseshoe Rapids, like a lost summer toy waiting to join the bodies and flotsam in Big Bass Eddy below the falls. "I was [watching] on top and saw it break apart before it went over," said Hill friend Frank Mancuso.

Wesley Hill:

> He thought the river wouldn't hurt him. I told him the barrel was too light. You're heavier than it is. If it hits rocks in the rapids and stops, you're going to shoot out of it like a ball out of a cannon, and he didn't put enough thought into what might happen in the upper rapids. Then, if you get over the falls, when it hits water at the bottom, the barrel will stop cold and you're gonna fly out . . .

There it is at the top of the devil's roller coaster.

"Oh, *Signore Gesù* [Oh, Lord Jesus]!" an Italian tourist screams.

And it disappears over the crest.

Bill is either dead or they'll slap him on the back and strike up "For He's a Jolly Good Fellow." And finally he will have some cash because Ma's fifty-ninth birthday is coming on August 21, and it will be nice for her to have a box of chocolates and a dozen roses. Boy, would he ever like to see Ma have a good laugh from the belly. Maybe there will even be enough money for a memorial to Pa, because there still was none along the river, and that was a travesty. Will the Hills be remembered?

It's over. Some witnesses say the barrel went over the falls at about the middle of the crest, just right of where he had hoped it would. They report seeing it hurled about twenty feet out from the precipice before it started its 165-foot drop, which should have been enough to avoid rocks Down There. Several people say it seemed to be intact when it hit the bottom, then flew apart as it bounded out of the water, perhaps after hitting a submerged rock. Whatever happened, the huge crowd falls mute, and the only sound, besides the falls, is Professor Robert B. Kleinschmidt's hymn from the Carillon Tower:

> There let the way appear
> Steps unto heaven,
> All that thou sendest me in mercy given
> Angels to beckon me
> Nearer, my God, to Thee

By this time, Sloggett is high up on the Falls View lookout, watching like a hawk with a pair of binoculars. He believes his cousin was still in the barrel when it catapulted over the edge, but it "probably came down on a pile of rocks. I turned and said to my brother [Jack], 'He's dead.'" But just a minute. Directly below the falls, on big rocks and wooden docks, thousands strain to see the barrel in the intense mist. A little farther downriver at the Maid of the Mist, Bill's sister, Margaret, had turned her head away when the barrel was right on the crest, but now she shouts, "Where is it? Where is he?" A small boat is launched, manned by Corky, Danny White, and others. In their desperate attempt to locate him, they nearly get into a terrible accident with the powerful *Maid of the Mist* tugboat near the base of the American Falls. Its captain, Clifford Keech, has to veer sharply to avoid cracking the smaller boat in two as both vessels come perilously close to killer rocks.

"*Sharooom!*" screeches the boat's whistle. "*Sharooom!*"

"What on earth are you doing?" Keech yells to the frightened men, his words as hot as the smoke coming out of the tugboat's stack. Another motorboat is so loaded with journalists trying to get close to *The Thing*, it almost swamps Corky's boat.

Finally, after a few agonizing minutes, Hill's barrel, or what is left of it, pops up in the lower river between the Canadian and American falls. Three tubes have fallen off, and ten are still loosely held together. Corky and those in his boat are the first to spot it, bobbing like a bunch of soggy doughnuts. As they row with purpose and panic, it becomes obvious that Bill is no longer inside; it's come apart under the strength of the water and has been reduced to a jumbled mess of rope and fishnet. The foam rubber mattress he had been stretched upon a few minutes before is spinning in the water like a demon let the air out of it. Looking through binoculars, Sloggett moans, close to weeping, "I told him the barrel was no good, that once it got wet it wouldn't stay together."

"He's not there!" Corky yells, his words carrying fright across the waters.

"He's not there! He's not in it!" Beatrice screams, wiping her spectacles. "My son, where is my son?"

"His shoes," one of the river rats groans. "The only thing in the barrel are his shoes."

"He's dead," Wesley says, holding his mother, failing to be matter-of-fact.

Also nowhere in sight are Bill's lucky charms, including his father's rabbit's foot. Spectators along the banks stop chucking pennies into the water for luck, and Edith and Margaret weep uncontrollably, followed by Beatrice and then Corky and Major, whose nice jacket and tie are falling apart. They know that, outside the barrel, there is little chance of survival in the strong undercurrents of the plunge pool close to the falls, even for as able-bodied a swimmer as Red Hill Jr. The only man who might rescue him is missing, and all that is left to look at is the rubber mess and cotton webbing that once had encircled the vessel. As the barrel's remains are brought to shore by Corky's boat, Bill's spaniel Pal jumps off the docks into the water and begins swimming around the crippled barrel, bewildered, looking for its owner. Family expects the worst. The Hills have recovered hundreds of bodies over the years. They know what the falls do to people. They don't want to see Bill as a floater.

"Where's Norm Chandler?" Corky shouts. "What about the puncture-proof tires? This isn't a river barrel, it's a fucking casket."

Chandler is already walking crookedly back up the gorge steps. He mumbles to those around him: "Why do I listen to people? Why? Why?"

"Well," sighs Danny White, "I guess *nobody* knows the river."

A ranting, impulsive Major slashes some of the barrel's tubes with a knife and forces his own head down into the water, hoping for the relief of suicide. The Maid landing becomes a three-ring circus as the large throng of spectators and reporters continues to gawk and gaze and take photographs of anything and everything, while the oblivious waterfall continues to plunge down in front of them in torrential quantities. Some of them start yelling, "Fake! He was never in the barrel! It was fake all along!" A local radio station broadcasts that Junior never got into the barrel and is hiding in Buffalo. The Hill brothers and some of the river rats want to punch up the critics, and they keep spinning in circles of emotion from rage to grief to helplessness.

"I'll kill anybody who says my brother wasn't in that barrel," Corky screams, as frothy as the suds washing up onshore. Asked if police believed he was in the barrel when it went over, an officer says, "He is not the kind of a guy to renege on that. He went over." Major can't make up his mind what he wants to do; one moment he's slashing tires and planning quick revenge on Niagara, trying to recruit enough good men to form his own crew to beat the falls, but then a different wave sweeps over him, and he thinks, "Dad had it right; stay away from that long, tall drink of water." Then he and Corky start sobbing again and vow to their mother right here and now that they will give up the river forever. Wesley is upset, too, but he had already announced to the family that he was not interested in becoming a daredevil, dead or alive; he had prepared for his brother's death long before it actually happened, and so his tears are dry on some fishing dock in the north country. Beatrice hugs her sons, but she is becoming angry with the missing William. How could he have put everyone in this position—didn't he love them, didn't he love her? Or did he love the river more? Just for once, she wishes, life could be simpler, as simple as it is, apparently, for other families.

A broken Edith looks at the base of the falls with drooping eyes. "Maybe he's with Lelawala," she says in a small, unconvincing voice.

Finally, police become involved, but call off the search after three hours, expecting Hill's body to show up later in quiet waters downstream, although floaters sometimes are not recovered for several days, if at all. Nobody knew that better than Red Hill Jr. Over at the Rapids Tavern, the celebration is canceled. "We don't feel much like it," waitress Alice Graham says. "He meant something to us all." Corky and Major go to the tavern, limp. "This has really done my mother in," Major says. "I'd say she has only a fifty-fifty chance of pulling through." Then he returns to the bowels of the gorge, where, long into Sunday night, he sits slumped on a dock, waiting for his brother's body in the dark. Several times, he yells "B-i-l-l!" across the shore to the United States, and it can be heard over the roar of the falls. Then he opens his trousers and leaks into the river. For the rest of the night, he counts every one of the stars in the sky. Bill is Major's rival no more. He is his brother.

***

Nobody wanted the sun to come up Monday morning, but it did, anyway—like God with a red eye. Shortly before seven, sixteen hours after he had begun his great, hopeful journey, William "Red" Hill was found 650 yards downstream from the Maid of the Mist landing. The river rats knew where to look. That's where he usually found them, anyway—most of the 210 bodies he'd recovered from the gorge. Unbelievably, his naked corpse was not battered, apart from a single gash on his forehead. A watch on his left wrist was still ticking, which likely would have amused Red because of its significance to the nine-to-five world, obviously carrying on without him. It was 6:50 a.m., nearly punch-in time for another week at Fleet. His body was recovered by a combination of river rats and Maid of the Mist workers—Mousie Sloggett, Phil Roberto, David Harrison, and Burt LeBlond, who looked at their friend's remains only when they had to. It made them even more nervous of the river, and they were careful not to fall out of the boat. The body was removed by truck to Morse and Son Funeral Home, which, really, was the only way Red Hill Jr. would ever leave the Niagara Gorge for good—in a box. The box looked very small. *The Thing* was also laid to rest as Corky and friends took it out into the country in a panel truck and burned it with matches and harsh words, although it took hours for the stench to dissipate. Family pressure was not so easy to burn.

As funerals go, Bill's was bizarre and complex, as everybody had a crack at writing his obit while huddled under a tarpaulin to protect the grave from drizzle at the Fairview Cemetery. Hands clasped behind their backs, many people were as sad for Bill's life as they were for his death, but perhaps they were the people who had not really understood him all the way along. Major stood up for his dead brother: "He put on a good show," he repeated to everyone he came across. "He picked the spot he wanted to live or die and he was watched by the biggest crowd ever—or one of the biggest. How many people watch a football game? A movie? And I'm sure most of the people who criticized him were there when his barrel went over." Others felt dirty, and no matter what they said to one another, they could not get clean, not even after collapsing across the flower-decked coffin before it was lowered into a place he wanted to spend eternity—beside his father, and not far from Franny. They put him and his questions into the ground pretty quickly. There was no money for a gravestone, just as there hadn't been for his father or Franny. Of course, there was the Anglican funeral at Christ Church, conducted by Canon Albert T. F. Holmes and attended by about 350 people. According to Anglican custom, there was no eulogy, only the singing of hymns by a white-decked choir and the reading of psalms:

> The Lord is my Shepherd
> I shall not want
> He leadeth me beside the still waters . . .

Corky wore dark sunglasses from the Niagara Parks Police lost and found, as if anything could hide his burning heartache. Beatrice traded her hospital gown for a black dress, and the only ones not at the funeral were two of the *whys* for Red's fatal quest, *that woman* (Alice) and their daughter, Sally. (Alice called *The Thing* That Thing and wanted nothing to do with the Hills.) Some people were still pissed off, others disillusioned, and some bitter—and none of their answers seemed to add up. "The cops didn't try that hard to stop him," Ken Sloggett said. Many called it suicide by a desperate man, or at least a boom or bust. And if you said softly that he passed away, somebody behind you might snarl: "Passed away? He had the life smashed out of him. Passed away to where?" Junior was a saint and a devil and a stupid man who should have known better than to let the coroner get hold of him before he was forty, many said, but in their cold science, coroners and old spinsters forgot an important fact about adventurers, Major opined—that two of the last things to die were dreams and ego. Despite Sloggett's bitterness, some detectives snooped around at the funeral, considering the possibility of laying a manslaughter charge if they could finger the men who pushed Red off on his one-way trip from Chippawa. No one dared be the rat. But soon after, Ontario premier Leslie Frost urged for stricter law enforcement of stunters on the river and for Criminal Code charges to be laid against them and those who help them. Frost said of Hill's ride, "In my opinion, such attempts are wholly undesirable from the standpoint of public interest. They add nothing to human knowledge." But he forgot to mention they *did* add tens of thousands of dollars, perhaps millions, to the coffers of the Niagara Parks Commission (owned by his provincial government), restaurants, and tourist establishments on both sides of the border that day, not to mention the incredible free publicity generated for Niagara Falls with the international stories and radio and television accounts of the Hill plunge and all the buzz around factories and offices. Wrote Sidney Katz in *Maclean's* magazine:

> The Niagara Parks Commission, opposed to stunting of all kinds, readily admits the Hill family has been responsible for a surprisingly high proportion of the press notices that have appeared throughout the world about Niagara Falls. Servicemen from Niagara Falls who came in contact with troops from many countries while overseas were surprised by the number of times they were asked about the Hills. They have added color and lore to the falls; they have welded a bond between the cold cruel waters of the Niagara and man.

Reacting to the publicity about Hill's death, an American pastor, Rev. Paul Whipple, said sarcastically,

> It must look beautiful with the blood of "Red" Hill in every merchant's window. But I suppose it paid off . . . If someone called your office and told you they were going to commit suicide you would call the police and stop him. But when some fool will do it the dramatic way, that will draw thousands to witness, you condone it.

When his tears had dried, Major tried to play cool: "When that big elevator from the sky stops, you gotta get on."

After Frost's announcement, police started cracking down and stopped two subsequent stunts, including Sander's. For now, Major postponed his own plans, thanks partly to his mother, wife, and sisters practically sitting on top of him; however, sixty-year-old Jean Lussier still schemed and was ready to increase the stakes and challenge the boulder-strewn American Falls, and Major's friend Philip A. Wessner Jr. of Reading, Pennsylvania, planned to go over the falls in a contraption similar to Junior's, saying he had an offer of $10,000 from an undisclosed source to make the attempt. It was not a dull week in Routinesville, was it, Red? For the next five nights, just as the weather office had predicated, meteors lit up the sky around Niagara.

CHAPTER EIGHTEEN
STUNTING GOES ON

Junior's death hit the family hard. Beatrice remained for some time in black—clothes and outlook—although she tried to keep everyone together with love and Protestant prayers. His four brothers (even Harry in Toledo) and three sisters were devastated. Bill had been a nice guy and a good brother. Major came out of the funk first; three weeks after his brother's death, he was in New Jersey, advising eighty-two-year-old Bernarr MacFadden, of New York, on the latter's proposed parachute jump into the river below Horseshoe Falls. Then Major revisited his own plans for going over, perhaps in a rebuilt *Jiggs' Jinx*. "I knew Major would get back into that stuff. It was too much in his blood," his mother said. "He'd already had a taste of it in his rapids trips and when he tried to go over the falls."

Corky was another matter. He'd just turned twenty-eight before Bill's death. Although he had never ridden a barrel in the river, Corky had a penchant for swimming in the dangerous waters below the falls, but the family didn't look upon Corky so much as daredevil as an outdoorsman, river rat, and rescuer, like his younger brother, Wesley—a backup singer in the Hill chorus. Along with Wesley, Corky was the baby boy of the family and was close to his ma, with whom he bowled on quiet nights, and his cribbage-partner sisters. Sometimes Beatrice still imagined him as the little four-year-old in the family album, all smart in a sailor's cap and suit, and she remembered him also for that day he was christened in 1939 by Rev. Wilmot at Christ Church. Oh, well, the boys were all christened, anyhow.

Corky hardly smoked or drank. He was such a good roller-skater and devoted husband to his wife, Joyce, that he refused a job as an instructor in New York City because it would have meant he would have to skate with another woman. But Bea wasn't so sure Corky wasn't a daredevil in waiting. Bill and Major hadn't become barrel jumpers until they were in their thirties, and she remembered that Corky had been fired from the Maid of the Mist in '48 while taking the day off to help Bill fly down the rapids. Corky had been on the rescue teams of Bill and Major for other barrel stunts, as well. With that in mind, right after Bill's very public death, Bea begged Corky to give up the river, to earn $4,000 a year like everybody else, and, lo and behold, he said he would try it. With a wife and two small sons to support, William Hill III, six, and four-year-old Chris, Corky had also held jobs as a steeplejack, conservationist, and construction worker. In April 1952, he signed on with the Rayner-Atlas Company on a hydroelectric expansion project to build a tunnel under the city of Niagara Falls, Ontario, for harnessing more of the river's great power.

In the early morning hours of Good Friday, April 11, 1952, Corky's sister, Edith, was working as an assistant at the Greater Niagara General Hospital in a job arranged for her by Bill's widow, Alice. Suddenly, an accident victim on a stretcher was rushed from an ambulance down the hall into an emergency room. "Nurses and doctors and ambulance people were all over the place," Edith recalled. "Blood was pouring out of his head and the [medics] were holding things over his head." When she got a good look at him, the man seemed to have a stone lodged in his throat. And, my God, it was her brother Corky. Less than three hours later, he was pronounced dead. Norman Hill was just twenty-eight. Corky had been on the night shift in a hydro tunnel (just his second day of work) when the accident struck.

At about twenty past seven in the morning, he was only ten minutes from finishing his shift, mucking rock in a loading bucket at the bottom of Shaft No. 2, when a stone three inches in diameter came hurtling 350 feet down the shaft and went right through his hard safety helmet. It was the second tragedy in three weeks at the site. Another sister, Margaret, recalled that Corky hadn't wanted to go to work that night; he would have rather stayed at her house playing cribbage, "but he said his wife would be mad if he didn't go." Solemn funeral services were held in the Morse and Son Funeral Home, where many bodies that Corky and his brothers and father had recovered had been embalmed over the years. One day not long after, little William III was found with flowers in Fairview Cemetery, near the graves of his father, uncle Bill, and grandfather Red Hill Sr. Another day, he wandered down to the Maid of the Mist docks, looking for Corky.

For months, Beatrice held her sons Major and Wesley close, as well as her three adult daughters. A budding writer, she published a poem in the *Evening Review*:

A Prayer that Was in Vain

I had four sons I loved so much
I prayed for them night and day
Then on that fatal day August fifth, 1951
I prayed to God to guide him but my prayer was in vain for,
God called my oldest son away
That left me with only three and then my prayer was
Not heard for on April eleventh, 1952, God took another son
    away from me and left me with only two
Now I pray with all my heart that
God will hear me and will not call another in 1953.

No other Hill died in 1953, but Major started planning about the falls again, even though there were now as many ghosts as people in the gorge. He wondered if there was a curse on the family. "You can't win," he said. "[Corky] quit the river because it was too dangerous . . . they say we take too many chances at the river, and then you go and get killed on a job underground." That year, Major was writing a book about his family, *Conquest of Niagara*, and looking for a publisher. He also got a job as a tour guide around Niagara Falls. He was friendly and personable, with tons of firsthand experiences to jabber about. Every stop by the bus brought a heartfelt story—in Chippawa was the launch point for so many heroes in barrels; closer to the falls was where his father rescued the sailors on the scow and where "yours truly" had been trapped in his barrel in a hydro pool. Oh, back in Chippawa, if he hadn't mentioned it, and he probably hadn't, was where his brother Norman was killed. Days with all-ears tourists were bittersweet for Major. He had his audience, but the stories were sometimes too agonizing.

As the decade wore on, though, he revived his own daredevil career, in which he had been so close to defeating the falls, or vice versa.

Speaking of Horseshoe, in the early 1950s, Lussier had reached his mid-sixties, but wouldn't quit on his dream to make his second trip, albeit he wanted three thousand bucks to make a new rubber ball and ten thousand to make the trip. "Show me the dough and I'll go, but it'll have to be this year or next; after that I'll be too old," he said. Lussier had plans for a three-layer ball around an aluminum frame. "I'll go over any waterfall in the world in a rubber ball. If the fall is too high, I'll put wings on the ball." Major liked reading about his rivals as much as he liked Russian literature. He went ahead and had an eight-foot barrel to challenge the falls built by Myer Delduca, who had constructed the *Torpedo* for his '49 rapids run. Delduca put more ballast (147 pounds) into this one to make it less susceptible to winds and currents. First, he had to test it in the lower rapids. In 1954, with a five-man team headed by Ken Sloggett, and wearing a white shirt and tie, the thirty-five-year-old Hill strapped his slender 126-pound frame into a parachute harness inside the barrel.

The first leg through the Whirlpool Rapids was, as usual, swift and stormy, and, par for the course, the Whirlpool snagged the barrel for ninety minutes. Inside the barrel, the heat reached 120 degrees; when it circled the outside of the Whirlpool, Hill opened the hatch to get some fresh air, and he waved a long arm to journalists, tourists, and police. With its iron ballast, the barrel didn't get jammed in eddies, as *Torpedo* had, but instead drifted to Thompson's Point, where Hill was to start the second leg of his trip to Queenston; however, police were waiting and arrested Hill, who suffered just a bruised side and ego. As officers escorted him away, Major, soaking wet, said, "They can't keep stopping me forever." The barrel was tied to the shore of the gorge, where he planned to retrieve it the following day. But, the next day while he was attending a square dance, the barrel broke loose from its moorings and went into the vortex of the Whirlpool like a mouse down a storm drain, and stayed there.

Perhaps the highlight of the 1950s for Major was his reception each summer at the Canadian National Exhibition, where he exhibited his barrels and stories, far from the distracting roar of the falls. Thousands of visitors filed past his barrels and seemed intrigued by his family tales of daring, especially a teenager from central Ontario, Dave Munday, who listened intently as Major fielded questions: What would you say is the most effective type of barrel for going over the falls? Could you describe the plunge pool below the falls and its dangers? Where is the best place to get a barrel into the river in order to avoid the police? Major took a liking to the otherwise-shy Munday, who was also interested in mechanics and, like Hill, parachuting. One day, he said, he would love to ride a barrel over the falls. His idol Major did not discourage him and laughed like Milton Berle when he said that maybe the two could go over together one day.

Back in Niagara Falls, Major continued to get the lion's share of attention for his barrel trips and falls plans . . . until July 9, 1960, when the unthinkable happened—seven-year-old Roger Woodward, of Niagara Falls, New York, became the first person to survive a plunge over Horseshoe Falls without a barrel. He was wearing only a life jacket, following a boating accident. His sister was rescued at the brink, but the boat operator perished. "Now, don't that beat all," Major said.

He and his brother Wesley believed that Woodward survived because he was caught up in a cushion of air over the falls and, due to his light weight, was tossed clear of rocks Down There, and if it hadn't been for his life jacket, he probably would have drowned or hit the rocks. Major wondered what might have happened if Bill had been wearing his life jacket when *The Thing* went over. Partly inspired by the Woodward accident, in 1961 Major and another man built a prototype of a twenty-six-foot steel boat powerful enough for rescue work in the Horseshoe Rapids above the falls, the *Rapids' Queen*, but they never got it into operation.

Also in 1961, William Fitzgerald, a maintenance man for International Business Machines in New York, suffered only minor injuries in going over Horseshoe in a big rubber ball. "I have just integrated Niagara Falls," said Fitzgerald, a black man, who first gave police the name Nathan Boya (taken from Thomas Mboya, one of his heroes, a former African labor leader). Fitzgerald wanted to bring attention to the discrimination against blacks in the United States. He went on to become a whistle-blower government research scientist, standing up for workers' rights. He said his stunt was also for a French woman he had met while serving with the US Army as a boxer in Paris in 1947; they had talked of marriage and spending their honeymoon in Niagara Falls. "I told her that men in this country do such things to prove their love—like the knights of old," he said. Fitzgerald was the first person to be fined under a new law in the Niagara Parks Act for performing a stunt without permission. He was fined the maximum one hundred dollars. Major acknowledged that he, too, did stunts to impress women. He had a new love in his life—local woman Winnie McIntyre, whom he planned to marry once he had gone over the falls. When Winnie was around, Major wore his blue flannel blazer, with a Legion 51 crest, and neatly creased gray trousers.

***

The Royal Canadian Legion Branch 51 was starting to get smoky one afternoon in 1970. Major Hill was sitting at a table, talking with a local newspaper reporter (the author) while his mother, Beatrice, sat in on the conversation. Major was decked out in his blue flannel blazer and a striped tie, almost the same as his father used to wear, but he wasn't going to marry Winnie McIntyre after all. Although he was skinny and sometimes tousled, his clothes were comfortable on him; with his short hair combed, he could've been a model for a department store catalog. These days, though, he wore forlorn best, head tilted right.

"Got a smoke?" Hill said. The reporter didn't, so Hill bummed one from a woman he knew, two tables down.

"Do you see yourself doing another daredevil event in the near future?" the reporter asked.

"Lemme smoke first. How 'bout a drink?"

The reporter ordered a jug of draught beer.

"None for me, thank you," Bea said, sipping 7UP, wearing a dark shawl and matching purse, held close to her. Her wrinkles were deep enough for troughs to catch rainwater.

An elderly man asked Major if he was buying. "Yeah." Major nodded. "You know, on my tab." The bartender wasn't laughing.

"Major drinks too much," Bea said to the reporter, her wrinkles in a dance. "He's only fifty-one. Does he look fifty-one to you?"

"Ma, I need one now and again," Major said, wincing as he touched the top of his right leg, which had been amputated below the knee just three years earlier from war wounds and too much river. The crease was gone from his trousers, and there was a small stain on his blazer. At one time, he would have been upset about such things, if he wasn't primed to become "the first one-legged man to beat the falls." When his mother finished her 7UP, he got up, wiped condensation off the table under the bottle, and took the empty to the bar. When he wasn't fussing over Beatrice, Major kept looking at the front door. "When's the photographer coming?" he said to the reporter, then he turned to his mother.

"This young man wants to know about me and the Horseshoe fall," he said, referring to the falls the old way.

"Lloyd, stop. Please, Lloyd, no more." She looked sorrowfully at the reporter and said to him, "Sorry, I'm here to give you the truth. Let's keep the Hills as a legend, like that spirit [Lelawala] going over in the canoe."

"That's only *part* of the truth," Major snapped. "No matter where you go, or what you think of the falls, you always come back to it. It's the heart that decides, not the mind . . . and we had more good times than bad—all those barrel trips . . . eleven of 'em."

"Eleven too many, if you ask your mother."

"Can't argue with the crowds we drew. Dad, seventy-five thousand, me three hundred thousand for my crack at the falls, and they got their money's worth, believe you me. Bill, maybe two hundred thousand a couple of times . . . We were in the *New York Times* and *Time* magazine." Major shuffled his fingers into his shirt pocket, looking for something.

Beatrice shook her head. "Water as thick as blood. A daredevil will never be as famous as the falls."

"Dad's in the wax museum down the street. You seen it? Life-size, but Dad is bigger than life. The Prince of Wales shook his hand!"

"Was." As a memory came down her cheek as a tear, she looked to the reporter for help. "That river is scary. Don't get me wrong—there were good times. They had good families."

"You betcha it's scary," Major said, raising his glass. "That's why we have a few beers first. You had to face every demon: claustrophobia inside the barrel, then fear of deep water and fear of heights and, of course, of gettin' yerself killed. If you're not scared, it's not worth it. Anyway, Wes doesn't want any part of it; I'm the only one left."

A tipsy man looked over at the table, where Major was holding court, and shouted, "Hey, Major, still livin' with your mum?"

Hill asked to be excused and went to the bathroom, limping, taking his sweet time. People watched him. His posture was going. A couple of old guys waved to him on his way past their tables, and he saluted them in an army way.

"No matter what you hear me or anybody else say about Major, he's still a gentleman," Mrs. Hill said. While he was away from the table, she stressed to the reporter that her son had never been the same since he'd come back from the war. "People in town say he's a drunk, a freeloader, but let me tell you, he's not the same Major. The war and the river took care of that."

A few minutes later, Major returned with a frothy glass of beer somebody had given him.

"You're limping more," his mother said. "See the doctor tomorrow."

"Lotsa miles left on this carcass, don't you worry, Ma. I could use some pain pills . . . I'm not done yet. Apart from these"—he displays his artificial leg and a large, stiff neck brace from a spinal injury, which he has hidden under the table—"I can still do it. My heart's good, no problems with the heart." He swigged beer and looked right through the floor. "I had a dream the other night where I was falling. It was real; my stomach was churning and the bottom was falling out of my world. I thought I was going to land lickety-split and die. I woke up just in time. Ever have that?"

The reporter nodded.

"Well, sir, some people think that dropping over them there falls is like that. I think, though, it's more like skydivin'. I've done a whole bunch of that in the army . . . it's quiet at first, except for your heart beating, then you feel like you're part of everything—the sky, the clouds, the wind, even the earth. You're not falling, you're flying. The wind is in your ears, but your stomach doesn't feel that hollow. You don't fall like you're going to be crushed at the bottom; it's like an elevator of air is lowering you. If you let yourself go and don't be scared, it can free your mind. Maybe that Greek fella, Strath . . . Stath . . ."

"Stathakis."

"Whatever . . . I think he had it right. You can think clearer; that's probably what it's like, going over the falls, from what I understand. I don't think it's like the falling nightmare I had the other night. They say if you don't wake up before you hit the ground, you die."

The reporter and Beatrice looked at one another. "He has dreams," she said. "When he wakes up, the sheets are soaked."

Suddenly, Major didn't need an audience; he started talking like no one was in the room. "Bill should still be here. *The Thing*!" He went quiet for thirty seconds. "*The Thing*! That's what's killing us. Dad died too young, Bill, well, and Corky was just a kid. Now it's after me . . . well, it ain't gettin' Major Hill. We're no quitters, this family. I'll be back; the Hills will be back. Just you wait and see. Red Hill will make it over the falls."

A waiter brought a warmed-up meat pie on a paper plate and a napkin for Mrs. Hill. "Compliments of the house, ma'am," he said.

"A meat pie?" Major frowned. He got up and replaced her plastic fork with a metal fork from the bar counter. "After what the Hills did in the army, they should be feeding us three-course meals at the Legion." Major and his mother were having trouble just paying the rent in a green frame house wedged between two buildings on Ferry Street, within the thunder of the falls. His war veteran's pension was just $105 monthly, plus $100 more annually for clothes. Her husband left Beatrice with just a $420 insurance policy, and she struggled with two government pensions, totaling $105.

"People think we made money off the stunts, but I can't even afford a monument for my husband's grave," she said.

"It's hard making any money these days," Major said. "Now they have helicopters to get floaters out of the gorge. There goes twenty-five bucks a corpse." He shook his head. "God, the *Maid of the Mist* isn't even a steamer anymore. Oh, well, I made three grand for my barrel lectures at the CNE. And I was adviser to that movie with Marilyn Monroe [*Niagara*]." He paused. "I stood next to her at the railing. She said she felt a strange lure to jump in."

Suddenly, a three-piece band burst into a polka, and several couples got up on a small dance floor. "In the old days, we could dance your socks off," Major said. "The Viennese waltz, roller-skating, the jive, square dance. With two legs, I was always the best dancer, Dad second."

Beatrice rolled her eyes and said to the reporter, "Sorry, I used to be more romantic. Major had so much talent—carpentry, electrical work, plumbing . . . that copper work he did of The Last Supper . . ."

"We have responsibilities at the river, Ma. Remember, Jesus saves, but the Hills save at Niagara. Oh, and if anybody's counting, I made the most barrel trips of Dad or Bill or anybody—five." Major frowned until he was sure the reporter had written that in his pad. The tips of his fingers were yellow; he used the cigarette machine so much, his mother said, he could play "You'll Never Walk Alone" on it to get it to chuck out a free pack at least once a month. "Oh, good golly, I forgot *Frigidaire Entertains*. That was another show I was on. It was a Friday evening show."

When the beer was gone, all three got up. Major pulled his neck brace from under the table and put it on for everyone to see. Beatrice adjusted her cane and thanked the reporter. "It's good for us to get out," she said. "All I do all day are chores and rocking in that chair. I'm too old to take care of Major anymore."

"I'll be fine," Major said. "Look—no crutches today." She kissed him on the cheek and left with a friend. "You'll be fine, Ma, as long as you can make aprons for people and those Aunt Jemima dolls."

When the reporter drove him home, Hill begged him to pull over across from an old warehouse. "Wait'll ya see this, buddy," Major said. There, limping to a big steel door, always conscious of his posture, he fiddled with a set of keys, but after a struggle he couldn't get it open. "Well, maybe another time. Hey, just write it down and I'll describe it for ya."

When they were both back in the car, the reporter got out his pad.

"Well, first of all, it's pear-shaped with a double hull. You know what that is? The interior is packed with Styrofoam. I call it my *Aqua Capsule*. Cost me a thousand smackeroos." Hill's hands became animated, holding an unlit cigarette. "If you can make a dollhouse, Dad once said, you can make a barrel." He put the keys in his pocket and lit the cigarette, puffing through the open passenger window. "This time, I'll pick a better launch point and go over the middle of the falls at seven thirty in the morning—there are no rocks below the middle of the falls, or currents to drive you back to shore. I'll ride in a sitting position when it goes over. Its weight will take me down, underwater, maybe fifty feet and bring me back to the surface two hundred feet downstream. I think I can make a safe prototype so that people can go over the falls every Sunday." As they passed the falls, Major went quiet, but suddenly said, beginning to slur, "They're saying these days the time of the daredevils is dead, a falls barrel once every ten or twenty years . . . I say it'll never be dead, as long as there's human spirit."

The following year, 1971, Major put a notice in the *Evening Review* that he was organizing a family reunion. "All relatives and anyone else who has partici-pated in the numerous adventures of the family are welcome," he wrote. The reunion would be held in conjunction with a television documentary about the Hill family. Before it aired, on Monday, June 14, 1971, Jean Lussier died of a heart attack at age seventy-nine in Niagara Falls, New York. The fourth person to go over the falls was nearly penniless and lived in a seniors' building after his apart-ment was destroyed by fire on Christmas 1970. Major fondly remembered that afternoon, forty-three years previous, when a roughed-up but grinning Lussier had emerged triumphantly from his crazy, oversize rubber ball, after beating

Horseshoe Falls and being rescued from drowning by Red Hill Sr. Major was nine at the time, and it was his first time to witness to a falls plunge.

Major read about Lussier's death in the papers and walked the streets of his hometown, Niagara Falls, shouting incoherently about Lussier and how he was now the last of the river men, and the falls would never get Red Hill. Major wasn't living with his mother lately and was lugging all of his belongings around in a shopping bag. To many people, it seemed like he was just drunk again. Although Major was drinking a lot lately, he was planning on becoming, in 1971, the first man to defeat the entire Niagara River in his *Aqua Capsule*. After walking the streets the night of Lussier's death, Major complained of pain in the stump in his right leg and went to Greater Niagara General Hospital, seeking painkillers, where he was given a shot of five milligrams of Valium (a muscle relaxant) and a vitamin shot. The unkempt Hill was reportedly in a snarly mood and being obnoxious to other patients, and so the cops were summoned. At first, they took him to a nursing home, where police were told he was no longer a resident, then they took him to an address he said was his home, but when they got there it turned out to be a restaurant that had been the Hill family home many years before; finally, he was taken to a police cell and charged with public intoxication. About eight hours later, at five in the morning, Major Lloyd Hill was found dead in his cell of unknown causes. Police said he had tried to kill himself on numerous previous occasions, twice with straps from his artificial leg. He was listed as having no fixed address.

Family members said that on the night of his arrest, Major had a mysterious bruise on the back of his neck, although no evidence of such was found during an autopsy, a coroner's inquest was told by investigators. There was no trace of alcohol in his blood and only a quarter of the amount of barbiturate it would have taken to kill him, leading to controversy and publicity in the press; however, any alcohol could have dissipated from his blood in the eight hours after his arrest, the inquest was told. A coroner's jury could find no cause of death. Major was fifty-two. Four of the Hill river men were now dead, including his father and two of his brothers; their average lifespan was forty-three. Major was survived by his estranged wife, daughter, three sisters, his adopted brother, his brother Corky's two sons, whom he had helped to raise, and a daughter he had with Corky's wife. (Major lived with her for a time after Corky died.) On September 25 of that year, a television special was aired about the Hill family, in the same time slot as *Cannon* and *Marcus Welby, M.D.*, in which the only surviving biological brother, Wesley, discussed the extreme highs and lows of his family at the falls. Upon Major's death, Beatrice was beside herself, and only the constant rocking in her living room chair kept her alive. "We shouldn't have to die young anymore. The diseases and epidemics are supposed to be under control," she said. "I guess there are some people who have a need to put their lives at risk to go against old Mother Nature." Three years later, Mrs. Hill was dead. They should have given her a medal for trying to save men from drowning.

CHAPTER NINETEEN
THE PROTÉGÉ

This story ends with inspiration few saw coming. The Hills finally made it over the falls, in a way. On an autumn morning in 1985, Dave Munday, the man who thirty years previously had idolized Major Hill and his barrel display at the Canadian National Exhibition, made the Big Splash over Horseshoe Falls and partly credited Major with his success. The forty-eight-year-old Munday, from rural Caistor Centre, Ontario, had a lot in common with Major—he was skilled with his hands as a diesel mechanic; had fourteen hundred parachute jumps as a skydiving instructor, and an obsession to go over the falls; and wound up with the same rescue man, Major's aging cousin, Ken Sloggett. "Major inspired me when I was a kid," said the introverted Munday, a simple father of two daughters who seemed on the outside to never get excited, who liked to bowl in his spare time. "If it wasn't for the Hills, I would never have gone to Niagara Falls." Unlike Major or most other Niagara daredevils, Munday sought no sensational head-lines, only personal satisfaction and thrills; in fact, he was more like Red Hill Sr.

Four days a week for six weeks, Munday drove thirty-five miles round trip from his home to the falls to watch the routines of police and find out when they took their doughnut breaks and shift changes. He selected a twelve-man crew, including electricians, mechanics, truck drivers, and the retired factory worker Sloggett, who was to direct the recovery. Munday picked a cold, rainy day, when police might not be as much on the lookout for a stunt; on Saturday, October

5, he confounded the cops and hydro authorities by having a truck deposit his barrel, with him strapped inside, over the railing only 150 yards from the brink of the falls, just before nine o'clock in the morning, as water levels were allowed to rise for the day. The one-thousand-pound barrel, made from a 450-gallon neoprene sprayer tank, was one of the more expensive Niagara vessels to date, about $16,000. *To Challenge Niagara* was seven feet long and three feet wide, lined with aluminum separated by ten inches of foam. After being dumped into the upper river, within seconds it hurtled over the falls before a small crowd to provide a first—with a video camera on board, it afforded a bird's-eye, if somewhat fuzzy, picture of the descent. Munday lost consciousness for a few minutes when the barrel landed below the falls and suffered bruises on his neck from his harness. For a time, the barrel was lodged in rocks at the base of Horseshoe, until the white-haired, sixty-nine-year-old Sloggett carefully climbed down and reached it; he knew that Munday was afraid of water and did not want him to panic, and he helped the daredevil get out of the barrel. On emerging, Munday was cheered by onlookers and media, who had been alerted only after it had been launched into the river. "I'm not a guy to get beat," the self-confessed loner said during a news conference he reluctantly attended several hours later. "Nothing ever beats me. I wouldn't have been able to live with myself if I had let Niagara Falls beat me . . . but I'm not a stuntman. I'm just an ordinary guy." He said he earned more respect for the falls: "I had no idea it was so violent. This was a very strong force, one I've never experienced. And the feeling of claustrophobia, being locked in that barrel, was frightening." Munday was the first Canadian-born daredevil to survive the plunge, but was fined $500 for stunting in the Niagara Parks and $1,000 more for breach of probation in Niagara Falls (Ontario) Provincial Court, in relation to an earlier failed attempt in which his barrel got stuck in shallow water. Munday told the judge it had been a "terrifying experience" and he was glad to come out of it alive. Because he promised he would not try the feat again, he avoided a possible thirty-day jail sentence, according to Corporal Fred Hollidge, a police spokesman. "You have to respect the ingenuity of his preparations and the dangerousness of the stunt," Hollidge said. "At the same time, he's breaking the law."

In a modern age of daredevils, Munday was one of six men and women to beat Horseshoe, mostly in high-tech barrels. In 1984, professional stuntman Karel Soucek, a former Czech tank commander, survived in a sophisticated plastic barrel, but later perished in the Houston Astrodome trying to re-create the event. The following year, Steven Trotter, a young bartender and stuntman from Providence, Rhode Island, who was inspired partly by Red Hill Jr., survived in two pickle barrels, fastened end to end and sealed with submarine-style twist caps and reinforced with fiberglass and balsa wood. (In 1995, Trotter plunged for the second time, in a barrel made from two hot water tanks and covered in Kevlar. Also with him in the barrel was his girlfriend, Lori Martin, a caterer from Georgia.) In 1989 Peter DeBernardi of Niagara Falls, Ontario, hoping to raise awareness about drug abuse, and student Jeffrey Petkovich of Ottawa, Ontario, became the first duo to survive in a reinforced steel barrel. In 1993, Munday was tired of others challenging the falls in high-tech equipment, so he conquered the falls for a second time in a decommissioned diving bell he bought from the Canadian Coast Guard. At age fifty-six, he was the first person to beat the falls twice, and the media dubbed him "Super Dave" Munday, referring to the television character and daredevil Super Dave Osborne. Somewhere, a Hill was finally resting in peace. Now, don't that beat all.

There were two fatalities of men who went over the falls in unusual devices—in 1990, Jesse Sharp, an unemployed bachelor from Ocoee, Tennessee, looking to further his daredevil career, died in a twelve-foot polyethylene kayak. His body was never found. In 1995, Robert Overacker, a stunt school graduate from Camarillo, California, raising awareness for the homeless, died on a personal watercraft after his rocket-propelled parachute failed to work. After 1995, police pressure and rising court costs kept daredevils from attempting the falls. The river and the falls apparently were changing—unbelievably, three men survived plunges over Horseshoe without aid of a device between 2003 and 2012. Kirk Jones of Canton, Michigan, survived with minor injuries after going over the falls without even a life jacket. His mother said he had been depressed over his life circumstances; prior to the plunge, the forty-five-year-old Jones had lost his job when his parents shut down the family business, making tools for auto parts manufacturers. Kirk was living in poverty with no wife, no children, and few friends. Jones himself told police it was a suicide attempt, but they arrested him and he was fined $3,000 for performing a banned stunt. Niagara Regional Police Sergeant Rick Berketa said that, at best, Jones' feat was a poorly planned stunt. "Daredevils take conscious risks with their lives with the emphasis on survival," Berketa said. "However, some risks are so great that the chances of survival based upon a balance of probabilities become so little that they become suicidal in nature. It may be a thin line of definition, but a line nonetheless . . . he did have a friend try to take a video of the incident."

Two unidentified men, apparently attempting suicide, survived plunges over Horseshoe, while suffering major injuries. One of them desperately swam ashore in the lower river and was rescued by firefighters. But dozens of others who jumped or fell into the river in suicides or accidents over that time perished, including in 2011, when Japanese exchange student Ayano Tokumasu, who climbed onto the railing at the falls to have her photo taken, lost her footing and was swept to her death. No one has ever survived a plunge over the rockier American Falls. Technology has allowed for commercial jet boats to carry tourists through the Devil's Hole Rapids, although the Whirlpool Rapids remains too dangerous. In 2012, Nik Wallenda, a seventh-generation member of the fabled Flying Wallendas high-wire professional family, was granted permission by governments on both sides of the Canada–US border to tightrope across Horseshoe Falls. An estimated one hundred thousand spectators watched, along with a record television audience of more than ten million viewers.

The real river men, however, have come and gone. In 2006, Wesley was the last of Red Hill's sons to die—of natural causes—at seventy-six.

Sadly, nowhere in Niagara Falls is a plaque honoring the Hill family. All that remains from the original age of daredevils are some of their barrels in museums and others at the bottom of the Whirlpool, and a badly rusted old scow, still sitting half a mile from the brink of Horseshoe. No one of the ilk of Red Hill Sr. or his sons remains to patrol the haunts, rapids, and slippery gorge of Niagara Falls, to go Down There. Apart from Wesley's sons, Red's grandchildren are not such risk takers or rescuers, but husbands and wives with interesting but yellowing albums and medals. Following his death, Red Jr.'s widow, Alice, kept her family from the Hills and returned Christmas presents sent to her daughter, Sally. "It was too painful for Alice; she didn't want to remember a lot of stuff," Sloggett said. But Sally became a hero on her mother's side of the family as a beloved nurse, and her son, Kelly Finn, became a US Army staff sergeant and fighter in the Iraq War in 2004, like his great-grandfather before him at Vimy Ridge.

Meanwhile, Niagara, the never-ending alpha seductress, rolls on with her fast water and deep drop, annually attracting millions of admirers, a few of whom inexplicably climb over a railing and leap into her waters. Every day of the year, within the rumble of Horseshoe Falls, tourist guides excite visitors from Hoboken to Hong Kong with tall tales of desperate men rescuing sailors from runaway barges, moonbows in the night sky melting honeymooners, and romantic fools who dare to become one with a magic river.

ACKNOWLEDGMENTS

Although I have a number of wonderful people to thank, some of this book comes from osmosis. From 1970 to 1990, I was a river rat, going into the Niagara Gorge for hikes, stories, and photos, and sometimes to recover bodies of suicide and accident victims with Wesley Hill, Ken Sloggett, and the Niagara Parks Police. In addition, I covered many daredevil stunts for newspapers and knew the river as well as anyone. Some of the daredevils and would-be daredevils from that era came to me for advice about going over Horseshoe Falls in barrels.

I began research in 1970 and have interviewed about 250 people over the years. Some of my research originally appeared in newspaper stories for the *Niagara Falls Review*, the *St. Catharines Standard*, the *Buffalo News*, and the *Toronto Star*, among others. Thank you to my editors and publisher, Gordon Murray, at the *Review* in the 1970s and the *Standard*, with managing editor Murray Thomson and publisher Henry Burgoyne, in the 1980s.

For the human side of daredevils, I'm indebted to three people in particular— Ken Sloggett, Edith (Hill) Powell, and Wesley Hill. From the mid-1970s until well into the 2000s, prior to their deaths, they provided me with hundreds of hours of interviews, making available family photos, old notes, diaries, albums, and other resources. Their insights into people's habits and personalities were invaluable. Dan Hill and Kelly Finn have been good recent contacts.

For historical information, I must thank the Niagara Falls Public Library (Ontario); the Niagara Falls Public Library (New York); the Francis J. Petrie Collection, the Buffalo & Erie County Public Library; the *Niagara Falls Review*;

the *Niagara (New York) Gazette*; the Niagara Falls City Directories (Ontario); the Niagara Parks Commission and its public relations director of many years, George Bailey; Niagara Parks Police (Ontario) and its chief for many years, Bill Derbyshire; and the New York State Park Police.

Background about what the Niagara River does to victims was provided in interviews with Derbyshire and Niagara coroner Dr. David Lorenzen.

Thank you to freelance writer Dwight Whalen, whose research and stories in the *Standard* and other publications shed new light on some of the old stunts and dispelled some myths and exaggerations. Also, thank you to George Seibel and Sherman Zavitz, historians of the City of Niagara Falls (Ontario), and Donald E. Loker, former city historian for Niagara Falls (New York).

Oh, yes, and who can forget the Internet? Invaluable resources include Google, YouTube, and NewspaperArchive.com.

This book is not intended to inspire future daredevils—the Niagara River remains dangerous and unpredictable, and the court costs for performing a banned stunt are substantial.

A final thank you to Amazon editors Dave Blum and Ali Castleman for believing in this work.

BIBLIOGRAPHY

ADEX News. "Man vs. River: Wesley Hill and the Niagara." June 1977.

Bailey, George. *Daredevils over Niagara*. Toronto: Royal Specialty Sales, 2005.

Belasco, Susan, ed. *Stowe: In Her Own Time*. Iowa City: University of Iowa Press, 2009.

Berton, Pierre. *Niagara: A History of the Falls*. Toronto: Penguin, 1998.

Cain, Stephen. "Tragedy at Niagara Falls." *Reader's Digest*, June 1958.

Clarkson, Michael. "River Rescue." *What's Up Niagara*, August 1988.

Dunlap, Orrin E. "Over Niagara in a Barrel." *The Wide World Magazine*, 1902.

Finn, Sally. *Niagara's Daughter: Memories of a Girl Named Sally*. Self-published, 2015.

Fitzgerald, William. "How I Went over Niagara Falls." *Science and Mechanics*, June 1962.

Graham, Lloyd. *Niagara County*. New York: Duell, Sloan and Pearce, 1949.

Gromosiak, Paul. *Daring Niagara: 50 Death-Defying Stunts at the Falls*. Buffalo: Meyer Enterprises, 1998.

———. *Water over the Falls: 101 of the Most Memorable Events at Niagara Falls*. Toronto: Royal Specialty Sales, 2006.

Healey, Roy. "Whirling Through the Whirlpool." Welland (ON) Chemical newsletter, July 19, 1945.

Hill, William Red, Jr. *True Facts of the Death Defying Barrel Trips*. Self-published, 1947.

Hill, William Red, Sr. *Red Hill: Hero of Niagara*. Niagara Falls: F. H. Leslie, circa 1941.

The Hills of Niagara. Documentary. Toronto: Canadian Broadcasting Corporation, September 21, 1971.

Hulbert, Archer Butler. *The Niagara River*. Forgotten Books, 2012.

Jackson, John N. *The Mighty Niagara*. Amherst, NY: Prometheus, 2003.

Katz, Sidney. "Why Red Hill Did It." *Maclean's*, November 1, 1951.

King, Paul. "Going Over that Edge Is the One Thing I Want to Do." *Canadian Magazine*, February 20, 1971.

Kiwanis Club of Stamford, Ontario. *Niagara Falls: Canada: A History of the City and the World Famous Beauty Spot*. Niagara Falls, ON: Kiwanis Club, 1967.

Kobler, John. "That Fatal Game at Niagara Falls." *Saturday Evening Post*, March 1952.

Kram, Mark. "To the Brink and Beyond." *Sports Illustrated*, July 12, 1971.

Kriner, T. W. *In the Mad Water*. Buffalo: J and J Publishing, 1999.

Lord, Walter. *The Good Years: From 1900 to the First World War*. New York: Harper and Brothers, 1960.

McConnell, Oviatt. "Red Hill, the Riverman: Jiu-Jitsu Tames Niagara." *Buffalo Times*, March 22, 1938.

———. "Through Niagara's Rapids in a Barrel." *Buffalo Times*, March 21, 1938.

McDermott, William F. "Niagara Daredevils." *Variety*, October 1942.

Moffett, Cleveland. "Leach over the Falls." *American Magazine*, May 1915.

Morden, James C. *Falls View Ice Bridge and Niagara Ice Bridges*. Niagara Falls: F. H. Leslie, 1938.

———. *Historic Niagara Falls*. Niagara Falls, ON: Lundy's Lane Historical Society, 1932.

Murray, Joan. *Queen of the Mist*. Boston: Beacon Press, 1999.

The Niagara Parks Act. Handbook of Regulations for the Niagara Parks Commission.

O'Brien, Andy. *Daredevils of Niagara*. Toronto: Ryerson Press, 1964.

"Over the Falls Alive." *Welland Tribune*, October 29, 1901.

"Over the Falls in a Barrel and Lives." *Daily Cataract Journal*, October 25, 1901.

Parish, Charles Carlin. *Queen of the Mist: The Story of Annie Edson Taylor, First Person Ever To Go Over Niagara Falls and Survive*. Interlaken, NY: Empire State Books, 1987.

Petrie, Francis. *Historical Flashback 1829–1979: 150 Years of Niagara Daredevils and Accidents.* Niagara Falls: self-published, 1979.

———. *Roll out the Barrel.* Erin, ON: Boston Mills Press, 1985.

Seibel, George A. *A Chronological Inventory of Daredevils and Stunters at Niagara Falls.* Niagara Falls, ON: G. A. Seibel, 1986.

———. *Niagara River of Fame.* Kitchener: Ainsworth, 1986.

Taylor, Annie Edson. *Over the Falls: Annie Edson Taylor's Story of Her Trip.* Self-published, June 1902.

Thoreau, David. *The Complete Works of Henry David Thoreau.* Amazon Kindle, 2012.

Van Allsburg, Chris. *Queen of the Falls.* Boston: Houghton Mifflin, 2011.

Whalen, Dwight. "Daredevils Bobby Leach and Red Hill Provided Niagara with Constant Series of Wild Escapades." *St. Catharines Standard,* August 18, 1984.

———. "The Fatal Philosophy of George Stathakis." *What's Up Niagara,* December 1987.

———. "I'll See You Below." *St. Catharines Standard,* March 19, 1988.

———. *The Lady Who Conquered Niagara.* Brewer, ME: EGA Books, 1990.

Young, Warren R. "A Family's Fate—to Battle Niagara." *Life,* September 29, 1961.

Zavitz, Sherman. *It Happened in Niagara.* Niagara Falls, ON: Lundy's Lane Historical Society, 2008.

———. *Niagara Falls: Historic Notes.* St. Catharines: Looking Back Press, 2008.

OTHER SOURCES ON THE WEB

http://www.niagarafrontier.com/

http://www.niagaraparks.com/ (Niagara Parks Commission)

http://www.nflibrary.ca/ (Niagara Falls, Ontario, Public library)

http://niagarafallspubliclib.org/ (Niagara Falls, New York, Public Library)

http://imaxniagara.com (Niagara IMAX Theatre Daredevil Exhibit)

http://bay-journal.com/ (*Bay Journal*, Michigan, Annie Taylor's hometown paper)

https://www.youtube.com/

GENERAL VIDEOS
ON NIAGARA DAREDEVILS

https://www.youtube.com/watch?v=u3-J_osprTw

https://www.youtube.com/watch?v=u3-J_osprTw

https://www.youtube.com/watch?v=6m9DUUjNITU

ALSO CONSULTED

Public Archives of Canada

Stories circulated through Associated Press, Canadian Press, United Press International, and Reuters

Niagara Falls (Ontario) Public Library's files on daredevils

Library and Archives Canada

During my many years of interviews, there were four people who gave good
information, but asked to remain anonymous for family reasons.

NOTES

CHAPTER ONE

For Hill's barrel plunge, I interviewed twenty-five people who were there, including most who are mentioned, apart from Hill himself, Alice (Sills) Hill, and their daughter, Sally. I was not there, but I believe I have painted a close picture of what happened, and how he was feeling. Many details and conversations were provided by Edith (Hill) Powell, Margaret (Hill) Genders, Major Hill, Wesley Hill, Ken Sloggett, his brother Jack Sloggett, and Beatrice (Clark) Hill; historian Francis Petrie; and journalists Ron Roels, Clive Jacklin, Nancy (Reynolds) Eidt, and John Fedor.

Other sources:
- Katz ("Why")
- King ("Going Over")
- Newspapers from August 6–7, 1951—the *Toronto Daily Star*, Niagara Falls *Evening Review*, *Niagara (New York) Gazette*, and *Buffalo Evening News*.

CHAPTERS TWO AND THREE

Information and quotes about Annie Edson Taylor's press conference and trip over the falls came from:

- *Daily Cataract Journal*
- Dunlap ("Over Niagara")
- Graham (*Niagara*)
- Kriner (*Mad Water*)
- Murray (*Queen*)
- Parish (*Queen*)
- Taylor (*Over the Falls*)
- Van Allsburg (*Queen of the Falls*)
- *Welland Tribune*
- Whalen (*The Lady*)
- *Suspension Bridge Journal*

The quotes, in italics, on her plunge came from Taylor (*Over the Falls*).

The information on the McKinley assassination came from Lord (*Good Years*).

Background on the Whirlpool Rapids stunters came from the files of Francis Petrie; the *Toronto Daily Mail and Empire*, July 10, 1900; and from a YouTube video on the *Fool Killer*: https://www.youtube.com/watch?v=nNikZiBT5Iw.

The quote by Graham that he had gone over the falls came from Kriner.

CHAPTER FOUR

The Thoreau quote came from Thoreau (his *Complete Works*).

Information on the early days of the Hills came from:

- Family albums, notes, and records provided by Beatrice Hill, Edith Powell, Wesley Hill, and Ken Sloggett
- Berton (*Niagara*)
- Drummond Hill Records of Morse and Son Funeral Home
- Niagara Falls City Directories

CHAPTER FIVE

Some information about Leach and his rivalry with Red Hill was from Whalen (*Leach and Hill*).

The daredevil history of the Whirlpool was taken from a number of books and from the *Geneva (NY) Daily Times*, December 13, 1910, and the *Gazette*, September 17, 1910.

The 1910 barrel trip by Leach, and then Hill, was taken from Whalen (*Leach and Hill*), *Popular Mechanics Magazine*, February 1911, several newspapers, including the *Geneva (NY) Daily Times*; and from Hill (*Hero*).

The courtship of Hill and Beatrice came from my interviews with Beatrice Hill, Edith Powell, Ken Sloggett, and Margaret Genders.

Leach's falls trip came from articles in the *Evening Review*, the *New York Times*, and the *Stevens Point (WI) Daily Journal*, July 26, 1911, the *Newark (OH) Advocate*, Whalen (*Leach and Hill*), Moffett ("Leach"), and Hill Sr. (*Hero*).

CHAPTER SIX

The section on the Niagara Ice Bridge collapse and rescue came from:

- Morden (*Falls View Ice Bridge*)
- Hill Sr. (*Hero*)
- Hill Jr. (*True Facts*)
- *New York Tribune*, February 5, 1912
- Cain ("Tragedy")
- Niagara Parks Commission records and press releases

The section on Vimy Ridge came from my interviews with, and letters, telegrams, and cables from, Ken Sloggett, Hill Sr. (*Hero*), and military records from the Canadian Department of Militia and Defense.

Hospital records for Hill were from the Princess Patricia Canadian Red Cross Special Hospital, Ramsgate, England.

The section on the scow came from my interviews with witnesses Edith Powell, Beatrice Hill, and Harry (Boltz) Hill, and the Niagara Parks Commission website; *What's Up Niagara* magazine; and reports from numerous newspapers in 1918, including the *Evening Review* and the *Buffalo Evening News*.

A video on the scow: https://www.youtube.com/watch?v=2nxeznO5D4s.

CHAPTER SEVEN

The information on Stephens's plunge came from the *New York Times*, July 12, 1920; the *Toronto Daily Star*, July 13, 1920; the *New York Tribune*, September 19, 1920; the *London Times*, April 6, 2002; the *Bristol (England) Evening Post*, October 28, 2003; Zavitz (*Happened*); and a feature article by Whalen ("I'll See You Below").

Beatrice's quote about Taylor was given to me in an interview.

CHAPTER EIGHT

Leach's falls plans came from the *Evening News*, Harrisburg, PA, August 26, 1920.

Reports on the Hills' domestic life came from my interviews with Beatrice Hill, Edith Powell, Harry Hill, Margaret Genders, and Ken Sloggett, and from Hill Sr. (*Hero*).

The info and quotes from the Houdini segment came from my interview with Beatrice and from the *Gazette*, May 6, 1921.

A YouTube clip from Houdini's Niagara scene: https://www.youtube.com/watch?v=E-po53jvj9Q.

The Leach-Hill swimming contest came from Hill Sr. (*Hero*), my interviews with Harry Hill and Ken Sloggett, and from local papers on September 7, 1925.

The death of Layfield came from obituaries in local papers and from my interviews with Ken Sloggett and Beatrice Hill.

CHAPTER NINE

The segment on the Lussier barrel viewing came from my interviews with Lussier, Ken Sloggett, Major Hill, and Winnifred Stokes.

Lussier's stunt came from my interviews with Lussier, Stokes, Cecil Burridge, Ken Sloggett, Beatrice Hill, and Major Hill, and from numerous newspapers, including the *Gazette* and the *Evening News*, July 4–5, 1928, Associated Press reports through NewspaperArchive.com, and an editorial in the *Pittsburgh Press*, July 6, 1928.

Video of the Lussier plunge: https://www.youtube.com/watch?v=qd-g_S_GHSY.

CHAPTER TEN

The quote from Susan Grove came from the *Jefferson City (MO) Post-Tribune* on August 5, 1929.

Info on Hill's 1930 barrel ride came from coverage in the *Daily Star*, May 30, 1930; Hill Sr. (*Hero*); and my interviews with Ken Sloggett, Major Hill, and Beatrice Hill (including her quote); and from these Internet videos:

- https://www.youtube.com/watch?v=1g2-S5lBKc8
- http://mirc.sc.edu/islandora/object/usc%3A18942

Information on Stathakis's plunge came from my interviews with Lussier, Major Hill, Edith Powell, Ken Sloggett and Stokes; Hill Sr. (*Hero*); the *Pittsburgh Post-Gazette*; the United Press; files from Francis Petrie, stories in the *Daily Star*; Whalen ("Fatal"); Kriner; and Internet videos:

- http://mirc.sc.edu/islandora/object/uscpercent3A18945
- https://www.youtube.com/watch?v=f85l8xyF16U.

The information on Sheep Hill came from interviews with Ken Sloggett, Edith Powell, Harry Hill, and Major Hill.

CHAPTER ELEVEN

Details were provided through my interviews with Jean Lussier, Beatrice Hill, Major Hill, Edith Powell, Harry Hill, Ken Sloggett, Jack Sloggett, Roy Healey, and Cecil Burridge, the pamphlets of Red Hill Sr. and Jr., and stories in the *Evening Review* and the *Gazette* on May 30, 1931, and the *Buffalo Times*, March 22, 1938.

CHAPTERS TWELVE AND THIRTEEN

I am indebted to the late Edith (Hill) Powell for the two chapters on Franny and scene-setting in the Niagara Gorge segment. She was her best friend and sister to Hill Jr. Some of the information and quotes she gave me appeared in a story I wrote in the *St. Catharines Standard*, August 26, 1987.

Also helpful were Margaret Genders, Max Jacobs, Harry and Beatrice Hill, Eileen Jackel, Frank Mancuso, Gus Mancuso, Catherine Hanna, Max Kaminsky, Alan Tustin, Agnes Tustin, Veronica Gardiner, the Ontario government's registry office, and St. Patrick's Church in Niagara Falls, Ontario.

For the information on Alice Sills, I thank her sister Agnes (Sills) Tustin, Alan Tustin, Edith Powell, Beatrice Hill, Major Hill, Wesley Hill, Kelly Finn, Ken Sloggett, Harry Hill, Margaret Genders, and Molly (Hill) Noyes, and the Finn book.

CHAPTER FOURTEEN

Details on Hill's death were from Ken Sloggett, Wesley Hill, Major Hill, Beatrice Hill, Edith Powell, the Morse and Son Funeral Home, and a story in the *Gazette* on May 14, 1942.

Junior's quote about his father came from his pamphlet.

The Hardwicke poem came from Edith Powell.

Sources for Major Hill's military history were from Major Hill, Ken Sloggett, family letters, and the Department of Veterans Affairs in Canada.

Information on Hill at Fleet came from Al Reid, Milf Zimmerman, Max Jacobs, Rusty Russ, Ralph Downs, and Ray Spear.

For Junior Hill's 1945 barrel trip, action sequences in italics were from his pamphlet. Other information came from my interviews with Niagara Parks Commission Chairman Max Gray, Roy Healey, Wesley Hill, Clive Jacklin, Nancy Eidt, Ken Sloggett, and Jack Sloggett, and from Roy Healey's story.

A video on Junior Hill's barrel trip: https://www.youtube.com/watch?v=eqj4dKmQEmo.

An Internet video showing the barrel ride, along with Stathakis's death plunge and Junior Hill's fatal 1951 barrel plunge over the falls: https://www.youtube.com/watch?v=SIy6RL7kpSI.

CHAPTER FIFTEEN

Information on Corky's swim came from my interviews with Wesley Hill, Major Hill, Beatrice Hill, Nancy Eidt, Ken Sloggett, and Max Gray, and from the *Daily Star*.

Details of prison time for Major and Junior Hill came from local newspapers and from Niagara parole officer P. A. Smith.

Sally's quote came from the Finn book.

Details of Junior Hill's 1948 rapids ride came from the *Evening Review* and my interviews. The segment on the souvenir store came from a story in the *Gazette* on November 6, 1948, and from my interviews with Ken Sloggett, Jack Sloggett, Wesley Hill, Nancy Eidt, Max Gray, Clive Jacklin, Edith Powell, and Beatrice Hill.

Ken Sloggett's quote on Major Hill came from my interview.

Major Hill's 1949 barrel trip came from my interviews with Ken Sloggett, Roy Healey, Molly Noyes, Clive Jacklin, Nancy Eidt, Max Gray, and Thomas Haymes; a story in the *Evening Review* on August 1, 1949, and an Internet video: http://www.shutterstock.com/video/clip-6267284-stock-footage-circa-s-major-lloyd-hill-attempts-to-barrel-down-niagara-falls-in.html.

CHAPTER SIXTEEN

From my interviews with Molly Noyes, Major Hill, Norm Cummings, Lou Pellet, Jiggs Rufrano, Vince Kerrio, Ken Sloggett, Junior Drylie, Jack Sloggett, Beatrice Hill, Edith Powell, Winnifred Stokes, Wesley Hill, Max Gray, Clive Jacklin, Nancy Eidt, and Jean Lussier, and from Kobler ("Fatal Game"), King ("Going Over"), and the *Toronto Telegram* on July 17, 1950.

CHAPTER SEVENTEEN

My sources for the plunge were the same as for chapter one.

The quote from Paul Whipple came from the *Gazette*, August 10, 1951.

Information on Hill's funeral came from the *Evening Review*, the *Gazette*, and my interviews with Ken Sloggett, Beatrice Hill, Max Gray, Margaret Genders, Vince Kerrio, Major Hill, Wesley Hill, Clive Jacklin, Nancy Eidt, and Edith Powell.

For descriptions of what it feels like to be inside a barrel on its way to the falls, I interviewed men who survived subsequent plunges—Jean Lussier, William Fitzgerald, Karel Soucek, Dave Munday, Steven Trotter, Peter DeBernardi, Jeffrey Petkovich, and Lori Martin. Otherwise, much of the info in this chapter was taken from the sources I mentioned above in chapter one.

Internet videos on the barrel plunge:

- https://www.youtube.com/watch?v=JAoCc82AG-E
- https://www.youtube.com/watch?v=FozejmaTfow
- https://www.youtube.com/watch?v=q8DhfOpkMUI

CHAPTER EIGHTEEN

Information on Corky's death came from my interviews with Edith Powell, Margaret Genders, Major Hill, Wesley Hill, Clive Jacklin, Nancy Eidt, Beatrice Hill, and Ken Sloggett.

Quotes from Major Hill and Jean Lussier came from my interviews with those men.

Information about William Fitzgerald came from my interviews with him. Other details came from Fitzgerald's article and from an Internet video: https://vimeo.com/39029110.

For the section on Major Hill and the Legion, I was there and recorded it with notes. Information also provided by Beatrice and Major Hill. The information on Major Hill's death came from police and coroner reports, my interviews with Beatrice Hill, Edith Powell, Ken Sloggett, Margaret Genders, Clive Jacklin, Nancy Eidt, and Wesley Hill, and from articles in local newspapers, including the *Hamilton Spectator*, June 16, 1971, and the *Evening Review*, July 8 and 20, 1971.

CHAPTER NINETEEN

Many details on Munday came from my numerous interviews with him.

The information on daredevils from 1984 to 1995 came mostly from my reporting, which included interviews with Karel Soucek, Steven Trotter, Peter DeBernardi, Jeffrey Petkovich, and Lori Martin, and from official reports of Niagara Parks Police and from an Internet video: http://channel.nationalgeographic.com/videos/niagara-barrels/. The information on Kirk Jones came from author interviews with police and newspaper reports.

A video of Dave Munday's 1985 barrel trip: https://www.youtube.com/watch?v=dDmw5HHnlkY.

ABOUT THE AUTHOR

Photo by Jennifer Clarkson

Michael Clarkson has been researching the story of the Niagara Falls daredevils since the 1970s, when he worked to help the Hills retrieve bodies from the gorge. He began his career as a police reporter for a local Niagara Falls newspaper, and his previous books include *The Secret Life of Glenn Gould* and *The Poltergeist Phenomenon*.